EQ
and Your Child

8 **Proven Skills To Increase Your Child's Emotional Intelligence**

Eileen D. Healy, MA, LMFT

Editor
Kimberly Healy Borg

Illustrator
Valerie Healy

Familypedia Publishing
San Carlos, CA 94070

Copyright© 2005 Familypedia Publishing

FAMILYPEDIA PUBLISHING
P.O. BOX # 1171
SAN CARLOS, CA 94070-1171
www.familypedia.com

First printing 2005

Library of Congress Cataloging-in Publication Data

Healy, Eileen D.
EQ and Your Child; 8 Proven Skills To Increase Your Child's Emotional Intelligence, first printing 2005.
ISBN 0-9770290-0-X

ATTENTION CORPORATIONS, UNIVERSITIES, COLLEGES, AND PROFESSIONAL ORGANIZATION: Quantity discounts are available on bulk purchases of this book for educational, gift purposes, or as premiums for increasing magazine subscriptions or renewals. Special books of book excerpts can be created to fit specific needs. For information please contact Familypedia Publishing, P.O. Box # 1171, San Carlos, CA 94070-1171; e-mail info@familypedia.com or 650-654-3125.

Visit us at www.familypedia.com

Dedication

This book is dedicated to my husband, Bill, who has been my best friend, loyal supporter, and co-parent for more than thirty years. To our three children Kimberly, Michael and Robert who have grown into wonderful high EQ (emotional intelligence) adults. Thank you for being a living testimony for this book.

CONTENTS

ACKNOWLEDGMENTS

This book has been writing itself throughout my personal and professional life for over thirty years. I thought it would be a relatively simple project to gather together everything pertaining to EQ that I had learned and observed during that time. I knew it was vitally important to combine my ongoing education, with my teaching experience, adding the knowledge I had gained from conducting twenty thousand counseling sessions to my personal life experiences of parenting my three children.

I WAS SO WRONG!!!

There was nothing simple about this project. Almost at the same moment I discovered I had everyone's support to write this book, I also discovered I am not a writer. I am a speaker! Boy was that an unexpected surprise, not to mention a serious disappointment to me. It presented a challenge I hadn't anticipated, a long three-year journey I hadn't planned, and many opportunities to test my own emotional intelligence.

I learned early in this project that determination, although it cannot create talent, could help find doors to open that lead to the talent you need. Whenever I became discouraged another door would open and through it would walk just the person I needed to move forward. Almost like an angel or the answer to a prayer.

I was told over and over again that this book needed to be written so all parents could be offered the opportunity to raise their child's EQ in a simple, easy way. I would not have succeeded with this project without the gifts and talents of all those wonderful individuals who were willing to walk through my doorway when it opened. It is these special people I want to take this opportunity to thank.

I would like to begin by thanking my husband Bill, who has been my unwavering supporter. He constantly reminded me of the value the completed book would bring to families. During my most discouraged moments, he would point out how every family deserved to feel as good as our family feels and that every parent would have what it takes to accomplish just that with EQ and Your Child.

Next, I want to thank our daughter and editor, Kimberly, who took all of my handwritten manuscripts, patiently deciphered them, put them into the computer, and edited them. I remember during her teen years thinking she had no patience when it came to research and term papers. She now has the patience of a saint. Not only did Kimberly transfer my scribble into a legible manuscript, but she challenged me every step of the way from her own life experience and the knowledge she gained from going through her own Masters Program in Counseling Psychology. But the most incredible thing is that while she was hard at work with this project, she and her husband became pregnant and delivered our first grandchild, a beautiful baby girl, Kaylene Rose. Needless to say new Mom, Dad, and Grandma were busy doing the suggested exercises with Kaylene while she was still in the hospital. The nurses were amazed at Kaylene's eye contact and awareness within the first twenty-four hours of life.

I want to thank my son-in-law, Chris, for being so patient and supportive during the hours and hours this project has taken away from his family.

Next, I want to acknowledge my daughter-in-law, Valerie, whose artistic talent and creativity can be seen throughout all the chapters. Val is a chemist by day and president and CEO of Sketch Concepts by night. Her illustrations bring life and humor to what otherwise could have become a very dry parent textbook.

I want to thank my son, Bob, whose contribution to this project has been invaluable. Just as when Bob was a child, he has respectfully challenged every aspect of this book from the research to the cover design until he felt fully satisfied that my message was clear and easily understandable to the busy parent. Bob, who is the CFO for Familypedia.com, will make sure that one dollar from every book sold is donated to charity, as our way of giving back for all our blessings.

I would like to thank my son, Michael, and my daughter-in-law, Caitlin, who have offered their support from the East Coast. The wonderful world of e-mail provided them the opportunity in their busy schedules to stay connected to this project. Their feedback and suggestions were greatly appreciated.

I'd also like to give special thanks to my colleague, Dr. Pamela Sudano-Ruegg, who has accompanied me along my professional journey since our Master's Program. Thank you for your constant support and encouragement.

I want to thank Kathy Wilson who helped launch this book with her enthusiasm, energy, ever-challenging questions, and input.

It is important to name each person who took part in our focus groups. Thank you for your time, your opinions, your suggestions, and your comments.

Your combined feedback moved this project from a dry clinical parent manual to the parent-friendly book it has become. I will be forever grateful.

Mimi Ahern	Dr. Pamela Sudano-Ruegg
Michelle Baeza	Karen Weber
Dawn Carroll	Dr. Peter Weber
Jessica Gatewood	Julie Wilcox
Sandra and Mark Grisedale	Dr. Michael Wilcox
Kerstin Goguen	Kathy Wilson
Michelle Lewis	Joseph Wolfe
Renee and Tyler Martin	Kathy Wright
Beth Sanchez	Regine Staufenberg

A special thank you to Sharon Branaman for taking notes for the focus groups and coming to the rescue during the last days of this project.

Jessica Gatewood, not only for the offered insight and feedback as the mother of a one-and-a-half-year-old son, but she became our grammar expert while she completed her Master's Program—thank you for all of your contributions.

Thanks to Mary Schwedhelm and Monika Kegel from Look Design in San Carlos, CA for our wonderful cover.

To all the children and their parents who have been in one of my classrooms, you have each taught me to be a better teacher.

To all the parents and children who have taken part in my Personal Skills Workshops or worked on raising their child's EQ in my office. I thank you for providing information, life experiences, and the research needed for this book.

To the girls from the St. Rose Healdsburg Birthday Gang, thank you for your opinions, encouragement, and cheerleading.

I would like to thank Christine and her daughter for putting a face to EQ. I smile each time I look at the cover. Our photograph says how good high emotional intelligence feels in a relationship. Thank you for providing me the usage of it.

I want to thank Laura Golden Bellotti, my developmental writer, who took the rough edges and smoothed them out with her expertise and professionalism.

And lastly, to all the women of WINGS (Women In God's Spirit) who have believed in me, prayed for me, and supported me through this long journey as I disappeared from their sight so I could spend time writing, I will always be appreciative.

INTRODUCTION

■　■　■

> Have you ever wondered why some children happily thrive despite the challenges that come their way, while other children fall apart under similar circumstances?
>
> Is it possible to teach your child to thrive?
>
> ## YES!
> Children with a high emotional intelligence thrive.

What Is Emotional Intelligence?

Emotional Intelligence is a person's ability to recognize one's own emotions and those of others and to respond appropriately to those emotions. If you're an emotionally intelligent person, you can tell the difference between feeling angry and feeling disappointed. You can pinpoint when you feel frustrated versus when you feel hurt. And you can sense when someone else is feeling worried, upset or sad. When you can accurately identify your own emotions and those of others, you can respond to life's unpredictable events and circumstances in an emotionally healthy way. This means you'll be much more likely to thrive in your relationships, your chosen field of work and in life.

In 1990, Peter Salovey, a Yale psychologist, and John Mayer, a psychologist from the University of New Hampshire, were the first to use the phrase emotional intelligence to refer to a person's ability to understand his or her own emotions and recognize emotions in others. Daniel Goleman's 1995 best-seller, <u>Emotional Intelligence: Why It Can Matter More than IQ</u> is often credited with introducing EQ to the general public.

As for the abbreviation EQ, it's based on the reference to IQ. Just as IQ refers to one's intelligence quotient or his or her measured intelligence, the common abbreviation for emotional intelligence is EQ, since we can now measure or attempt to measure this newly identified type of intelligence.

You might be wondering why there is a need for a book like this if EQ is something you're simply born with or not. Even though EQ is the result of several factors—including gender, birth order, personality, preferences, genetics, environment, role modeling, and emotional coaching—research has shown that emotional intelligence can be increased at any time during a person's life. It's never too late—or too early—to help your child raise his EQ.

Parenting is a difficult challenge at best, but when children have a high EQ, family life is so much easier! The household is calmer. Communication is clearer. Chores and homework time do not turn into a battleground. When a family is made up of members with high EQ, everyone enjoys a closer emotional connection, and children feel loving support as they grow and take risks in the world and within relationships.

As a Licensed Marriage and Family Therapist, California credentialed teacher, and the founder and developer of Personal Skills Workshops Program for Children, I have come to a simple yet profound realization: Children who have a positive attitude toward life's challenges share certain characteristics, which are recognized as the strengths of a person with a high emotional intelligence.

For over thirty years, I have worked with children ages three through seventeen to help them deal with the problems life sends their way. When I have worked with these children and taught them the *8 Proven Skills* found in this book, their self-acceptance, self-confidence, and life satisfaction have soared as well as their abilities to handle life's difficulties. Their parents are always delighted and amazed with the positive changes in their children.

These *8 Proven Skills* can radically change a child's life. Children who are shy become more outgoing. Those who are unmotivated and resistant to learning become more willing to approach tasks and succeed. Children who whine or are overly dependent become problem-solvers and achievers. The *8 Proven Skills* help them become more adept at understanding their own feelings and those of other people, which results in deeper, more satisfying relationships with family members, friends, and others.

I found that it didn't matter whether I taught these skills in a classroom of thirty-five, in a group of six in my Personal Skills Workshops, or in my counseling office one-on-one; children's EQ always increased.

What I do in my counseling office or did in a classroom is not magical or even that difficult, but it has been extremely effective with thousands of children. This is why my clients, friends, and family encouraged me to write this book. EQ and Your Child is written with the hope that every child who has at least one person in his or her life willing to spend the time with him or her working on these exercises will experience a life-changing transformation—and enjoy a happier, more fulfilling life.

My husband and I worked these exercises with our own children, from their infancy through their teens, with great success. We have a daughter and two sons. They are each so incredibly different that it always amazes me how they started from identical genetic pools!!! But every parent of more than one child knows that siblings can be different, whether it is their strengths, skills, and interests or simply their perception of the same problem. Bill and I learned soon after our second child was born that the only thing that is consistent about children is their inconsistency.

The great news is that all children respond positively to the exercises in this book. And every child has the ability to build the eight skills. Children respond in their own ways, but they will respond—and their EQ will increase.

Probably the most powerful reason you will want to help your child do the exercises in this book is that, as your child's EQ increases, you both will feel a greater emotional connection to each other. Not only that, but you'll be opening the door for your child to relate to others in an emotionally authentic way. Your child will be comfortable talking about feelings and problems rather than sweeping them under the rug or using them as fuel for conflict.

I wrote this book so you can help your child increase his or her emotional intelligence and enjoy the benefits that come with it. If I can work with a child in my office and make a huge impact in a short amount of time, why shouldn't you, the parent (or grandparent, aunt, uncle, or caring person), be given the life-changing lesson plan I use? Why shouldn't you receive the respect and trust that children give me when I work on these 8 Proven Skills with them? Can you imagine how much better for children to work on increasing their EQ with someone who loves them!

This book will help you evaluate your current approach to parenting and strengthen the positive effects it is having on your family and your children. As you gain powerful insights into how emotions work, you'll be offered practical strategies to help your child grow into a happy, fulfilled, high EQ adult.

You And Other Members Of Your Family Will Receive These Bonuses As You Work The Exercises:

- Your own personal EQ will increase.
- Your family's EQ will increase.
- Your child will learn to emotionally trust and connect with you in a deeper way.
- You will be the one who gives the precious gift of a strong, healthy life foundation to your child as you prepare her or him to be a high EQ adult!

-1-

WHY IS MY CHILD'S EMOTIONAL INTELLIGENCE SO IMPORTANT?

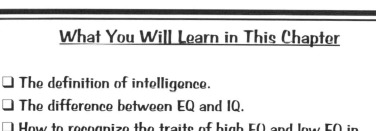

> ## What You Will Learn in This Chapter
>
> ❑ The definition of intelligence.
> ❑ The difference between EQ and IQ.
> ❑ How to recognize the traits of high EQ and low EQ in children.
> ❑ How to recognize the difference and connection between EQ and common sense.
> ❑ The benefits for a child with a high EQ.

What Is Intelligence (IQ Vs. EQ)?

Webster's Dictionary defines intelligence as the ability to acquire and retain knowledge and IQ (Intelligence Quotient) as a number showing how intelligent you are compared to others. We are all born with a certain IQ. Although there have been experiments demonstrating that IQ can be raised a few points with concentrated effort at a young age, on the whole IQ doesn't vary much throughout a person's lifetime. One's emotional intelligence or EQ, on the other hand, can be raised at anytime throughout one's lifetime. Your commitment to helping your children raise theirs will benefit them in countless ways, as you are about to discover. By reading this book, you'll find that your own EQ will be raised as well. Trust me, this always happens!

What Does EQ Involve?

Emotional Intelligence (EQ) involves two fundamental skills: the ability to recognize your own emotions and respond appropriately in any given situation, and the ability to recognize other people's emotions and respond to them in a healthy way. People with high EQ—whether they're children or adults—can manage their emotions so life doesn't overwhelm them. Because they can identify what other people are feeling, they have a fairly easy time forming and sustaining healthy relationships.

People with high EQ can motivate themselves to set life goals, learn, grow, and be productive. They are also more emotionally resilient, which means they can bounce back from life's rough spots. When life throws them a curve ball—whether it's a serious crisis or an everyday problem—people with high EQ draw on their inner confidence and skills. They have an inner voice that tells them, "I can face this crisis or overcome this obstacle and move on. I will survive it!"

How Can Parents Tell The Difference Between A High And Low EQ In Their Child?

For years now, in my roles as educator, school counselor, family therapist, and parent, I have been observing what high and low EQ looks like in children. Regardless of the setting, my observations have been consistent.

A high EQ child is not afraid of constructive criticism or of taking risks.

Children with high EQ come across as more content, fulfilled, and optimistic. They accept themselves—both their weaknesses and their strengths. They are not afraid of either constructive criticism or taking risks. A high EQ child has little fear of speaking in front of the class or an assembly because he knows intrinsically that growth is good, nervousness is natural, and no matter what happens, he will survive the experience.

High EQ children have more friends because they know how to be a friend. They don't panic over tests because they are more organized when it comes to studying, completing projects, and doing their homework. Because they have a strong sense of self-esteem and self-confidence, the learning process is interesting, fun, and rewarding—rather than frustrating and overwhelming. They have learned to thrive on growth and success and to weather disappointments and failure.

Typical High EQ Characteristics

- Capable of picking up on Mom and Dad's emotions
- Inquisitive, curious, and anxious to learn new things
- Handles or responds to change in plans without falling apart
- Demonstrates high self-esteem and high self-confidence
- Keeps temper tantrums to a minimum
- Accepts who she is and feels comfortable with her strengths and weaknesses
- Knows how to be a friend
- Knows how to enjoy success and survive disappointment
- Not put off by the hard work needed to accomplish goals
- Has the confidence to take a risk
- Not offended by constructive criticism or overly thrown by a lack of success
- Takes responsibility for his own actions
- Takes the normal frustrations of life in stride

On the other hand, children with low EQ often let life's problems pull them down. Rather than stopping to think before taking action, they tend to overreact emotionally. They frequently come across as angry, sad, out of control, lonely, unmotivated, overly aggressive, or shy. They can be emotionally fragile, dependent, and needy and tend to fall apart when other children do not. They feel stuck when faced with change or disappointment and often whine, blame others, or come up with excuses when something goes wrong. Children with low EQ may exhibit poor sportsmanship and characteristically have few long-term friends.

Low EQ children often let life's problems pull them down.

Typical Low EQ Characteristics

- Lacks resilience when change or disappointment occurs
- Uses unhealthy behavior to get needs met (i.e., threats, temper tantrums, whining)
- Defensive: uses excuses or blames others when something goes wrong
- Doesn't make friends easily
- Not very motivated or focused
- Can be overly shy or overly aggressive (a bully)
- Self-absorbed, entitled, shows lack of empathy
- Lacking in self-discipline
- Often ignores social conventions and rules (i.e., interrupts conversations, disrupts in class, cuts into lines, disrespects property)
- Resistant to new experiences
- Exhibits poor sportsmanship

How Does IQ Relate To EQ?

Perhaps you're asking yourself, "If high EQ is going to make my child's life and mine so much better, what's the significance of IQ?" In his essay published in 1995, *Cracking Open the IQ Box,* Howard Gardner presented the latest research regarding the power and influence of IQ in predicting a person's success in life. His statistical research attributes 20% of success in life to IQ and the remaining 80% to other factors, of which EQ was found to be a primary contributor. What does this mean in terms of your child—and the man or woman he or she may grow up to be? Let's take a look at some high IQ, low EQ scenarios.

A man might be a world authority on political theory, but have few friends because he lacks social skills. A woman might give a brilliant speech on nanotechnology, but not be able to carry on a simple conversation with those who attend the reception following her presentation. A renowned professor might be able to explain complex theories of relatively to his students, but be unable to develop or maintain a meaningful relationship with a partner.

Knowing how to interact with people—how to empathize, how to listen, and how to share opinions, thoughts, and feelings—is the hallmark of high EQ individuals. It is also a life skill that we need in order to be happy and successful. People with high EQ can succeed even with an average IQ because their exceptional people skills make them highly valued co-workers, partners, friends, and parents.

Can A Child With High EQ Have A Bad Day? YES!

Jonathan's Story

Having a highly developed emotional intelligence doesn't mean your child will never be in a bad mood, yell at his sister, or get his feelings hurt. Everyone experiences moments of low EQ when they feel out of control or overreact emotionally, rather than considering both their feelings and their rational thoughts.

Let's take a look at Jonathan on one of his bad days. Jonathan is a seven-year-old who demonstrates a high EQ on a regular basis in response to life's difficulties. So on the day of Justin's fourth birthday party, Jason's younger brother, Mom and Dad were both surprised and disappointed with Jonathan's behavior throughout most of the day. Jonathan had been involved in the planning of Justin's party. He had not only helped to choose the theme and the decorations, but had also helped fill the party bags the day before the party. With a smile on his face, he told Justin four or five times how much fun the party was going to be. On the morning of the party, however, Jonathan started whining about a tummy ache and saying he couldn't get out of bed. Mom took his temp-erature and found that Jonathan wasn't running a fever. In fact, he didn't have any flu or stomach illness symptoms. When he asked in an "I think I'm going to die" voice if Mom could make him some pancakes and come read him a book, Mom looked at him like he had lost his mind. She reminded him that today was Justin's party and she could really use Jonathan's help blowing up balloons while she finished the cake. When Jonathan yelled back at his mom that he wouldn't blow up balloons, in fact, he wasn't even going to go to "Justin's stupid party," Mom was more shocked than ever. What happened to that sweet little boy who had been so helpful in the planning stages of his brother's party?

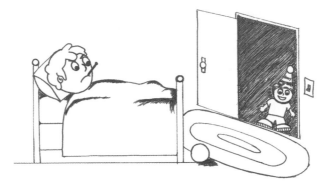

Even high EQ children have low EQ days.

I don't need to tell anyone with two children that Jonathan's temperament didn't improve as the day went along. Mom, Dad, and Jonathan had planned well for the party, but they had forgotten to plan for sibling envy on the party day. Jonathan knew how much attention Justin would get that day and how terrific all the presents would be from his friends and family. Just thinking about this made Jonathan jealous and upset. The more upset he got, the more his emotions overwhelmed his ability to think rationally. He simply wanted to wish the day away. And so it was a definite low EQ day for Jonathan!

Ideally, high EQ individuals like Jonathan balance their thinking brain (IQ) with their emotional brain (EQ). In other words, they can balance their emo-tional awareness of themselves and others with their knowledge and the ability to rationally process their thoughts. Their EQ acts as their compass, and their IQ steers them to make wise, informed decisions. On days like the one Jonathan was having, that compass can be temporarily malfunctioning.

When parents experience their child having a low EQ day, it is important to use it in the future as a wonderful teaching moment for the parent and a learning moment for the child. In Jonathan's case, it would be important for either Mom or Dad to follow up days later by exploring with Jonathan what he thought of his little brother's birthday. His parents would want to talk about what Jonathan thought happened that day to make him so grumpy, to ask him what he wished had happened that day, and if there is anything he might do differently next year on his little brother's birthday.

If Jonathan struggles to come up with an understanding of what happened or a future plan, his mom and dad can then make some suggestions and tell Jonathan they'll talk about it again before his brother's next birthday. In this way, his parents will begin to implement Jonathan's problem-solving skills.

How Does EQ Relate To Common Sense?

When I was first introduced to the term emotional intelligence, I found myself confusing it with common sense. I think it might be helpful to explain the difference.

Webster's dictionary defines common sense as "ordinary good sense or sound practical judgment." Emotional intelligence, on the other hand, is the ability to recognize and label what one is feeling at any given moment, and to make a reasonable guess about what others are feeling. Simply by labeling one's emotions a person actually feels a sense of control over those emotions. When you name your emotions, you own them instead of the emotions owning you! Once you have labeled and acknowledged your emotions, you are ready to access your common sense. Your EQ response comes into play first, and then your common sense follows.

IQ contributes to common sense. In order to make a sound practical judgment, people need to be able to access their cognitive brain so they can think through a problem. When a person has low EQ, his decisions are usually driven by whatever emotions arise in the moment. His emotions control him, and this rarely results in good practical judgment or common sense actions. People with high EQ on the other hand, are able to make sound practical judgments because (a) they recognize their own emotions and the emotions of others, (b) they consider how their emotions will affect them and others, and (c) they can balance their EQ and IQ to form an appropriate response to the situation.

Children with high EQ are able to remain calm in the face of a crisis because they have emotional self-knowledge and are in tune with the feelings of those around them. When difficult situations arise, they stop and think before responding with either words or actions. As a result, they are generally able to use their common sense to get through a tough emotional situation, as five-year-old Katie did.

Katie's Story

Katie and her mom shared this story with me about using EQ and common sense. They had worked on the skills in this book and thought I'd be thrilled to hear about the results of their efforts. They both reminded me that one of the Problem-Solving Skills exercises they had worked on the year before in my office involved devising a plan to keep them both from getting overwhelmed if they ever got separated in a large store.

So here's their story: Mom and Katie had gone into Target together. After about a half-hour, they became separated. Needless to say, Mom started to panic—a mother's worst nightmare! Katie told me she was scared, but she also knew that her mom was looking for her—because they had a plan. They had set up their plan when Katie was four years old, and it covered what they would do if they ever got separated in a large store. The plan was that Katie and Mom would both ask a store clerk where children go when they got lost.

Because of her high EQ, Katie was able to access her common sense and keep herself from panicking . She remembered the plan that she and her mom had talked about a year before and had reviewed on and off during the year. She told herself to look for a store clerk. She could tell who was a store clerk because they wore red vests and badges. She told me she kept reminding herself that her mom was looking for her, and that kept her from getting really scared.

Mom and Katie told me that when they met up in the store manager's office they gave each other a big hug. They also decided to come up with a new plan to avoid getting lost in the future.

This new plan will contribute to solving the problem of Katie being lost from her mother. One of the reasons this little girl was able to formulate such practical, common sense thoughts is because her emotions didn't erase her ability to think in what could normally be a panic situation. Someone with high EQ can draw upon his or her common sense at any given moment, in order to make a good decision or begin to problem-solve. Someone with low EQ would not be able to access her common sense because her overblown emotions would get in the way.

What Benefits Will Your Children Enjoy With A High EQ?

- They'll be able to <u>recognize their own emotions and talk about them</u>.

- They'll be able to <u>make better decisions based on a clearer understanding of their feelings</u>.

- They'll be able to <u>slow down their responses to emotional situations, rather than "flying off the handle."</u>

- They'll come to know that, <u>whatever the problem</u> they are dealing with at the moment, <u>there will be a solution</u>.
- They'll learn that, because there are always solutions to problems, <u>they won't feel bad forever.</u> In other words, they won't become hopeless.
- They'll learn to <u>deal positively with the inevitable disappointments</u> in life.
- They'll be better able to resolve conflicts with their parents, siblings, and friends because they will have learned to <u>consider the feelings of others</u> and <u>weigh the consequences</u> of their behavior.

ARE WE OR ARE WE NOT IN CONTROL OF OUR EMOTIONS? IN THE NEXT CHAPTER, WE'LL EXPLORE JUST HOW OUR EMOTIONS WORK.

-2-

HOW DO EMOTIONS WORK?

■ ■ ■

```
┌─────────────────────────────────────────────────┐
│                                                   │
│        What You Will Learn in This Chapter        │
│                                                   │
│  ❏ Emotions are physiological.                    │
│  ❏ There are several theories on how emotions work.│
│  ❏ There are basic emotions common to all human beings.│
│  ❏ How external stimuli produce our emotions.     │
│  ❏ A simplified explanation of what happens when we│
│     respond emotionally.                          │
│  ❏ Our brain seems to have two memory banks: one for│
│     emotions and one for factual information.     │
│                                                   │
└─────────────────────────────────────────────────┘
```

How Emotions Work

To help your child increase his EQ, it is important for you to have an understanding of how our emotions work. While we're not always aware of it, our emotions are essentially physiological. That is, they stem from a physical and psychological process that our bodies go through in response to every life situation. Emotions can be triggered by external stimuli perceived through our senses (sight, sound, touch, smell, and taste), by internal stimuli from our self-dialogue and thoughts, or by a combination of both.

Sometimes our emotions feel voluntary and sometimes they feel involuntary. Here's a familiar example of an involuntary type of emotional response: Your four-year-old son, Bobby, is quietly playing on the floor with his colorful Lego® building blocks. He is relaxed and content as he builds the tallest tower possible, and he feels proud of his accomplishment. Then out of the blue, your two-year-old son runs by the tower of blocks and knocks them down. Bobby's heart starts to race. He jumps up off the floor and starts chasing his little brother, yelling "Mom!!" As he pursues his brother through the house, Bobby is angry, upset, hurt, and frustrated, just to name a few of his emotions. His whole body is reacting emotionally, and he wants retribution now!

Emotions can be triggered by an unexpected external event.

This is just one example of emotions being triggered by an unexpected external event. Bobby was surprised by his little brother's action of knocking down the blocks and didn't plan for the immediate physical and emotional reactions that followed. His body went from relaxed to completely agitated in less than five seconds.

Here is a slightly different example: In this case, your daughter, Jennifer, is anticipating feeling apprehensive on the first day of kindergarten, so you have worked with her on and off throughout the summer to prepare her. You have walked her to school from your house, shown her where her classroom is, and talked to her about what kindergarten will be like. You've told her what to expect from the teacher and from her classmates, and what school activities she'll be doing. You've also talked with Jennifer about how she might feel on her first day of school. She knows you will take her there and pick her up right outside of her classroom when her school day is finished. You have planned something to do after school on the first day, so she will have something special to look forward to. You have even helped her pick out the clothes she wants to wear the first day.

So it was a complete surprise to both you and Jennifer when she started to cry at her classroom door and said she didn't want to go inside. As she grabbed on to your hand like a lifeline, you found yourself wondering, "What just happened? This day was supposed to be calm and smooth." You both experienced a swell of emotions you had planned so carefully to avoid.

In both of these examples, we can see that emotions can be complex and that an emotional response can occur even when we are prepared for a situation. This might give you some insight into why so many researchers can't agree on just one theory explaining how emotions work in our bodies and brains. Some theorists believe that our emotions are the result of external stimuli sending a message to our brain. Others contend that emotions are caused by our thoughts or internal stimuli. A third group of researchers believes the cognitive part of our brain interacts with the emotional part of our brain to produce our emotions. Still others believe that there is no interaction between the cognitive and emotional parts of the brain and that these two areas work independently of each other. The good news for parents is that you don't need to understand what the major researchers and theorists are struggling to understand in order to help increase your child's EQ. You only need to be willing to learn and understand the *8 Proven* Skills in this book. But before we get to those, we need to familiarize ourselves with the range of emotions we commonly experience.

To make our understanding even more complex, the leading researchers in emotional intelligence have not even agreed on a definition of emotions versus feelings. Six Seconds, a wonderful nonprofit organization dedicated to helping educate and inform the public on emotional intelligence, interviewed six EQ experts and published the interviews on their website EQ Today (www.eqtoday.com). Each of the experts was asked identical questions, one of which was, "What is the difference between emotions and feelings?" I thoroughly enjoyed Maurice Elias' answer. He is the co-author of Emotionally Intelligent Parents. He said, "I have no idea, and you can quote me!" Thank you, Maurice Elias. I just did! In this book, I am going to use emotions and feelings interchangeably.

A Wide Spectrum Of Emotions

It is important for all of us to be aware of our own emotions. This means recognizing them and being able to label, validate, and acknowledge them. Some emotions are so intense that there is no way you can miss or misread them. Others are subtle and may exist in the background of our experiences. Researchers all agree about one thing: we are always experiencing emotions.

For example, as you sit reading this book, you are experiencing at least three or four emotions at once. You may not be aware of them because they are not as intense as those described in earlier examples. However, you might be feeling:

- curious
- concerned
- hopeful
- encouraged

Think for a moment of a child's kaleidoscope, with its hundreds of small pieces continuously turning and forming new patterns. Each of us has hundreds of emotions that are continuously felt in our bodies, and they constantly change whether we are aware of the process or not.

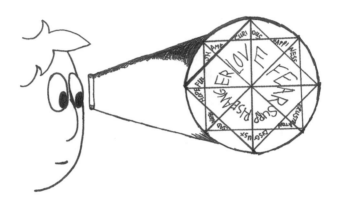

Our emotions are continuously changing like small pieces in a kaleidoscope.

Although top researchers in this field disagree as to a definitive list of primary emotions, Daniel Goleman lists in his book what he considers to be the eight main categories of emotions:

- Anger
- Fear
- Shame
- Disgust
- Sadness
- Love
- Enjoyment
- Surprise

Just as secondary colors build on primary colors, Goleman believes that all other emotions, of which there are hundreds, can be categorized under these eight primary ones.

Paul Ekman, head of the Human Interaction Laboratory at the University of California, San Francisco, has also done extensive research on facial expressions as they relate to emotions. He lists four basic emotions (fear, anger, sadness, and enjoyment) that he believes are common to all people across every culture throughout the world. To come up with this finding, he and his research group studied diverse populations, including primitive people who had no access to TV, movies, or other modern day influences. His research tells us that certain core emotions are not taught; rather, they are part of our shared human condition.

> What is your child's response when he notices a dog playing nearby at the park? Perhaps his heart starts pounding. He may experience anything from excitement to surprise to fear to panic, and his body reacts by jumping up, freezing where he is, perhaps running towards or away from the dog.

Our Body's 4-Step Response Process To Our Emotions

The following is a simplified explanation of what the various researchers in the field generally agree happens as we emotionally respond to life. When emotions occur, our bodies go through a 4-Step Process that involves three distinct parts of the brain—the *thalamus*, the *amygdala*, and the *neocortex*.

Our Body's 4-Step Emotional Response

1. One or more of our senses (smelling, seeing, hearing, touching, and tasting) transmits information to a part of our brain called the thalamus.

2. The *thalamus* passes the transmitted information to two other parts of our brain, the amygdala that receives it first and the neocortex that receives the transmitted information milliseconds later.

3. Our *amygdala*, which is part of the limbic system, reacts with emotions to the information sent by the thalamus.

4. Our *neocortex* pulls up reference information that relates to the message sent by the thalamus.

Let's Look At These 4 Steps In A Little More Detail

Step #1

The thalamus continuously receives information from our five senses. For example, a child is playing at the park. He sees a dog. The information, "I see a dog," is sent from the vision sense to the thalamus.

Our thalamus continually receives information from our five senses.

Step #2

The thalamus then acts as a 9-1-1 dispatcher and sends on the information, "I see a dog," to both the amygdala and the neocortex. It is a shorter route (by milliseconds) to the amygdala than to the neocortex, so the information arrives at the amygdala first. As it turns out, this delay proves to be extremely important.

Some messages received and sent to the amygdala produce little reaction. In fact, we don't even notice them. Other messages received by the thalamus and sent on to the amygdala have such an intense reaction that we feel it throughout our whole body. The amygdala and the neocortex react differently to the information they receive.

Step #3

The amygdala acts as our "emotional hard drive." It holds all the emotions we have ever experienced and the intensity of those emotions, but it doesn't include specific information about the events that triggered each emotion. In this case, the amygdala would hold all emotions about dogs that your child has ever experienced, as well as all emotions about every other experience your child has ever had that produced similar emotions. The amygdala doesn't decipher fear, anger, or joy over a dog-related situation he had in kindergarten from fear, anger, or joy over a non-dog related situation he had in third grade. To the amygdala, fear is fear, anger is anger, joy is joy, and these emotional experiences are all equally weighted. There is no chronology of emotions in the amygdala.

The amygdala provides our initial *whoosh* of emotion. This unfiltered emotional response is based on the amygdala's data bank of past emotional experiences. Research has shown that it is the amygdala that produces the "fight or flight" response that we share when facing a dangerous or threatening situation.

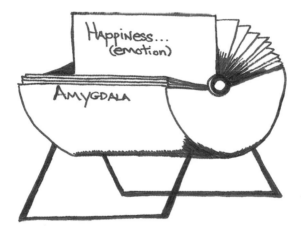

**Our amygdala holds all of the emotions we have ever experienced
and can pull them up at any time.**

Step #4

Milliseconds after the amygdala receives the message, "I see a dog," from the thalamus, the neocortex receives the same message. If the amygdala is our "emotional hard drive," the neocortex is our "informational hard drive." The neocortex is the holder of all the information we have that relates to a particular subject. In our example of the child responding to seeing a dog at the park, the neocortex would recognize dog, then pull up all the information the child has about dogs; for example, what to expect from a dog when it is growling, playing, eating, or barking. Such information helps the child make a more rational decision that considers the possible consequences of his actions. For instance, "Should I stay and continue to play near the dog, or should I run to a parent for protection?" Or, "Are dogs friendly? Can they be dangerous? Are there visible signs of danger or friendliness I should be looking for in a dog?"

In a real sense, our brain has two different memory banks. One holds all our emotional experiences and the other holds all of our factual information. Our emotional data bank defines our emotions, while our informational data bank helps us sort out a variety of information in order to make rational decisions. Research shows that the best decisions come from a harmony between our emotional brain and our cognitive brain—in other words from a balance between our EQ and our IQ.

Helping your child develop emotional intelligence involves helping her to recognize her emotions and to make sure that her rational brain guides her decision making process. As you will see in the following chapters, this combination of thinking and feeling holds the key to a healthy EQ.

HAVE YOU EVER MADE A DECISION BASED ON AN IRRATIONAL THOUGHT? IN THE NEXT CHAPTER, YOU WILL DISCOVER JUST HOW POWERFUL OUR THOUGHTS CAN BE.

-3-

CAN THOUGHTS PRODUCE EMOTIONS?

■ ■ ■

<u>What You Will Learn in This Chapter</u>

❑ How our thoughts can produce emotions.

❑ How important *self-talk* is.

❑ The power of our perceptions.

❑ The power and influence of our thoughts—both rational and irrational.

❑ Our perception becomes our belief, and our belief creates our reality.

Can Thoughts Produce Emotions?

The simple answer is **yes!** As you think about your child's EQ, it is important to understand the relationship between her thoughts and her emotions. In the last chapter, we talked about how emotions are a response to both internal and external stimuli and we considered examples of how a child responds emotionally to external stimuli, such as a dog playing nearby in the park.

Again with thoughts, the thalamus acts as a 9-1-1 dispatcher, forwards the message received from your child's thoughts to both the amygdala and the neocortex. Since the amygdala is closer to the thalamus, it produces an immediate emotional response. The neocortex receives the same information milliseconds later and begins to pull up the factual information about the thought. In the next step, the neocortex, with the emotional help from the amygdala, thinks about the information it has and comes to a decision concerning the original message it received and the consequences of different actions that could be taken.

Thoughts -> Emotional Response

Human beings talk to themselves on a regular basis. We talk to ourselves about how we look and feel every morning. We talk to ourselves about the other drivers on the freeway or the other commuters we observe on the subway, train, or bus. We talk to ourselves about our work, our co-workers, our children, and our spouses—the list goes on and on. This ongoing dialogue is what I refer to as *self-talk*. Self-talk is what creates our thoughts.

Michelle's Story

Take for example the case of Michelle, an eleven-month-old. She is happily playing on the family room floor with her toys, while Mom is within sight preparing dinner in the kitchen. Mom hears the buzzer go off in the laundry room and leaves to get the clothes out of the dryer. Michelle looks up and doesn't see her mom. She panics and starts to cry. What happened?

Michelle's awareness is the early stage of self-talk.

Even though Michelle isn't yet aware of her self-talk, she noticed Mom was no longer in the kitchen, and in her own way said to herself, "Where's Mom? I'm alone! I'm scared!" Michelle's thoughts caused her emotional response, and she began to cry.

Mom runs back into the family room expecting to see Michelle hurt, and to her surprise, her daughter is just sitting there crying. Mom realizes that Michelle noticed she was gone and became frightened, so she picks Michelle up and soothes her with a calm reassuring voice. Then she puts a reassured Michelle back on the floor and life goes back to normal.

Mom is a little confused, though, because just a week ago, she could go into the laundry room and come right back without her daughter having such an intense reaction. What Mom is unaware of is that little Michelle is beginning to connect emotional patterns, such as, "I feel good when Mom is in the room, and I don't feel good when I am alone." This is the beginning of self-talk.

Vincent's Story

Another example of how self-talk produces emotions is the case of six-year-old Vincent, who patiently waited an hour for his father to come home from work play catch with him in the front yard. This father-son playtime had become a pattern in Vincent's life over the last couple of weeks. On this partic-ular evening, though, Dad had a bad day at work and just wanted to come home, change his clothes, and relax. Or perhaps he wanted to share his bad day with his wife if the house was calm enough. When Vincent ran up to Dad before he was barely out of the car and said, "Here's your mitt , Daddy. Let's play catch," Dad responded with, "I'm sorry Vincent, not tonight. Daddy's really tired." Dad was polite as he offered an explanation about why he wasn't going to play to-night. Still, the outcome of Vincent's evening was determined by his own follow up self-talk.

Here are several different self-talk possibilities for Vincent, along with the actions that might follow:

#1: "Wow, my dad's really tired. I hope he's not sick. He'll probably play with me tomorrow. I'm really disappointed, but I know Daddy usually likes to play with me, so he must be having a really bad day. I guess I'll play something else." Vince gets on his Razor® and rides around his driveway.

#2: "Why isn't Daddy playing catch with me? I'm really mad. I waited for an hour to play. It's not fair! I'm really mad." Vincent goes into the house, slams the door, goes into his room, and throws his toys around.

#3: "My dad must be really mad at me if he doesn't want to play with me. I wonder what I did wrong. Maybe he thinks I'm a really bad catcher. Maybe I'm terrible at baseball and he won't ever want to play with me again." Vincent starts to panic and his self-esteem is shaken.

All the above perceptions, as seen in Vincent's self-talk, are possible from a six-year-old. At that age, children feel their emotions and begin to self-talk. Sometimes the self-talk is positive, and sometimes it's negative.

So, what happened between Vincent and his dad? In this case, Dad did everything right. He was tired, and after a bad day at work he needed to take care of his own emotional needs. What Dad had to do later that evening was to check in, one-on-one, with Vincent to see if he understood why they hadn't played catch earlier that afternoon. It was important for Dad to spend five or ten minutes exploring Vincent's perception of what happened earlier. Because Vincent's mom and dad had taken one of my seminars, Dad knew how to interact with his six-year-old when a situation created an unexpected disappointment.

Later that evening, Dad discovered that Vincent believed Dad didn't think he was any good at baseball. He was scared that Dad wasn't going to play baseball with him again. In a one-on-one talk with Vincent, his dad was able to help change his young son's understanding of what had happened, and they set up a time to practice catch later that week. Dad and Vincent also talked about feelings.

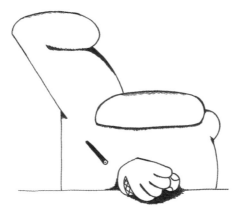

**It is important to explore our children's
perceptions of their negative experiences.**

Sensing that his son was disappointed and hurt, Dad asked Vincent to always talk to him when he feels hurt by anything Dad says. By encouraging his son to talk about his feelings—and by explaining his own feelings to his son—this dad is paving the way for his son's high EQ.

Thoughts And Perceptions

Have you ever noticed how you silently talk to yourself? Our thoughts come from an internal dialogue, which goes on within each of us throughout the day. Self-talk is a normal process, and it's how our thoughts are created.

When we have an experience and have had the time to think about it afterward, what we tell ourselves about that experience—our self-talk or thoughts—creates our *perception*. A perception is an understanding or an awareness, which we reach after thinking about something. This is how we form an idea. Have you ever had the experience of working yourself up into an intense emotional state as a result of your self-talk? Or, on the other hand, have you ever been aware of talking yourself out of a heightened emotional state?

Our internal dialogue plays an extremely powerful role in producing our emotions. The challenge for our children, and for us, is to be able to tell whether we are sending our brains rational or irrational thoughts. When our children are upset, how can we help them to understand what they're feeling and to then respond appropriately? It is best to start by helping them to explore their perceptions of the event, situation, or person that produced the upset. Next, you can help them move beyond their initial negative emotional response to a more rational perspective. This will then lead to constructive problem-solving.

As you begin to explore how your child's thoughts produce emotions, a word of caution: don't expect their perceptions to be as sophisticated as yours. Their ability to process their thoughts into wise perceptions is naturally limited by their age and life experiences.

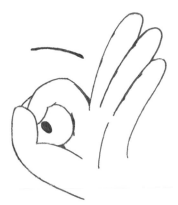

Children have a limited understanding and knowledge of how the world works.

Do you want to gain an immediate sense of how your child's perceptions differ from yours? Try this experiment (as shown above): Curl your pointer finger and your thumb into a circle and then look through them while closing your other eye. Your vision is narrowed when looking through this small circle, right? This gives you some sense of the limited understanding and knowledge our children have. That circle expands as they grow, so be patient.

Matt's Story

Six-year-old Matt came home from school one day and told his mom that he hated Johnny because Johnny was mean to him. In fact, Johnny and Matt had never even talked to each other, but Matt had convinced himself that Johnny was mean because he had never talked to Matt. Matt thus felt angry and hurt. After careful questioning and sensitive listening, Matt's mom discovered that because Matt and Johnny had not yet played together, Matt believed Johnny didn't like him. Matt's perception, while not based on the facts, produced intense negative feelings.

> **Perception -> Belief -> Reality**

Matt and his mom talked about some things that Matt could do with Johnny at school the following day. They decided that Matt would bring a ball to school and invite Johnny to play with him.

The next afternoon, Matt came home with a big smile on his face. He announced to his mom that Johnny was his new best friend—they had laughed and played ball together before school and at recess. Matt's story shows how powerful our thoughts can be. When Matt thought Johnny didn't like him because he didn't play with him, he hated Johnny. Then Matt problem-solved with his mom and asked Johnny to play with him. When Johnny accepted, Matt's perception—and emotions—changed.

Matt's mother knew enough to understand the limits of her six-year-old son's perceptions and was able to decipher how his internal thoughts produced a negative emotional response. She then helped him transform that negative response into a positive one. Let's take a look at what happened

Rational And Irrational Perceptions

Just like Matt, your child's thoughts can produce either rational or irrational perceptions, which then go on to produce either rational or irrational beliefs. A belief is anything believed or accepted as true, even though there may be an absence of any evidence. When a child's perceptions result in rational beliefs, he will likely go on to make rational decisions. Rational beliefs produce an emotional response, but one that is reasonable or appropriate.

On the other hand, when your child's thoughts, perceptions, and beliefs are irrational, they can often result in an emotional response of anger, hurt, resentment, guilt, shame, anxiety, and depression. Irrational beliefs can cause your children to head down a bumpier life path and to make decisions that are not in their best interests.

The good news is that even young children, with our help, have the power to change their irrational thoughts into rational ones—and to feel much better in the process. Throughout this book you'll learn how to teach your child to think in a healthy way so, rather than being defeated by their self-talk, they can be encouraged, challenged, and inspired by their own thoughts.

> HAS YOUR CHILD EVER SHARED A THOUGHT OR IDEA WITH YOU, AFTER
> WHICH YOU FOUND YOURSELF WONDERING, "WHAT ARE YOU
> THINKING?" OR "WHERE DID THAT COME FROM?" IN THE NEXT
> CHAPTER, YOU WILL LEARN THE SIGNIFICANCE OF IRRATIONAL BELIEFS
> AND HOW TO CHANGE THEM.

-4-

CAN IRRATIONAL BELIEFS INHIBIT YOUR CHILD'S EQ?

What You Will Learn in This Chapter

❏ How irrational beliefs can become part of your child's belief system.

❏ Examples of children's irrational beliefs.

❏ What an unconscious belief is and how it affects your child.

❏ The difference between "must" beliefs and "preferred" beliefs.

❏ Simple ways to change "must" beliefs.

Can Irrational Beliefs Inhibit Your Child's EQ?

In the last chapter, we learned that thoughts produce emotions—and also that thoughts produce perceptions which in turn solidify into beliefs. In this chapter, we are going to consider the role that your child's irrational beliefs can play and how these can inhibit his emotional intelligence. Once we're aware of how this process works, we can help our children avoid this life-narrowing trap.

Your child—like all of us—makes decisions based on her beliefs. She also praises or criticizes herself based on those beliefs. In other words, her successes and failures are measured according to her particular beliefs. But...

What If Your Child's Beliefs Are Wrong?

What if your son's or daughter's belief is built on an irrational thought, which is inhibiting them from putting forth his or her best effort, from making new friends or from enjoying life to its fullest? Unfortunately, this happens all the time, even to bright, high EQ children. Their perceptions are not based on any concrete evidence; perhaps there is not even logical, but somehow they end up in their belief systems as a truth.

Allana's Story

Take the example of Allana, an eight-year-old girl, who refused to go on a camping trip with her family to Yellowstone National Park. Allana's family had been planning their trip for six months. They planned to travel with two other families whom they had known for years, but as the time drew closer to leaving, Allana started crying and yelling that she wasn't going with them. In fact, Allana, who normally displayed a high EQ, told her mom and dad she would call Grandma and ask if she could stay with her during the two weeks her family would be on vacation. Allana's mom and dad were baffled. They had always camped once or twice a year with Allana and her younger brother. They could not figure out what was wrong.

In desperation, they called me and set up an appointment. I explored the family's experience with camping and spent the session trying to hear anything that might explain Allana's resistance to the upcoming family vacation. At the end of the session with the parents, we decided to set up a session with just Allana and me. Her mom and dad were to come in for the first five minutes of the session with Allana. During that time, they encouraged Allana to share with me her reasons for not wanting to go camping with them.

When Allana and I were alone, I asked her to tell me about her previous camping experiences. She talked about them positively. She had had fun and she would go camping to those other places again. The more we talked, I began to realize her resistance was not about camping in general; it was about camping in Yellowstone National Park. The more we explored what she knew about Yellowstone, I discovered some very interesting information. It turned out that Allana hadn't known much about Yellowstone Park until she was at her friend Sarah's house two months earlier. While she and Sarah were in the kitchen having a snack, Sarah's thirteen-year-old brother, Kevin, came in and overheard Allana talking about camping at Yellowstone with her family and friends. The thirteen-year-old brother jumped into the conversation and, from what I could tell, had great fun scaring Allana with gruesome stories about whole families being eaten by bears as they slept in their tents at Yellowstone. He even added that if the bears weren't too hungry, they only ate the little girls and left the parents and boys alone. As more and more stories unraveled, it was easy to understand why Allana was resistant to the camping trip. She believed that if she went to Yellowstone a bear would eat her.

Mom and Dad's challenge was clear: they needed to convince Allana that she and her family would be safe. They started with the thirteen-year-old, who was told by his parents to explain to Allana he had made up all the stories he told her. He told her that he was just having fun with her, just like telling her ghost stories. In the end, Allana's fears were quelled and she joined her family for the two-week vacation.

I met with Allana after they returned to check in with her. Allana told me she had a good time, but she would never go back. Although her parents had explained to her that no families had ever been eaten by bears at Yellowstone Park, Allana still felt nervous about the bears at this particular location.

As with Allana, even after a parent has helped a child change an irrational belief (Bears will eat me in Yellowstone) to a rational one (My parents know what to do to keep me safe in Yellowstone), the child often has lingering emotions that accompanied the irrational belief.

Have You Ever Jumped To A Conclusion?

Have you ever jumped to a conclusion about somebody or something without all the information and later realized that you had jumped to the wrong conclusion? A person with high EQ has learned to slow down the thought process before it runs wild. They have the ability to explore whatever emotions arise from a given situation, consider if those emotions are based on rational thoughts, and then respond accordingly. As parents, we can help our children through this "slowing down" process to make sure that their negative self-talk doesn't turn into negative beliefs about their ability to deal with the world.

We learned from Matt, the six-year-old boy in Chapter Three, that when he changed his thought from "Johnny is mean" to "I'll ask Johnny to play with me," he changed his emotional response from anger and hurt ("I hate Johnny") to happiness and contentment ("Johnny's my new best friend").

Everyone engages in self-talk, and, as a parent, it's important to become aware of the ways your child might be developing beliefs based on his own self-talk. Whenever I ask a young child in my office what they are thinking about, I am always amazed at the beliefs they share with me.

Andrew's Story

For instance, Andrew's father brought four-year-old Andrew into my office because Andrew had refused to go to his dad's house anymore. He would cry every time his dad came to pick him up. Both Dad and Mom were confused at what was happening with Andrew. They had been divorced since Andrew was a year-old, and every other weekend and Tuesday night since then Andrew had slept at his dad's house. So neither parent could figure out why Andrew was refusing to go to Dad's house now.

I met with Andrew's dad to get a history of his relationship with his son. I explored with Dad any changes that had happened recently or were about to happen. The biggest one that Dad could think of was his upcoming marriage, but Andrew was going to be part of the ceremony and seemed excited about it. Andrew also seemed to have a good relationship with Darlene, his father's fiancée.

I explored further for any changes in the family. I asked the dad about Andrew's bedtime routine. Dad said that for years he simply put Andrew to sleep in his bed and then some nights moved Andrew to his own bed, but more often than not Andrew would sleep through the night with his dad. I asked what was going to happen after the marriage and was informed that Darlene had moved in three weeks ago, and was sleeping in bed with him. When I asked how this changed Andrew's bedtime routine, Dad said that he was now putting Andrew to bed in his own bed. Andrew's room was just down the hallway from his. Dad didn't think this was the problem.

Dad and Andrew came up with a plan to make them both feel good.

We set up an appointment for me to meet with Andrew. Dad sat with Andrew for the first five minutes. Dad looked at Andrew and said that he had talked to me and that he trusted me. Dad asked Andrew to please talk to Eileen [that's me] about what was making him so sad about coming to his house.

When Andrew and I started to talk, I asked him questions about his mom and dad: what he likes best about them, what activities he liked to do with them. He answered that what he liked best was when they laughed and giggled together. Then I asked him about Darlene. He said he liked her and that she was really nice, but his whole body language changed. So this was where I would find the answer! I then asked Andrew to share with me how things were different since Darlene moved into his daddy's house. Our conversation went like this:

Andrew: My daddy doesn't love me as much as he used to.

Eileen: Wow, I bet that really hurts your feelings.

Andrew: Yes, that makes me really sad.

Eileen: Really sad. I think I'd be mad too!

Andrew: I am sad and mad and I don't want to go over to my dad's anymore because it makes me feel really bad.

Eileen: Andrew, what made you figure out that your dad doesn't love you as much anymore?

Andrew: Because Darlene sleeps in his bed now and I don't anymore.

Eileen: When you used to sleep with your dad in his big bed, you knew he loved you and now that you don't, you know he doesn't love you as much?

Andrew: He loves Darlene more than he loves me. That really makes me sad because I love my dad the same!

Eileen: Your dad told me he really really loves you a whole lot! Could we bring him in my office and tell him you don't think he loves you as much as he used to because he makes you sleep in your own room instead of his big bed?

Andrew: No, because I don't want to make him mad at me.

Eileen: Well, I don't think he'll be mad at you because he asked me to help figure out what makes you so sad; but you know what? We don't need to bring him in right now.

Andrew: (Sigh of relief.)

Eileen: Andrew, do you love anyone besides your daddy?

Andrew: Yes. I love my mom, my grandma Mary and my grandpa Joe and my Nonie and Papa. Oh yeah, my dog, Harley.

Eileen: Wow, so you love a lot of people.

Andrew: Yes.

Eileen: Do you love your mom more than your dad?

Andrew: No, I love them the same.

Eileen: So, you can love two people the same. Do you love your grandmas more than your grandpas?

Andrew: No, I love them the same.

Eileen: So, a person can love lots of people the same. You love lots of people the same. Especially your mom and dad?

Andrew: Yes.

Eileen: Do you think it's possible that your daddy still loves you the same and now loves Darlene too?

Andrew: I guess.

Eileen: Do you think maybe your daddy thought you might want to sleep in your own bed because you just turned four, and four years old is pretty old? And lots and lots of four-year-olds like to sleep in their own bed in their own room?

Andrew: I guess.

Eileen: I'm wondering if your daddy had any idea that he hurt your feelings by having you sleep in your own bed. I have a feeling your daddy didn't mean to hurt your feelings and that he's going to feel bad when he finds out. I bet this has been a big misunderstanding and that your dad loves you as much as ever and will always love you as much as ever.

Andrew: Maybe.

Eileen: I think we should ask him in my office, and why don't I do the talking.

Andrew: Okay.

Four-year-olds are great! They have so much four-year-old wisdom and logic. They talk to themselves all the time and come up with their own logical conclusions. They then buy into their own wisdom because they believe they are right. They rarely check out their conclusion; they just accept it.

Andrew's story went on to have a happy ending because he succeeded in changing his <u>irrational thought</u>:

> "Daddy doesn't love me as much anymore because he doesn't want me to sleep in his bed."

to a <u>rational thought</u>:

> "My daddy loves me as much as ever. He just thought because I'm four now I would want to sleep in my own big boy bed."

Dad and Andrew came up with a good plan to make them both feel okay through the transition of Darlene moving in and marrying Dad. Dad and Andrew decided that Andrew would sleep in his own "big boy bed" when he was at his dad's, but he would start out in Dad's big bed like always. Later in the evening, Dad would move him to his own bedroom.

They put that plan into effect about six months ago. Dad checks in with me every couple of months and it seems like all is going well. Dad and Mom have both learned to look for irrational beliefs when there is an obvious change in Andrew's behavior.

When You Need To Play Detective

In this case, a child who normally exhibited a high EQ for a four-year-old was reacting with low EQ in this particular situation because of an irrational belief ("My daddy doesn't love me as much anymore") that he had convinced himself was true. There will be times when parents need to step into the role of a detective to get at the root cause of an irrational belief—namely, his father's decision to not allow him in his bed any longer.

When you find yourself needing to step into this role of a detective, follow these simple guidelines:

1. Begin your role as a detective with an open mind so you will be able to listen to your child without any preconceived ideas.

2. Ask exploring questions. These usually begin with: "What do you think...?", "How does it...?", or "When do you...?"

3. Avoid interrogation questions. These usually begin with: "WHY are you...?", or "WHY do you...?"

What might be another example of a common irrational belief? One need not be an ace detective to figure out that two- or three-year-olds reacting to a new baby in their house might hold the irrational belief that Mom or Dad doesn't love them as much as the new baby. Cognitively, two- or three-year-olds derive their thoughts from their feelings. If a situation feels good or bad, their thoughts about it are directly affected. For example, a three-year-old who has always had Mom or Dad's undivided attention may want to like their new little brother, but may feel left out and lonely every time Mom feeds the baby. Feeling sad and left out may start them on the pathway of believing that "Mom loves the baby more than me because she spends so much time with him," or "Mom must love him more than me because otherwise I wouldn't feel so bad when she's holding him."

A three-year-old's worried, sad, and angry feelings about being displaced by a new baby in the house can sometimes lead to an escalation of irrational thoughts from "Mom loves the baby more than me," to "I hate the baby." We know the kind of behavior that might follow. This is one of those irrational beliefs that new parents want to watch for so they can help change their young child's perspective as soon as possible. When parents don't take action with this particular irrational belief, it can cause some intense, even ugly, sibling rivalry. Having the kind of conversation I had with Andrew, in which the older sister or brother can talk about his or her feelings about the new baby, is the most direct way to nip this irrational belief in the bud.

"Mom loves the baby more than me because she spends so much time with him."

What Is An Unconscious Belief?

To make things just a little more complicated, most research tells us that all human beings have various levels of consciousness, ranging from conscious to unconscious. Webster's Dictionary defines *the unconscious* as "the sum of all thoughts, memories, impulses, desires, and feelings, of which the individual is not conscious, but which influences their emotions and behaviors."

Remember in Chapter Three we learned that our thoughts create our perceptions. Our perceptions then become our beliefs. Our beliefs produce our reality. It is no different in the world of our unconscious. Our unconscious thoughts create unconscious perceptions, which in turn become unconscious beliefs that are incredibly influential in our conscious reality although we are not even aware that these beliefs exist.

Most of our self-talk goes on at our conscious level. That is, we are aware of what we are saying to ourselves, whether we are decision-making, problem-solving, or debating both sides of a question. Often, however, our insights are the result of a blending of conscious and unconscious thoughts. Those unconscious thoughts—many of which grow into unconscious beliefs—may have been stored in our minds for decades. A number of them may be irrational.

Dr. T. Berry Brazelton, a well-known author and pediatrician, has done extensive research on newborn infants and found that they begin to input their observations of the world from birth. It is fascinating to watch a newborn infant look around and begin to use his senses to develop an awareness of the world. While the newborn lacks the cognitive ability to engage in self-talk, he is actively engaged in storing information. In other words, he is inputting into his memory feelings, experiences, and responses to people and to the environment around him.

As the infant grows, he continues to input observable and sensory information into all levels of his consciousness, especially into his unconscious. In fact, an infant begins to form life beliefs based on this information at a very young age. For example, based on his experience of interacting with the people in his immediate world, an infant might form such beliefs as "If I cry, someone will pick me up, change my diaper, or feed me." Or, "When my big brother picks me up, he smiles, and I feel good." Or, "When my Uncle Al picks me up, it feels rough—and I don't like how it feels." Or, "When my dog licks my face, it tickles and makes me laugh."

As an infant grows, he continues to input observable and sensory information.

Rudolf Driekurs, a well-known psychologist from the 1950s, once said in his book, <u>Children: The Challenge</u>, **"Children are great perceivers of emotions, but poor interpreters."** As a family therapist, I have observed over and over again the truth of this statement. Almost from birth, children can feel happiness, love, and safety (security). They can also feel the stress, tension, and anger in their home. They sense such emotion and take it in, but they don't understand it. The emotion doesn't evaporate. It's stored in their amygdala. If the emotion they're holding onto is the stress they've experienced in their family, and if that family stress continues, a very young child can become filled with anxiety—even clinically depressed. They may not be aware of the stress in their family, but they develop an unconscious belief that families can cause unhappiness and stress. They may even avoid marrying and having their own children later in life because they want to avoid the stress and anxiety they associate with family.

As we continue to grow, we are constantly inputting observable inform-ation—our perceptions, reactions, memories, learned behaviors, desires, and feelings—into our unconscious. A young child inputs how her mom mothers, how her dad fathers, how her mom and dad treat each other, and how her family communicates, disagrees, and plays together. Young children often input information about their family's way of doing things, as if it's the only correct way.

Perhaps your child has come home after having dinner at a friend's house and said something like, "At Mike's house they leave the TV on while they eat." Or "Mike's mom and dad didn't sit with us when we ate dinner." The implication is that, from your child's perspective, Mike's family doesn't have dinner the right way because it's not the way your family does it. Until they're about eight to ten years old, children often believe the way things are done at their house is the way things are done everywhere—and, of course, it's the right way. (Then by age thirteen, often nothing's right at our house!! But that's the next book). The point is that the unconscious part of your child's brain is always active and exerting a powerful influence on his thoughts.

"Dad, at Mike's house they leave the TV on while they eat."

How Can You Recognize Your Child's Irrational Beliefs?

One of our primary jobs as parents is to help our children identify and rethink their irrational beliefs. One surefire way of recognizing an irrational belief, either in ourselves or in our children, is if we hear a statement with the words "MUST", "SHOULD", or "HAVE TO". For example: "I should not ask for help....", "I have to get invited to Sarah's Party....", "I must get an 'A' on my math test....", or "Mom has to kiss me goodnight every night....".
Whenever a person says, "I must", it is always followed with an irrational belief. For instance:

- "I must have that toy, and if Mom doesn't buy it for me, I will be miserable forever."

- "I have to get invited to Sarah's party because otherwise everyone will think I'm an unpopular nerd."

- "Mom has to kiss me goodnight every night or it means she doesn't love me."

What Is Wrong With The Word "Must"?

The word "must" in anyone's belief system represents *Absolute Thinking*. Absolute Thinking declares that what I am saying must happen, and if it doesn't, my world will not be okay. When these words are a part of anyone's core belief system, they set up the person for disappointment.

There are three types of *MUST BELIEFS*—and holding any one of them is certain to result in frustration, regret, and dissatisfaction.

The "I must..." Belief:

- "I must be held by Mom as long as she holds the baby, and if I'm not, it means she loves the baby more."

- "I must make the team, and if I don't, my life will be miserable and everyone will call me a loser."

- "I must get invited to Sarah's party, and if I don't, no one will like me and I won't have any friends."

- "I must get that new toy, and if I don't get it, my life will be unbearable."

When a child holds an "I must..." belief, she sets herself up to fail because the word 'must' is an absolute, and there are no absolutes in the universe or they would already be happening. The child is guaranteed to be let down. When she experiences the let down, she views it as a failure. An "I must..." belief sets a child up emotionally to feel embarrassed, ashamed, disrespected, hurt, less than, not good enough, and guilty—rather than valuable.

The "You must..." Belief:

- "You must praise me for everything I do well, and if you don't, you don't love me and I will be hurt and angry."

- "You must read me a book and kiss me every night before I go to sleep, and if you don't, it means you don't love me and I will be angry and hurt."

- "You must buy me the toy I want, and if you don't, it means you don't like me and I will be angry and resentful."

- "You must spend as much time with me as you do with the baby, and if you don't, it means you love the baby more and I will feel angry and resentful and hurt."

A "You must..." belief requires that someone else live up to your expectations, and if they don't, it is a perceived failure for you. A "You must..." belief sets you up emotionally to feel anger, hurt, and resentment towards the person who did not meet your expectations.

The "Life must..." Belief:

- "'Life must treat me fairly, and when it doesn't, I can't bear it."

- "Life must turn out the way I want it to, and if it doesn't, it will be too painful."

- "Life must be happy all the time because I hate to feel bad, and if it isn't happy, I will do whatever I can to avoid the feel bad feelings."

If children are doomed to be disappointed by the "I must..." or the "You must..." beliefs, the "Life must..." beliefs are devastating. Life will do what life will do. A "Life must..." belief sets a person up emotionally to want to avoid the pain of being let down by life. Children with this belief are afraid to try new things for fear of failing. Teenagers with "Life must..." beliefs will often use drugs or alcohol to avoid the perceived pain of life not being fair. As adults, "Life must..." beliefs often cause Clinical Depression.

One of the most valuable gifts that we can give our children is to help them identify their "must" beliefs and transform them into hopes, plans, and goals. In this way, we'll be helping them plan for a fulfilling future rather than a disappointing one.

Flexible Thinking = A Healthy Emotional Response = High EQ

Children with high EQ have learned to stop and think about what they are saying to themselves. They have learned to avoid *Absolute Thinking* and to replace it with *Flexible Thinking*. A high EQ child knows she can change her way of thinking—and in so doing, can change her emotional outlook on life.

Children with high EQ learn to stop and think about what they are saying to themselves.

WHAT WE PERCEIVE -> WE BELIEVE ->
WHAT WE BELIEVE -> BECOMES OUR REALITY

One simple way to change irrational absolute thinking into rational thinking is to change the word "MUST" to the word "PREFER". When we help our children to do this, we help them change the belief that's sent to their brain, as well as the emotional response they'll have toward that belief. Here's how this life-changing process works:

MUST BELIEFS/ ABSOLUTE THINKING	Vs.	PREFERRED BELIEFS/ FLEXIBLE THINKING
#1. "I must be invited to Sarah's party, and if I'm not my world will be miserable forever."	Vs.	#1. "I would prefer being invited to Sarah's party, but if I'm not I will survive and next week I may even start making some new friends who I can count on..."
#2. "You must respect me and if you don't I'll have to take some revenge because my life will be miserable."	Vs.	#2. "I would prefer you to respect me, but if you don't I will continue to respect myself by taking care of myself."
#3. "You must buy me that toy that I want now and if you don't I will be angry and resentful."	Vs.	#3. "I would prefer you buy me that toy that I want now, but I have learned that if you don't buy me what I want today sometimes you might buy it for me later—so I'm going to do my best to be patient and not cry or have a temper tantrum."
#4. "You must let me stay at the park longer because I'm having fun and if you don't I am going to be angry and resent you (and have a temper tantrum)."	Vs.	#4. "I would prefer staying at the park longer, but I have learned that if I fight you will make me take a long nap when I get home and if I don't fight you might bring me back to the park for awhile."
#5. "Life must treat me fairly, and if it doesn't it will be too unbearable—so I won't even try."	Vs.	#5. "I would prefer life to be fair, but if it isn't, I will survive and look for people and experiences that make me feel good."

Irrational Beliefs Can Become Rational Beliefs

How does an irrational thought become an irrational belief—and how might that affect your child's EQ? Remember, we've been inputting perceptions into our unconscious nonstop from birth. Children don't always have the chance to check out whether there's another way to look at life, one that differs from the information stored in their conscious and unconscious minds as beliefs.

So, just as Allana's and Andrew's parents were, it is imperative that parents are vigilant about their children's irrational beliefs. Look for an abrupt change of behavior or mood shift towards a particular person, event, or situation. When you notice this change, especially with a child who normally displays a high EQ, you want to have a one-on-one conversation with him and listen for any irrational thoughts, the way I did with Allana and Andrew. Or, like Michelle's mom did, stop and think about changes in the family, the routine, the household, or your child's ages and stages. Then, if you recognize an irrational belief, begin to explore with your child how he came to this belief. Next, challenge the belief with another way of thinking, a more rational way. By shifting to this new perspective, you can change your child's irrational belief to a rational one.

As you work through the lessons in the second half of this book, you will learn the skills needed to explore your child's perceptions and core beliefs. By helping them develop healthy beliefs, you'll be preparing your child to confidently and optimistically face life's challenges. Life will always put up roadblocks and speed bumps, but a child with a high EQ knows he can maneuver around them and happily reach his destination.

HAVE YOU EVER WONDERED WHAT KEY NEEDS MOTIVATE A PERSON TO MOVE TOWARDS SUCCESS IN LIFE? IN THE NEXT CHAPTER, YOU WILL LEARN ABOUT OUR GREATEST EMOTIONAL NEEDS.

-5-

YOUR CHILD'S GREATEST EMOTIONAL NEEDS

■ ■ ■

What You Will Learn in This Chapter

❑ The greatest emotional needs that all human beings strive to meet.

❑ The three prerequisites for meeting these needs.

❑ When these needs are not met, children can become depressed, even suicidal. They might withdraw from family and friends or begin acting out in ways that bring negative attention.

What Are These Greatest Needs?

Every human being constantly strives to fulfill two fundamental emotional needs. Whether a person is young or old, male or female, rich or poor, educated or not, they are in search of whatever will satisfy these needs.

So what are these greatest emotional human needs?

1. A Feeling of Belonging

2. A Feeling of Worth and Significance

When these emotional needs are not met, a child or an adult will withdraw from life, become depressed, and may even give up the will to live. More than

80% of teen suicides are attributed to these two fundamental needs not being met. More than 50% of failed marriages occur because of these needs not being met for one or both partners. These emotional needs also explain why a teenage girl with no husband or sufficient means of support chooses to get pregnant and keep her baby. Her baby grants her the status of Mom which brings worth and significance to her life. The baby's unconditional love gives her a sense of belonging and acceptance.

Every human being strives to have their emotional needs met.

As a school counselor, I spent many hours explaining to teachers and school administrators that the children who were the most difficult and needy were those not having these emotional needs met. Once this was understood, it took little effort to turn a child's behavior around. The child simply needed to feel a sense of worth, significance, and belonging.

Children from as young as three years old are innately aware when these needs are not being met. They will act out in ways that attract the attention of those around them. Their acting out is often met with a negative response. For a child who does not feel a sense of worth or significance, the attention he receives as a result of his negative behavior is better than no attention and he is willing to pay the price of the consequence. In a young child's belief system, receiving attention often becomes equated with significance and worth.

As adults, we often talk about life's meaning and purpose. We may believe that our notion of life's purpose changes overtime, but it doesn't. All that changes is the way we talk about it. The one thing that is necessary to feel that our life has a purpose is the sense that we have something of worth and significance to contribute in our relationships and in life. Young children also need to feel that sense of contributing. For a three-year-old, it may be something as simple as putting out the napkins on the dinner table and being told what a big help he is.

As you work through this book to raise your child's EQ, you will be increasing your child's sense of belonging, worth, and significance. You will be helping your child meet his greatest emotional needs. Research has identified three prerequisites necessary to meet these needs for our children and for ourselves.

The Prerequisites Are:

1. To be Actively Listened to in such a way that we know the listener is trying to understand what we are saying.

2. To be Respected for our feelings, thoughts, and ideas.

3. To be Appreciated and Valued for Our Contributions.

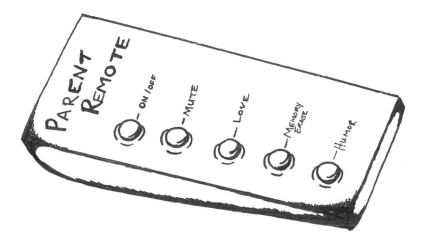

Genuinely listen and respect your child.

As you go through the *8 Proven Skills* with your child, you will be listening to her or him in a way you might not have done before (Actively Listening to your child). You will be asking questions about what your child is feeling and thinking (Respecting your child). As research tells us, the best way to send the message to someone that you are genuinely listening and that you want to understand what they are saying is to ask questions that explore what they have just said. You will learn how to do this in the Communication Chapter. Lastly, as you work the *8 Proven Skills,* you will be noticing and acknowledging in a consistent way your child's contributions. By doing this, you'll be sending your child the message that they are of worth and significance in the family (Appreciating and Valuing your child).

As a preview, here are two exploring statements you can say to your child to make them feel that you want to respect and understand them:

1. "Let me make sure I understand what I think you just said...."

2. "Help me to understand what you just said...."

When people hear these statements (an adult or child), they are left with a feeling that the listener is truly listening and is trying to understand them. In fact, during the last twenty-five years while raising our family, Bill and I have incorporated the following mantra into our communication skills:

> ## "When In Doubt, Check It Out!"

In my therapy practice, my goal is to get every one of my clients to incorporate these three prerequisites permanently into their relationships. Couples and families would reduce the stress and tension in their relationships by 100% almost immediately by just doing: 1) Active Listening, 2) Respect for ideas, feelings, and thoughts, and 3) Appreciation and Value for contributions.

The *8 Proven Skills* chapters will not only increase your EQ and that of your child, but will teach you how to meet your child's greatest emotional needs along the way. It couldn't be more powerful or easier.

> **ARE YOU READY TO TAKE A CLOSER LOOK AT YOUR CHILD? IN THE NEXT CHAPTER, YOU WILL EXPLORE WHAT HIGH EQ AND LOW EQ LOOK LIKE FROM BIRTH THROUGH AGE TEN.**

-6-

DEVELOPING EQ FROM BIRTH TO TEN

■　■　■

What You Will Learn in This Chapter

❑ How your child's EQ is developing from birth.
❑ How to recognize signs of high and low EQ at individual ages and stages.
❑ How the Limbic System works and why it's important.
❑ The importance of eye contact and using calm, soothing techniques during the first three years of your child's life.
❑ Helpful parent-child interactions that will increase your child's EQ at each age and stage.

Overview Of EQ From Birth To Ten

This chapter will give you an overview of how emotional intelligence develops from birth to ten years old. It will offer you insights into your child's world regardless of his or her age. I will also suggest some helpful parent-child interactions that you can begin today, even if your child is only a month old.

It is especially important for a parent of more than one child to remember that, even though you have done everything successfully with your first child, you can't rest on your laurels with your second. Your interactive parenting behaviors might not seem as exciting as they were with your first child, but remember that everything is a first for your second child. Your second child doesn't learn from your interaction with his older sibling; he learns from his interaction with you. Everything is new and exciting for him. So in your tired moments, consider how the time you invested with your first child paid off, and commit to giving that same time and quality attention to your second child or third. You are their number one teacher and role model!

As you read through this chapter, you will notice I have not described any signs of low EQ until the age of two. During the first two years of your infant's life, he is reacting to life everyday. He is learning how to respond to you and those around him. Although he is already developing his EQ, there is no reason to be concerned about low EQ during the stages of birth to two years. Your job during these stages is to continue to get to know your infant, to continue to make his world feel safe and secure, and to continue to follow the suggestions offered in this book. Relax...and enjoy these stages!

Birth To Six Months

Research over the last twenty years has given us tremendous insight into how a baby begins to develop his beliefs about life, his ability to self-regulate his emotions, and the powerful effect a parent's interaction has on a child's long-term EQ. It is during these very important early years of your child's life that the circuits in the brain are being developed with a personality that will last a lifetime. The interaction an infant receives from a parent or caretaker during this time produces an emotional connection and a stimulation response that brings alive thousands of circuits in an infant's brain.

**An infant is aware of how different love, laughter, and smiles
are from stress, tension, and anger.**

Dr. T. Berry Brazelton and Dr. Stanley Greenspan, both leading child psychiatrists, have each presented research showing that infants begin to relate to the world from the instant they are born. During the first six months, the infant shows an active interest in his surroundings. His senses are inputting into his brain responses to everyday sights and sounds. He is also inputting emotional responses to his world. An infant is not capable of labeling emotions, but he is already aware of how different love, laughter, and smiles feel in comparison to stress, tension, and anger in a household.

During these first six months, an infant is also beginning to interact with the people around him. All you need to do is watch a five-month-old's response to your funny faces or peek-a-boo game to verify what the experts tell us about a baby's ability to engage in relationships.

Research has also discovered that a very young child is capable of learning how to calm himself down and regulate his emotions during the first three years of his life. It is during this time that an infant inputs into his brain his initial responses to his world, which then create the emotional foundation that he carries with him throughout his life. His parents play a paramount role in this process.

Remember the amygdala is the holder of all of our emotional experiences and the neocortex is the holder of the factual information. To help you understand what is happening during these early years of a child's life, it is essential to realize that the infant's brain is continuously developing and growing.

The emotional part of the brain, including the amygdala, is called the Limbic System. This is important for you to know because your initial emotional interactions with your infant contribute to his permanent Limbic System.

Think of the brain as the receiver in a home stereo system where everything is interconnected—where one unit, the television, is connected to the same receiver as the VCR and the DVD player. Connected to the Limbic System and starting at the base of the brain is a large nerve called the vagus nerve. Its job is to support the functions of our digestion, respiration, and heart rate. Because it is located in the emotional part of the brain, it is affected by our emotional responses. The interconnectedness in this particular part of our brain helps us understand why we have a physical response to our emotions. When the amygdala experiences fear, for example—which is part of the Limbic System—the vagus nerve sends a response down to the nervous system. As a result, and thanks to the interconnectedness of all your circuits, your heart might start pounding, you might experience shortness of breath, or you might get a stomachache.

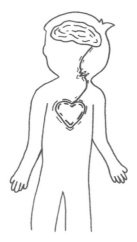

When an infant is startled by a loud noise, all circuits are activated.

During the first years of your child's life, your job is to help him learn to self-soothe. You accomplish this through your emotional interactions with him, which are key in his ability to develop a high EQ.

For instance, when an infant is startled by a loud noise, all circuits are activated. His heart might pound and he might begin to breathe more rapidly. If you notice that your baby has become upset in this way, hold him and talk calmly to him. When you do this, you'll be teaching him about self-soothing. He is learning that a calm voice, perhaps a gentle rubbing or rocking motion, even quietly singing to him will help him to calm down. In other words, we can say the child experiences what is referred to as *rupture* (fear and intense body reaction) and *repair* (soothing and calming the body's response). To better understand rupture, think of a young child having a temper tantrum. For instance, three-month-old Stevie is lying contently in his Fisher-Price® Bouncer when, without any warning, he begins to scream. Going from content-ment to screaming in a manner of seconds is what I am describing as a rupture. Stevie's mom goes to him immediately, picks him up, and rubs his back while she rocks back and forth gently. This calming action is what I refer to as a repair. Think of a teakettle whistling on the stove. As you lift it off the burner, the whistling subsides.

The most important thing a parent can do during the first six months of their infant's life is to give the child positive emotional feedback. Some examples of this would include a soothing voice, smiling, making eye contact, and face-to-face interactions. During these months, new parents learn to pick up cues from their infant regarding his needs and then learn to respond to those needs. Con-necting with your infant can be as simple as noticing that your child is looking at you and then looking back at him and smiling. You can also connect with your baby by engaging him in conversation. The sounds a child makes at this age may sound like babbling, but they are an infant's way of copying or mirroring you. When you babble back in a positive tone, you will encourage your infant to feel valued, nurtured, and supported.

Your positive interactions with your baby are critical for him to develop the ability to self-regulate and to increase his emotional intelligence. If a baby's needs are responded to in a positive way, he learns: "When I feel bad, something can be done about it and I can feel good again. Mom or Dad will notice my signals of distress and take an action so I'll feel better." Whether the distress is caused by hunger, a wet diaper, feeling sick, or feeling scared, when a baby learns there is a solution to particular problems, he develops confidence and emotional intelligence.

When you respond to your infant with positive communication, you are preparing him for self-soothing and the self-regulation of emotions that is at the core of high EQ.

Look for opportunities to have positive eye-to-eye contact. Play with your child whenever possible during bath time, diapering, and feeding. Hear yourself laugh and feel yourself smile. All of these actions lay the foundations for your child's ability to connect emotionally in future relationships.

The following are some signs that your baby is beginning to develop high EQ:

- He smiles back when you smile at him. (No, it's not always gas!)

- She follows you with her eyes and watches what you are doing.

- He drops a toy, then holds it and drops it again if you give him back the toy; in other words, he trusts that you'll pick up the toy and give it back to him.

- He recognizes how he feels. Example: He knows that he feels good, content, and safe when he is being fed.

- She recognizes that she doesn't feel good when she is wet or hungry.

Six Months To One-Year-Old

At this stage, your baby is learning how the world works. Everyday (twenty-four hours a day, seven days a week, fifty-two weeks a year) nonstop she is inputting information about life. She doesn't understand cognitively, but she is inputting sensory perception at a rapid speed and is already beginning to form a response to the world. She is also beginning to use her emotions to get her needs met. For instance if she is hungry, she might cry until she is fed. If she is tired, she might cry until she is rocked. In her own way, she is aware that she is getting her needs met as a result of communicating her feelings to you.

It is important that you consistently use eye contact, a calming voice, and soothing body movements such as rubbing, gentle patting, and rocking in your arms at this stage in your baby's life. Your positive communication during this time is crucial. An infant at this age takes on his parents' emotions and behaviors as his own. If Mom or Dad responds to the baby when upset with calming and soothing motions, it teaches him that his emotions are of value. He learns to connect his parents' presence to calming his upset. Remember, your infant is inputting how his world works minute-to-minute. When you are calm and soothing while your child is upset, you are helping him develop coping mechanisms he will use for a lifetime. You are also role modeling that when you are upset, you don't need to be emotionally overwhelmed by your feelings.

At this age, you can begin to talk about feelings and even name them. Your infant won't understand cognitively what you are saying, but it will help you begin to be comfortable talking about feelings.

All of these suggested parenting behaviors lay a positive emotional foundation between you and your child, help you to build intimacy between the two of you, and help him on the pathway to developing a High EQ.

The following are some signs that your six-month-old to one-year is developing high EQ:

- He watches your reaction to him.

- She interacts in relationships—smiles, makes eye contact, etc.

- She processes what's going on around her even though she may not understand it.

- He takes time to examine a new toy or object—touches, probes, and inspects it, rather than just throwing it down. Example: He can be fascinated with a piece of paper for two or more minutes.

- She expresses her emotions to communicate basic needs. Example: She cries to let you know she's hungry, has a wet diaper, or is hurting.

- He recognizes and responds to your soothing actions which you have been using since his birth.

One-Year-Old To Two Years Old

A one-year-old is not only trying to walk and explore his surroundings, he is also trying to talk and connect emotionally with his caretakers. This is the time for you to begin to help your toddler talk through his emotions. You can begin to label various emotions by name as you are calming your child down from an upset or tantrum. For example, you might say, "I can see that you are feeling sad about having to leave the park now...." Continue to be aware of your voice, as it is the key in teaching your child to self-soothe. Our children begin to challenge us during this year with their behavior, but they are only exploring their world to find out how it works. This is the year to begin to set limits. So expect some confusion and resistance.

Positive interactions are critical for your child in order to develop self-regulation and a high EQ.

The following are some signs that your one-year-old is developing high EQ:

- He tries to figure out the meaning of no. When you tell him "No" he might:
  - stop his behavior and look at you, perhaps in a puzzled way.
  - repeat the action that caused you to say "No" to verify what you mean.
  - move on to another activity.
  - repeat the word no back to you.
- She communicates her needs by crying, using body language, by pointing, by pulling you, and by using primitive sentences or single words. Examples:

- To communicate that she is unhappy about being put in her crib with the door shut, a one-year-old might cry or scream.

- To communicate that she is happy that Mom is holding her, she might smile, and make positive sounds.

- He begins to understand that his emotions have a purpose and power. Example: He cries when his older sibling takes away his toy. And if Mom comes to give the toy back, the one-year-old learns that crying has positive results.

Two Years Old To Three Years Old

This is a year of experimenting with behavior, pushing limits, and learning boundaries. During the year, you will notice your child experiencing a number of rupture emotions (tantrums) and an equal number of repair opportunities to teach herself to self-soothe and self-regulate her emotions.

It is especially important to be consistent in your expectations of your two-year-old. Otherwise, you'll send mixed messages to your child. This is a good time to think about what you want to teach your child so you can follow a consistent plan. Also, this a good time to talk with your co-parent to make sure you are both on the same page in regard to the expectations. For instance, if you want to continue to teach your child to self-soothe and self-regulate her emotions, you'll need to continue role modeling self-soothing.

You'll also need to remember to continue labeling your feelings and those of your two-year-old so he learns more about what you're communicating and what he is experiencing as well. For example, if you notice that your child is pouting, you might say, "I can see that you're feeling sad or disappointed."

If your two-year-old has a melt down, which he will at one time or another, stay calm and continue to use a calming voice. Give him positive body contact such as holding him gently or rocking him in your arms. <u>You do not want to match his intensity with your own.</u> Remember: don't take your child's be-havior personally; it is not about you.

What is a tantrum about—and how does it relate to EQ? A tantrum is about testing the boundaries placed in your child's world. All two-year-olds test the boundaries; it is part of their learning process. It is normal at age two for a child to resist a parent's no if it means the child doesn't get what she wants. Remember a typical two-year-old is egocentric or self-centered. It is part of who she is at age two. Our job as the parent is to understand and accept a child as a typical two-year-old and help her move through this developmental stage without enabling her to get stuck in some of her negative behaviors.

It only takes one or two wins for our two-year-olds to hold on to the belief that "If I cry and carry on long enough, I will get what I want." Once they experience a win, most two-year-olds will continue pursuing the behavior they want to get away with, ignoring their parents' emotions. If they win even one out of every ten times, their belief becomes: "If I keep up the behavior that it takes to get what I want—even if my parents seem not to like it—I will eventually win." When children hold this belief, it keeps their EQ low because they remain focu-sed on getting what they want rather than taking into consideration the feelings of others. Also, their belief that "I must win or I will not be happy" limits their ability to roll with the punches—which is another sign of high EQ. Remember the Absolutes in Chapter Four: when a child believes "I must..." he is developing an irrational belief, which will ultimately set him up for failure. You want to explore the belief with your two-year-old and redirect it.

If you're having a hard time saying "No" to your two-year-old, don't panic. But do take this opportunity to help him change his belief from "I can't be happy unless I get what I want!" to "I can be happy without always getting my way." Again, it only takes one or two wins early in a child's life to develop the behavior that leads to self-centeredness and lack of empathy for others.

So how do you change your two-year-old's insistence on always getting his own way, even when you tell him "No"? You begin by changing his belief in the unspoken message you may have sent over the last two years—that "No actually means Yes—if you cry or whine long enough." Parents who refuse to consistently set boundaries for their young children don't realize that they are teaching them that rules can be ignored. Setting boundaries and role modeling for your child that there are rules they have to follow is one of a parent's most important jobs. You have to perform that job every single day—even when you're standing in a checkout line with a cranky child.

For example, one day when I was running into Costco on my lunch break, I stood in line to get a yogurt and a soda. There was a young mom in front of me with a three-year-old son sitting in her shopping cart. While I was behind her, her son asked for a churro, six different times. Each time the little boy asked in a louder and whinier voice. And each time the mom's no became stronger. The mom stuck to her no, holding her ground as her son became louder and more demanding, I thought to myself, "Go Mom—You are doing a great job of teaching boundaries and the value of no."

But that wasn't the end of the story. When the mom finally got to the front of the line, her little boy continued to plead for what he wanted. So she ordered—

you guessed it—a churro for her son! The little boy beamed. He had gotten what he wanted after all, despite all of his mom's adamant, but meaningless no's!

Children learn very young the meaning of no.

All I could think of was "Oh Lady, you have just taught your son that a no doesn't really mean <u>no</u>—in fact it often means <u>yes</u>." That is now your little boy's belief. The mom smiled as she gave her son the churro. If she continues to teach him that no has no meaning, she will live to regret the life lesson she just taught him. When he's a teenager and she tells him, "Be home by 10 pm", "No Drinking", or "Get your homework done first", does she really think he'll pay serious attention to her rules?

<u>You can teach your child that "No Means No" by following these simple steps:</u>

> **<u>Step 1:</u>** Be aware of how many times a day you say no. No can be camouflaged as a "Stop that....", "Don't do....", or "I've told you before you shouldn't...."

> **<u>Step 2:</u>** Notice whether you mean what you say when you tell your child no, or whether you're okay with the behavior in which they're engaged.

> **<u>Step 3:</u>** Notice whether you follow through with your no or change your mind and let the behavior go on. When you say, "Stop teasing your sister" or "Stop running in the house," but don't follow it up with a consequence, your child learns that such statements don't mean no. Instead, he forms a belief that no just means that Mom or Dad is recommending that I stop my behavior. If your child's

belief is "A no doesn't always mean no—in fact, sometimes it means yes", it's time to change his belief to: "When Mom or Dad says no, they mean no!"

When you've completed Steps 1, 2, and 3, you'll be aware of how often you say "No"," Stop", or "Don't" without any follow through. Your job now is to only say "No", "Stop", or "Don't" when you mean it and are willing to follow through...with Step 4.

Step 4: Choose one or two behaviors you want your child to change. For one week, these are the only behaviors you are going to say no to. AND... you are only going to say no when you mean it. This means that when your child doesn't follow your direction, you must give him some kind of consequence so he believes that "No Means No!"—and not "Yes, if you pester me enough." Consequences can range from a firm "I'm really disappointed in you!" to removing a toy, to a time-out, to loss of something special (like dessert, a TV show, or game time). Remember, the purpose of the consequence is to teach a lesson. The consequence must fit the behavior.

That's it—that's all you need to do! However, saying no only when you mean it, and following up with a consequence, is not as simple as it sounds. If your child has had success getting his way, be prepared for resistance. It may take more than a few times of following up your no with a consequence before he really believes that "No Means No!" When your child learns to accept your no, he begins to realize that his parents have feelings. Becoming aware of other people's emotions is a clear sign on the road to high EQ.

The following are some signs of high EQ in a two-year-old:

- She resists a no with crying and pouting for fewer than ten minutes.

- He resists a no by trying another tactic to get the parent to say "Yes."

- She shows her disappointment at not getting what she wants and then moves on to something else.

- He comes to you for a hug or snuggle when he is feeling sad or hurt.

- She begins to recognize when she is frustrated or upset.

- He sits and enjoys stories that involve feelings.

<u>The following are some signs of low EQ in a two-year-old:</u>

- She yells, screams, or carries on for ten minutes or more.

- He kicks or hits siblings, Mom ,or Dad when his parent tells him "No."

- When her feelings are hurt, she withdraws and cries for a half hour or screams for more than ten minutes.

- When there is a change in plans that he doesn't like, he gets angry or pouts for more than ten minutes, screams and yells, or refuses to go along with the plan.

Three Years Old To Four Years Old

Three years old is the Year of Autonomy, when children learn they are no longer connected to Mom. They are becoming independent and begin to explore the world beyond Mom.

**It takes courage to branch out after spending the first
two years of life connected to Mom.**

It takes courage to branch out after spending the first two years of life be-lieving you are connected to Mom and therefore are always safe. Age three is a year of exploring, testing the world, and then coming back to Mom for emotional security and safety. During this time, a three-year-old starts connecting with his emotions. That is, he begins to name a few of his emotions and talk about them.

To continue teaching your child to self-regulate his emotions, which in turn increases his EQ, it is important to talk about feelings even more frequently than during the first two years. Current research is finding the more you talk about emotions with your child during these years, the more able he will be to consider the emotions of others by age six.

So, talk about your feelings and encourage your child to talk about hers. A perfect time to talk about your child's emotions is a few hours—or even the next day—after a temper tantrum. Remember to just explore with your child what she thought happened. For example, three-year-old Emma and her friend, Lisa, were on a play date at the park. When Emma's mom, Carol, announced it was time to pack up all their toys to go home, Emma started yelling, "No, I'm not leaving. You can't make me!!!" Lisa just stood and watched Emma yelling at her mom.

Carol, being a high EQ mom, simply said good-bye to Lisa and her mom, picked up Emma who was still yelling and screaming, put her in her car seat, and headed home. Emma cried most of the way home, but Carol never raised her voice or made threats. When they got home, Emma was much calmer. Still, Carol knew this wasn't the time to talk about what happened at the park.

A few hours later, when Emma had been calm for quite a while, Carol made a healthy snack and asked Emma to join her. In a pleasant mood now, Emma had moved beyond her temper tantrum, which had probably been motivated by the belief, "I must stay at the park for the rest of the day, or I will be miserable." When Mom and daughter finally sat down to explore what Emma thought had caused her to be so upset at the park, Emma's irrational belief had been disproved. Emma was not miserable for the rest of the day.

When you are in this situation, you might ask your child, "What do you wish had happened instead of the temper tantrum?" or, "What would make it better next time?" However your child answers such questions—even if you don't agree with the responses—the process of examining her feelings helps her on the road to positive problem-solving and self-regulating her emotions.

It is important to encourage children to try new tasks and to acknowledge their successes.

The following are some signs of high EQ in a three-year-old:

- She complains and pouts when she hears "No", but she doesn't yell or scream.

- He may cry for a few minutes when he hears "No", but then moves on.

- She might be unhappy and temporarily resistant to a change of plans she was looking forward to, but is developing a willingness to be flexible.

- He is willing to try to share his feelings with you.

The following are some signs of low EQ in a three-year-old:

- She cries, screams, or yells at Mom or Dad for more than ten minutes when told "No."

- He hits Mom or Dad when told "No."

- When his feelings are hurt, he yells and screams at Mom, Dad, or siblings more than ten minutes.

- She hits or kicks when expressing anger.

- When he's in a "down mood," he withdraws and is sad for more than a half hour or refuses the offer of encouragement.

- When presented with a change in plans, she yells or screams for more than ten minutes or refuses to go along with new plans.

Four Years Old To Five Years Old

Four years old is the Year of Independence—Year of Motivation. This is one of the most important years in preparing for a child's future academic success. It is during this year that a child begins to develop his motivation while experiencing an emotional response to trying new tasks. These can be as simple as dressing himself, making the bed, or setting the table. They can also be as involved as learning to count, learning the alphabet, learning another family's rules when visiting friends, learning to get along with a group of peers at preschool, and developing friendships through play groups.

A parent's job is to encourage their children to continue to try new tasks, and to help them recognize their successes and accomplishments. It is the identification with this sense of pride which will motivate them later in school (and in life) to continue with an assignment knowing they will feel good about themselves once it is accomplished.

When a child tries a task at age four and is unduly corrected or criticized, they soon become discouraged about trying any new task. At four years old, it doesn't feel good to try to accomplish something, to think you're successful, and then to be told by your parent that you failed.

Don't panic—almost all parents do this at one time or another. Once or twice is not going to doom your child to academic failure. On the other hand, if you criticize your child's attempts at a new task on a regular basis, you will have some serious rebuilding to do.

Let me tell you how I did it wrong with our first two children before I did it right:

Our first two children are eleven-and-a-half months apart, so I made all the mistakes most parents make with their first child with our first and second children. This is also why I know that you can correct any mistakes you make.

At three and four, Kimberly and Michael were eager to get themselves dressed for preschool. They were proud of their accomplishments and would rush out of their bedrooms all ready to go to school. On those days—and there were many—when they mixed stripes with plaid, or one striped sock with one plain one, I would say. "You look great, but do you mind putting on two socks that match?" or, "Could you go change your striped shirt to a plain one?"

**Parental criticism, when inappropriate, can undermine
a child's growth and motivation.**

Looking back, I realize that my children's body language showed me they were discouraged and disappointed because I didn't approve of the way they had accomplished the task of dressing themselves. I made them feel badly about a job that they thought they had done well. I didn't stop to think that the fashion sense of a three- or four-year-old is pretty limited. So I was criticizing them for something they didn't know anything about and then having them correct a mistake they didn't even realize they had made. With a little more parenting experience and a lot more parenting education under my belt, by our third child I only bought socks without stripes and solid color pants. I realized the "fashion problem" was mine, not our children's.

Whenever we can, we should offer our children tasks at which they have a good chance of success. Experiencing the feeling of success motivates children to want to accomplish more. It is equally important, however, to face disappointment and failure when they inevitably occur. When a four-year-old experiences disappointment or failure, it is often the result of inexperience. Our job as parents is to help self-soothe our children by talking with them in a calming voice. As we explain life's lesson that things don't always go the way we want them to, it is important to follow-up with exploring questions. For example:

1. <u>What</u> do you think happened?

2. <u>How</u> do you wish it had happened?

3. <u>What</u> would you do differently next time?

<u>The following are some signs of high EQ in a four-year-old:</u>

- She shows disappointment or anger by stomping her feet, but doesn't cry, yell, and scream.

- His pouting and stomping only lasts a few minutes.

- She is willing to talk about how she is feeling.

- He is building extensive feelings vocabulary. You will learn more about this in Chapter Ten.

- Although resistant to a change of plans, she will usually go along with them even if she sulks.

- If there is a younger sibling, he may name the sibling's feelings.

<u>The following are some signs of low EQ in a four-year-old:</u>

- When told "No," he yells and screams at parent, kicks, and bangs door more than five minutes, cries for twenty or more minutes.

- She grabs toy away from younger sibling when angry.

- When his feelings are hurt, he cries more than thirty minutes or withdraws for more than an hour.

- She turns hurt into anger by breaking or destroying something, writing on wall.

- In response to change of plans, he yells at his parent, saying, "I hate you!" for longer than fifteen minutes.

- She refuses to talk about the new plan, yelling at her parent each time a discussion is attempted.

- He physically refuses to go along with the new plan, refuses to change clothes, or get into car.

Five Years Old To Six Years Old

Five-year-olds have usually begun kindergarten, and parents now have a new co-parent in the classroom teacher. This is going to be a wonderful help as you continue to work on setting rules and expectations in your child's life.

Year five in a child's life, if all is going well, can bring a new respect for expectations and rules. A child often begins to comply where he used to resist. He is ready to take on some responsibilities. Again, it's an important time to remind yourself not to say "No" unless you mean it. And with that short reminder, let's take a look at what high and low EQ looks like in a five-year-old.

The following are some signs of high EQ in a five-year-old:

- He is beginning to accept and recognize that his feelings are unique to himself—they can be different from his parents.

- When she's upset with her sibling, she is more likely to use her words than to try to hit her brother or sister.

- He is becoming more flexible with a change of plans.

- When he is upset, he is more likely to talk to you or withdraw and be alone rather than yelling and screaming.

- She's upset for two or three minutes when told "No" and then lets it go and moves on to another way to get you to change your mind. Ultimately, she can pick up that you are serious and that you are not going to budge from your position.

The following are some signs of low EQ in a five-year-old:

- He yells, screams, even stomps his foot for ten minutes when told "No."

- She yells, screams, and cries when she is upset.

- He may add, "I hate you!" as a ploy to get his way.

- She may cry anywhere from fifteen minutes up to an hour, or stay in a sullen or sad mood most of the day when told "No."

- He resists encouragement to come out of the sad mood or even smile. (Some children are authentically stuck in the sadness, others like the attention. Knowing which is happening is part of a parent's job!)

- When faced with a change in plans, she yells and screams for up to ten minutes.

- He offers another plan and then threatens you or tries to intimidate you into undertaking his new plan.

- She may go to her room and refuse to leave until her needs are met.

Six Years Old To Seven Years Old

A six-year-old is learning new skills. She is willing to try new experiences and likes to be in charge. She likes to win and have her own way, whether it's with a sibling, friend, or parent. At the same time, she has a new grasp on reality vs. fantasy. Personal fears begin to evolve. One great fear of six-year-olds is wetting their pants in public. Another is being afraid of punishment by parents, teachers, or other adults. They are often afraid of loud noises. Again, a six-year-old's mood can shift in less than a minute, like an adolescent's. This often causes them to seem egocentric, even selfish.

Six-year-olds now perceive themselves to be at the center of their world, rather than their parents. It is important that you continue to set boundaries and limits—but if your child resists, show empathy while enforcing those limits. Children need the consistency and structure in the boundaries you set. It offers them a sense of security to know how things are supposed to work in their family. As you increase the structure and expectations in the areas of responsibility and academics, look for opportunities for your child to have some control over their own life. You accomplish this by offering them choices you can live with.

One great fear of six-year-olds is wetting their pants in public.

The following are some signs of high EQ in a six-year-old:

- When he hears "No," he is likely to try to talk you out of it.

- She is willing to talk about her feelings.

- He may point out how he thinks other people are feeling.

- She is becoming aware of others' feelings and may ask how you are feeling.

- He is disappointed with a change of plans, but is becoming more flexible in his response.

- If she is angry, she may try to talk you into what she wants you to say "Yes" to rather than kicking and screaming. Her persistence may seem like it's never going to end, but don't give up or give in.

The following are some signs of low EQ in a six-year-old:

- She yells, screams, kicks, or carries on for more than ten minutes when told "No."

- When his feelings are hurt, he cries for a half hour or more.

- When her feelings are hurt, she is angry for a half hour or more.

- He takes his anger out on a younger sibling by hitting or taking something away from them.

- When she is faced with a change of plans, she yells and screams for ten minutes.

- He refuses to hear about new plans.

- She goes to her bedroom, shuts the door, and refuses to go along with new plans.

Seven Years Old To Eight Years Old

Age seven is usually a mellow year. This is because the child is moving into a new cognitive stage of development called the *Concrete Operational Stage*. This is the stage at which your child is beginning to think and solve problems logically. A seven-year-old may complain more often than a six-year-old, but he is also more willing to do household chores. He is beginning to show more empathy towards others. He even cooperates with his friends and peers on a more regular basis. Taking school more seriously, he sometimes worries that he won't be smart enough to understand what the teacher is presenting. If you are a family that attends any religious services, this is the year that your child will start to ask you questions about your religious beliefs. He also begins to question his own place in the world.

A seven-year-old is beginning to show more interest in helping Mom or Dad around the house. Do not let this opportunity pass by. Find things that your child can do to contribute to the running of the house. Make sure the jobs are age appropriate and then acknowledge and show appreciation for his contributions. I have included a Household Chores Chart in Chapter Sixteen. You might want to refer to it. It presents the research on age appropriate chores. It will help you be realistic about your expectations of your child. Your child is moving from his self-centeredness to gaining an interest in others.

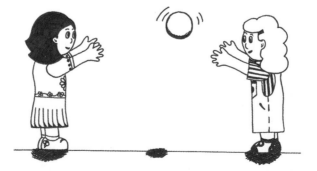

A seven-year-old cooperates with friends on a more regular basis.

The following are some signs of high EQ in a seven-year-old:

- When she's told "No," she uses her new abilities of rationalization to get you to change the "No" to a "Yes."

- When plans are changed, he offers other suggestions rather than getting upset or angry.

- When her feelings are hurt, she is willing to talk about them and discuss a plan to help her feel better.

- He is recognizing and beginning to read other people's body language.

- She expresses sadness and disappointment when her feelings are hurt. She may become withdrawn and quiet, but can be encouraged out of it.

The following are some signs of low EQ in a seven-year-old:

- When she is told "No", she may:

  - withdraws from the family or yell at parents.

  - gets angry and stay angry with a parent for a longer period of time.

  - shuts down and not talk about the reason the no.

  - turns being told "No" into a catastrophe.

- He claims no one else understands when his feelings are hurt.

- She gets into a bad mood when her feelings are hurt and sometimes stays in it all-day.

- He screams and yells his disagreement about a change of plans for more than ten to fifteen minutes.

- She refuses to budge from her position of "No, I won't go along with new plans" for more than a half hour.

- He refuses to be talked into a new plan by Mom or Dad.

Eight Years Old To Nine Years Old

Eight-year-olds are ready to take on the world. They feel confident and are open to try new experiences, whether it's soccer, scouts, ballet, piano, computer, etc. They are cooperative at school and even more considerate at home. They are learning to be in healthy relationships both at home and at school. As they work on improving their skills, they feel good about their progress. Their common fears are being chosen last on a team, not being liked by their teacher, and not having enough time to finish their schoolwork.

Eight-year-olds are ready to take on the world.

The following are some signs of high EQ in an eight-year-old:

- For the most part, he is willing to talk about his feelings when he feels hurt or upset. He may want to talk to someone other than Mom or Dad. (Don't take this personally.)

- Once she has opened up about her feelings to another person, she is ready to work on a plan to help her feel better.

- Even the highest EQ eight-year-olds can break down and cry or refuse to talk to a supportive, helpful parent.

- He takes his relationships with friends seriously.

- She thinks about other's feelings and is more sensitive to being hurt by her friends.

- When he's angry with Mom or Dad, he is willing and capable of disagreeing with them, but in a respectful way.

The following are some signs of low EQ in an eight-year-old:

- She yells at her parent when told "No," and responds with "I don't care what you say; I'm doing it anyway!"

- When his parent tells him "No," he screams that the parent is an "awful person."

- When she is told "No," she withdraws in anger and refuses to talk to her parent for a half hour or more.

- When his feelings are hurt, he withdraws and refuses to talk to parents for an hour or more.

- She takes out her anger on another family member when her feelings are hurt.

- He yells, screams, and refuses to go along with a change of plans.

- She physically refuses to move when her parents or family are ready to go with the new plan.

- He proposes an unrealistic plan of his own and yells or tries to intimidate everyone into accepting it.

Nine Years Old To Ten Years Old

Nine-year-olds show greater self-confidence. There is a new bounce in their step that says, "I can do it!" They work on more projects outside school with their friends and in school with classmates. They are cooperative both at school and at home. Parents often begin to think, "Gee, parenting isn't so difficult after all."

Nine-year-olds have a bounce in their step as they show greater self-confidence.

Nine-year-olds are pleasant to be around. They're logical, able to problem-solve, and enjoy challenges. They take on new responsibilities and enjoy a new sense of independence. Their fears are centered around their friends. They have begun to share feelings and secrets with friends, and now they begin to fear that their friends might choose a new friend and tell their secrets. They also fear being teased or made fun of by their classmates or even by their teachers and coaches.

The following are some signs of high EQ in a nine-year-old:

- He uses his new ability to rationalize to disagree with parents rather than yell.

- She uses her new logical ability to try to change a parent's no into a yes.

- He often shares his feelings, especially with the same sex parent. He is looking for support and understanding.

- She doesn't show emotions of hurt and anger in public, holds more inside so classmates and friends won't criticize her. However, she still recognizes her emotions and needs to talk about them.

- Boys begin to feel more intense anger. They will need to talk about the anger so they don't suppress it and then explode. With the help of parents who role model how to express anger in a healthy way, they can practice healthy ways of expressing their anger. This will be addressed in more detail in Chapter Fifteen.

- They take disappointments and change of plans with less intensity than even a year before.

The following are some signs of low EQ in a nine-year-old:

- She yells at a parent for up to five minutes when told "No."

- He hits a sibling because he's mad.

- She breaks something to express anger.

- He speaks disrespectfully to Mom or Dad to defy them.

- When her feelings are hurt, she withdraws or is sullen for hours.

- He turns his hurt feelings into anger or disrespect directed at family members.

- She refuses to adjust to a change of plans, yells for ten minutes.

- When there is a change of plans, he shuts down and withdraws from family or is disrespectful to parents.

- She reacts physically to a change in plans by refusing to move, making her body rigid.

Ten Years Old

Ten-year-olds are like the calm before the storm of puberty. At this stage in his life, a child is generally happy with himself and with the world. No longer feeling like a child, he takes pride in fulfilling the responsibilities he is given, in his academic accomplishments, and in developing particular skills—whether they are musical, athletic, scouting, or dancing. His fears still center around friendships: losing a best friend or having his secrets told to others is a nightmare. Instead of being fearful of being chosen last for a team, he fears being chosen first and embarrassing himself. For example, being first up to bat and striking out.

At ten, your child will begin to imitate the same sex parent and want to play primarily with same sex peers. Sexual questions at this important age are centered around sexual identity—Who am I? How am I supposed to act? It is also important that the child is encouraged to have a relationship with the opposite sex parent. Books about healthy relationships should be introduced at this age.

The following are some signs of high EQ in a ten-year-old:

- When disappointed and upset by a no from Mom or Dad, he let's his parents know in a respectful way.

- She tries to use logic and rationalization to get parents to change a no into a yes.

- He is willing to talk about his anger or hurt.

- She often needs time alone after being upset and then can rejoin family in a positive mood.

- He can be coaxed back into family activity after experiencing anger, hurt, or any negative emotions.

- She is willing to listen to parent's feedback or observations about disappointment or perceived failure.

- He is willing to work on a plan to move beyond a negative situation or event.

- She is beginning to recognize there is more than one-way to look at a situation.

- He recognizes when his emotions feel like they could overwhelm him.

- He often reaches out to help others.

The following are some signs of low EQ in a ten-year-old:

- She yells and screams at Mom or Dad in a disrespectful tone of voice when told "No" or calls the parents disrespectful names in the hope of intimidating them into changing their mind.

- After being told "No," he threatens or intimidates parent for hours.

- When her feelings are hurt, she may:

  - withdraw and shut down for hours.

  - refuse to talk about it with parent.

  - display intense sadness or despair.

- He turns hurt feelings into anger and disrespect expressed toward family members.

- When told of a change in plans, she may:

  - yell and scream for five to ten minutes.

  - refuse to discuss alternate plans.

  - physically refuse to take part in a new plan.

  - be disrespectful as she tries to intimidate parents into accepting the old plan.

HAVE YOU EVER WONDERED HOW WE BECAME WHO WE ARE TODAY? IN THE NEXT CHAPTER, I WILL ASK YOU TO TAKE A LOOK BACK AT YOUR LIFE EXPERIENCE IN YOUR FAMILY OF ORIGIN.

-7-

REMEMBERING YOUR OWN CHILDHOOD

■　　■　　■

<u>What You Will Learn in This Chapter</u>

❏ The families we grew up in have a tremendous influence on us as adults.

❏ You can decide which family behaviors (that you learned in your *family of origin*) you want to keep—and which you want to let go of.

❏ You have the power to change any behavior you want to change.

❏ You will discover where some of your responses originate.

❏ You can consciously choose how you want to interact with your family.

Family Of Origin

Try not to rush through this chapter. Take the time to look back at your family of origin to understand how you came to be the individual you are today. When you go through this process, your self-awareness and thus your EQ will be enhanced, which will in turn benefit your entire family.

How we think and behave is in large part due to the accumulation of experiences we had in the family we grew up in, our family of origin (FYO). We can make the choice to take control of our own destiny and make changes in how we act and think. We do not need to remain an emotional prisoner of our family of origin.

To understand yourself more clearly, sometimes you need to look back to see where you came from. As I mentioned earlier, when we are children we assume every family is just like ours. That every family does things just like we do in our family—otherwise they must be doing things the wrong way. We form our belief systems when we are children and take these with us into adulthood. We don't even question our fundamental beliefs until we are about twelve, at which point we don't usually have the skills to change them.

How things happened in our families growing up has a powerful influence on the way we do things as adults. For instance, we often parent the way our parents parented us. But when we are willing to take an in-depth look at our childhood, we begin to understand our families and ourselves more clearly. We also learn that life is constantly about choices. We can choose to continue some of the behaviors and traditions from our family of origin. We can keep the things we enjoyed about our families and that had a positive effect in our lives. We can also choose to create our own way of doing things. In other words, we can empower ourselves to make needed changes in how we act and think.

**How things happened in our families growing up has a
powerful influence on the way we do things as adults.**

If you are married become aware that each spouse brings to a marriage different life experiences, some positive and some negative. With an understanding of yourselves and the families in which you each were raised, the two of you can talk about the family life you want to create together. And you can come up with a plan to make your vision a reality.

When moms and dads hold the same vision or goals for their own family, they usually feel like they are on the "same page" and work better as a team. They are aware of what actions they need to take to continuously move towards forming the family they envision. This shared vision, goal setting, and a plan of action for forming a healthy family contribute to creating a high EQ family.

I had never gone through the process of exploring my family history until I was in graduate school. I was so resistant at first! I didn't want to understand me any better—I liked myself just fine. So you'll understand what a shock it was for me to find out that I had grown up as an ACA (Adult Child of an Alcoholic). Even though my dad had died right before my eighth birthday, I already had the survival coping skills of an ACA at that young age. I had always thought that certain traits were just the way I was: stubborn, independent, private, and a caregiver resistant to receiving help from someone else. I'd listen to every one else's problems, but mine remained secret.

The list of ACA characteristics goes on and on. The point is because I explored my childhood as I am now asking you to do, I was able to get to know myself on a deeper level. Although I discovered that I was disappointed and at times angry at some of the ways my family had interacted, exploring my family history never resulted in loving my parents any less. It was about discovering who I was and then deciding if the ways in which I was raised were how I now wanted to raise my own children.

If you find that you want to raise your children in the exact way your family raised you—hurray for you! If not, by the end of this chapter, you will be aware of the things you want to change. You have the power to change any patterns you want to by simply giving yourself permission to do so. And, of course, you also have the power to keep any of those wonderful traditions you want to incorporate into your own family. You are in control.

Bill and I could never have been as genuine and effective as parents if we had not taken the time to get to know ourselves by understanding how we became who we were. Go through this chapter at your own pace. By exploring your past, you'll be giving yourself and your children a powerful gift. Even if your significant other does not wish to do this (yet), don't be discouraged—don't let that hold you back!

Since we are our child's most important teacher and role model, it is essential that we know ourselves. And much of that self-knowledge comes from reflecting on how your mom, dad, siblings, and others in your family interacted with each other and with you when you were growing up. This awareness will help you understand who you are—and how you want to parent your own children.

Relax and have fun with the questions. They are all about discovery and decision-making. If you come up with your own questions, write them in the margins. Or, scratch out my questions and write your own. Whether you simply read the questions and think about them, or take the time to write a response with a few words or an entire essay, completing this chapter will give you a better understanding of how your family of origin influenced your beliefs, values, morals, and behavior. You can then take the time to think about which of those you'd like to keep and those you'd like to change.

Remembering...

1a. What did you like about your family? _____

_____

1b. Why did you like it? _____

_____

2a. What didn't you like about your family?_____

_____

2b. How would you have done it differently?_____

_____

3. <u>When did you feel...?</u> (Name a specific time, such as "I felt loved when I brought home good grades and my dad congratulated me." Don't just say, "I just knew it." There may not be an answer. If your answer is "I never felt

loved," this is more common than you can imagine.)

a. loved? _____

_____

b. loved by Dad?_____

_____

c. loved by Mom? _____

_____

d. loved by others? _____

_____

e. a sense of belonging?_____

_____

f. appreciated? _____

_____

g. angry? _____

_____

h. hurt? _____

_____

i. like an outsider? _____

_____

j. lonely? _____

_____

k. laughed at? _____

_____

l. misunderstood? _____

_____

m. ignored? _____

_____

n. successful? _____

_____

o. like a failure? _____

_____

4. When did you laugh? _____

_____

5. What made you laugh? (belly laugh) _____

_____

6. Did Mom and Dad role model encouragement?

How?_____

_____

7. Did Mom and Dad role model patience?

How?_____

_____

8. How did your family:

Communicate? _____

Listen? _____

Solve Problems? _____

Make decisions? _____

Fight? _____

Disagree? _____

Play together? _____

9. What was one unspoken rule in your family of origin that you never broke? (i.e., "Don't lie.")

_____

_____

10. How was this rule enforced?

_____

_____

11a. How did Dad express his anger? _____

_____

11b. How did Dad discipline? _____

_____

11c. How did Mom express her anger? _____

_____

11d. How did Mom discipline? _____

_____

12. What was more important in your family...

   a. How things looked to others? _____

_____

b. How things really were? _____

_____

13. What are some of your favorite memories?

    1._____

    2. _____

    3. _____

14. What are some of your worst memories?

    1._____

    2. _____

    3. _____

15. What did you promise yourself you would never...

    ...do to your children: _____

_____

    ...say to your children: _____

...say to your spouse (significant others, etc.): _____

Family Secrets...

Family secrets (such as alcoholism, child abuse, etc.) can be TOXIC. As long as you must keep a SECRET, it can never be a PROBLEM that you can resolve, learn from, or accept. Also, keeping secrets creates a tremendous amount of stress.

16. Did your family have a family secret? Drugs, Drinking, Abuse, Emotional absence, rage, etc.

---

17. What were the secrets? Why were they a secret?

---

18. Do these secrets still exist today?

Household Routines...

Remember your...

Dinner Table?

Who was there?

_____

_____

What did it feel like?

_____

_____

What would you have done differently if you could have?

_____

_____

Bedtime?

Who helped?

_____

_____

What was the routine?

_____

_____

What worked?

_____

_____

Didn't work?

_____

_____

Homework?

What was the routine? Was it loose or structured?

_____

_____

What did it feel like?

_____

_____

What did you like or not like about the routine?

_____

_____

Were you a good student?

_____

_____

What helped?

_____

_____

What do you wish had been different?

_____

_____

One-on-One Time?

What was your favorite time with your mom?

_____

_____

When?

_____

_____

What was your favorite time with your dad?

_____

_____

When?

_____

_____

Vacations?

Favorite?

_____

_____

Least favorite?

_____

_____

WOULDN'T IT BE WONDERFUL TO LEAD A SATISFIED LIFE WITH A CLEAR ROAD MAP OF WHAT'S RIGHT OR WRONG? IN THE NEXT CHAPTER, YOU WILL EXPLORE THE IMPORTANCE OF CONSISTENT MORALS AND ETHICS.

-8-

MORALS, ETHICS, AND VALUES

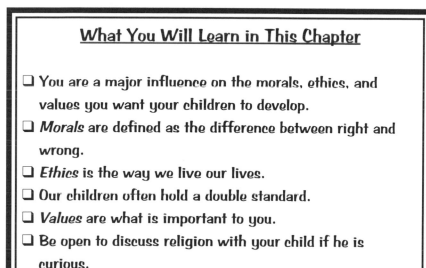

What You Will Learn in This Chapter

❏ You are a major influence on the morals, ethics, and values you want your children to develop.
❏ *Morals* are defined as the difference between right and wrong.
❏ *Ethics* is the way we live our lives.
❏ Our children often hold a double standard.
❏ *Values* are what is important to you.
❏ Be open to discuss religion with your child if he is curious.

Every Family Is It's Own Culture

As your child's EQ increases, you will notice his awareness of other people's emotions and his responses to them. Young children tend to be egocentric, self-absorbed, and focused on their own needs and wants; as our children grow, they begin to reach out beyond their personal world into their surrounding communities. They enter relationships and interactions beyond Mom, Dad, and family, and they encounter differences.

Every family is a culture unto itself, with its own beliefs, patterns, customs, and traditions. Children are brought up in their family cultures and take on the morals, ethics, and values that are presented to them early in their lives. As young children, they believe that every family's culture is the same as theirs. When they venture outside their family and are met with the unavoidable differences and diversity that exists in the world, these core morals, ethics, and values are challenged.

When a child is raised in a family where morals are clearly taught and role modeled, it is like giving the child a road map to follow as he explores his way along his life's journey. The road map is laid with a solid foundation of what's right and what's wrong. When a child ventures off the main road and begins to get lost and overwhelmed by life, he can use his map to get back to the main road. When a high EQ child has been given this strong foundation it makes it easier for him to move into dialogue about his challenges in life with both parents and other trusted adults.

With their road map of high EQ, children, teens, and young adults can steer themselves more clearly toward problem-solving issues that arise. Their self-acceptance remains high because they make healthy decisions based on an inherent moral code that leaves them feeling satisfied with their choices. A high EQ child with a strong moral foundation will be drawn into relationships with other children who have similar morals and ethics.

And lastly, a high EQ child with a strong moral foundation will feel good about the choices he makes, especially throughout his teen years.

This chapter focuses on morals, ethics, and values.

Morals

Morals are defined as the difference between right and wrong.

- Lying is wrong

- Cheating is wrong

- Murder is wrong

- Slander is wrong

- Hurting someone is wrong

- Embezzlement is wrong

- Destroying someone's property is wrong

- Stealing is wrong

Research has found that 80% of children's morals are set by the age of ten. At that early stage of their life, they already know the difference between right and wrong. The remaining 20% of their morals are developed by their mid-twenties as a result of life experiences.

So our teaching and role modeling is important in the first ten years. After age ten, most of our parental lectures are tuned out on a regular basis, because our children have already heard the sermon and don't want to hear it again. It is at this time in a child's life that he begins observing his parents and taking mental notes on his mom and dad's behavior. Children at this stage will look to see if their parents "practice what they preach"—if they role model what they have been lecturing about for the last ten years.

80% of children's morals are set by age ten.

Ethics

Ethics is the way we live our lives. How do we apply the morals we have learned in our childhood to the actions we take in life? Does the end justify the means? Is it okay to lie and cheat to succeed in something?

As parents, we need to consider how morals enter our daily lives, not only for our own sake, but also for the sake of our children. What might they be learning from us when we act the way we do? Have we developed a code of ethics that we live by no matter what situation is thrown our way? Do we change our ethics according to circumstances? What are we role modeling for our children?

If you want to role model to your children a particular code of ethics, you must live it consistently. If you tell your children to always tell the truth and they overhear you tell even a white lie—they will believe it's okay to lie sometimes. In the movie <u>Liar Liar</u>, Jim Carrey's character tries to defend his habitual lying by explaining to his son, "Everybody lies, everybody lies!!!" All his young son can do at that point is look at him in disbelief.

My husband and I were asked to present a workshop on Morals and Ethics to fifty teenagers in a Christian youth group a couple of years ago. We divided the presentation into two parts: Part One was an exploration of morals, ethics, and values; Part Two consisted of choices, responsibility, and accountability. At our first session, we asked the teens to fill out a questionnaire, which would remain anonymous. We asked them to be as honest as they could be and told them we would give them a copy of the results the following week when we met for session two.

What we learned surprised us. We discovered that for many teens there is a different moral code applied to their friends than to their parents, teachers, and coaches.

<u>Here are the results of our workshop questionnaires:</u>

- 61% of the teens said it was okay to lie to their parents, teachers, and coaches in order to not get in trouble or to get out of work

- 74% had lied for such reasons

- 100% of the teens said it was not okay to lie to your friends

- 100% said it was not okay for their parents, teachers, or coaches to lie to them

- 65% of the teens said it was okay to copy a friend's homework (cheat) if you forgot to do an assignment—in order not to get in trouble

- 82% said it was not okay to cheat while you were playing a game—they also said that it was never okay for their parents to cheat

- 63% said it was okay to pass on a rumor about somebody you didn't know, but...

- 85% said it was not okay to pass on a rumor about somebody you did know

- 97% said they hated it when their parents talked about them to their friends

- 90% believed in God

• 100% believed they knew the difference between right and wrong

What this experience taught us is something we had known as teens. There is a teen double standard of morality. It is okay for teens to lie and cheat in certain circumstances, but it is never okay for parents to do so.

Our children hold us to a higher standard, a stricter moral code. They are constantly watching and testing us to see if we live what we say. When they test us and we fail, they use our hypocrisy as a justification for engaging in negative behaviors themselves.

I mention this to remind you how <u>powerful a parent's role modeling is in forming a child's moral code, which he will then take with him into adulthood</u>. Simply telling your children how they should behave isn't enough; we must show them what good behavior looks like by consistently engaging in it.

Parents often bring me their children and ask me to fix their bad behavior. Parents who swear at their children will ask me to help their children become respectful toward them... <u>I start with the parents</u>. Parents who spank their children will ask me to help their children stop hitting each other... <u>I start with the parents</u>. Parents who lie will ask me to help their children to stop lying... <u>I start with the parents</u>. In each of these cases...<u>I start with the parents</u>.

Ethics is the way we live out our morals. If our children see us living by our morals when it's easy, but then bending under pressure—for example, if we lie to get out of a commitment to a friend, cheat on our income taxes, or gossip about a neighbor—they will enter their adult lives with weak ethics. This means they're likely to have a difficult time surviving the challenges life throws their way. Our children will take on these beliefs: 1) I can't trust what my parents say is true, and 2) I can ignore my morals whenever it is too inconvenient to adhere to them.

Values

Values are different from morals and ethics in that they vary according to what is important to each family and individual. For example, if you grew up in a family where money was tight, you might learn to value your belongings more than someone who grew up in an affluent home. If you grew up in a family where Dad was always away on business or in the military, you might place more value on spending time with him than someone whose father came home every night after work. If your family engaged in most of their family fun outdoors, chances are you'll place a high value on spending a lot of time outdoors. Whereas, if your family's idea of fun was to go to museums or films, those are the activities you're likely to value most.

Our values include not only the activities, interests, and material goods that are most important to us, but also the personality and character traits we like best in people. Respect, a sense of fairness, honesty, and living up to commitments are all examples of personal values that steer our lives.

As parents, we are in the position to help influence our children's values as they are growing up. A person's values are not right or wrong. They are just what's important to that person as a result of life experience and culture. If a person holds gaining wealth as an important value, he might direct his life towards that goal. The same goes for education. The only way values can get complicated is if the value causes a person to live his life in an unethical way. For instance, if someone embezzles money or robs a bank to become wealthy, then the value has become a negative influence, which can damage that person's life, as well as the lives of others.

**If your family engaged in most of their family fun outdoors,
you might place a high value on outdoor activities.**

Simple differences in values can create a need for compromise or negotiation in a relationship. For example, if a husband grew up valuing hiking, camping, and outdoor sports as the way to enjoy a vacation, and his wife grew up valuing visits to museums and historic sites as the way to enjoy leisure time, what is important to each of them will likely clash when they set out to plan a vacation.

If you want to get in touch with some of your most deeply held personal values, try this exercise:

Ask yourself, "What makes me angry?"

- Is it being treated unfairly?

- If so, fairness is a value for you!

• Is it being disrespected?

    • Then, respect is a value for you!

• Is it being lied to?

    • Honesty is a value for you!

Now observe what makes your child consistently angry, and you will have an insight into your child's emerging values. These character values are the ones that run the deepest in each of you.

World Religions

A child's willingness to talk about a higher being—for instance, God, Buddha, the Enlightened One—is another aspect of his developing morals, ethics, and values. Even if you are a parent who questions whether a higher being exists, your child is exposed regularly to other children and adults who not only believe in a higher being, but attend church or a service regularly.

Children have a natural curiosity about God, Heaven, and church. If you do not belong to a church or a particular religion, I would suggest that when your child begins asking religious questions, you go to your nearest library or bookstore and look in the children's section. You will be amazed at how many children's books there are about religions and a higher being. They are as diverse as there are religions and cultures in the world. I define religion as the way you worship whether it is Presbyterian, Methodist, Mormon, Catholic, Baptist, Jewish, Muslim, Buddhist, Christian, Non-Christian...the list goes on. I think of spirituality as your personal relationship with God or a higher being.

For any parent who belongs to a particular religion, I recommend that you take your child on a regular basis either to a Sunday school program or to the church service—or both. You will be giving your child an additional opportunity to feel a sense of belonging. Remember the sense of belonging is one of our greatest emotional needs.

Teaching your children to pray is another priceless gift, which you can give to a child as young as two years old. Praying can offer them a sense of connection to, and protection and support from, God or their higher power. It gives them a powerful force to which they can connect when they are lonely, sad, or scared.

When you give your child a religious foundation, you are offering them an additional support system to which they can always turn in troubled times. If there is no such foundation established at a young age, there is no sense of belonging to God or to a spiritual home.

I am always surprised when I work with young adults in their late twenties or early thirties who resent their parents for not giving them some kind of religious foundation. Not just a spiritual one, but also a religious foundation. Even teenagers who complain to their parents about going to church tell me in session that they like going to the church youth group activities. Again, it offers them a sense of belonging. They are too proud to say they want to go, but they often tell me they are disappointed when their parents give in to their complaining. The bottom line is that most children and teens are more than willing to go because of the sense of community and belonging that churchgoing provides.

Praying can offer our children a sense of belonging and support.

The other valuable lesson for our children, which is taught by most religions, is forgiveness. At the heart of most religions is the idea that God is a forgiving God who understands that we "blow it" at times and that we are human. Most religions teach that when we are sorry, God is always there, ready to forgive us. In this way, children learn from most religions that it is normal for all humans to make mistakes. Religion teaches that God, like our parents, will always forgive our bad choices, because, like our parents, God loves us.

Religion often helps us to co-parent by asking our children to live an ethical life guided by their morals. It supports the parents by teaching their children, through stories and parables, to make responsible decisions and to then follow through on the decisions they make. The teens that make it through the adolescent years with their relationships to their parents intact are usually the ones who know that if they make bad choices, they can ask their parents for forgiveness, serve their consequences, and move on. They have learned very early that being given a consequence and serving it feels like forgiveness and a fresh start or a clean slate with their parents.

Just recently I attended a seminar at Santa Clara University in California. In the lobby of the Graduate Studies Building, there was a display comparing the major religions of the world. The display described Hinduism, Jainism, Buddhism, Chinese Religion, Judaism, Islam, and Christianity. I learned as I read though all the information that a common link among each of these religions was a similarity in their code of ethics. Each religion had a version of the Golden Rule. I found this fascinating, given the vast differences in culture.

The following is a worlds-eye view of the Golden Rule:

1. Hinduism (MAHABHARATE X111.114.8)

   "This is the sum of duty: do nothing to others which would cause pain if done to you."

2. Jainism (SUTRAKRITANGA 1.11.33)

   "A person should treat all creatures as he himself would be treated."

3. Buddhism (SAMYUTTA NIKAYA V 353.35-354.Z)

   "A state that is not pleasant or delightful to me must be so for him also; and a state which is not pleasant or delightful for me, how could I inflict that on another."

4. Chinese Religion (CONFUCIUS ANALECTS 15.23)

   "Do not do to others what you do not want them to do to you."

5. Judaism (RABBI HILLEL SHABBOT 31a)

   "Do not do to others what you would not want them to do to you."

6. Islam (Sayings of 40 HADITH MUHAMMAD OF AN_NAWAI 13)

   "No one of you is a believer until he desires for his brother that which he desires for himself."

7. Christianity (MATTHEW 7:12; LUKE 6:13)

   "In everything, do to others as you would have them do to you."

Once again, if you belong to a religion and make it a positive part of your child's life, he will have another place in which to feel a sense of belonging, self-worth, and significance. And when he does occasionally get stuck in life, he will have a safe, supportive, forgiving place to return to.

There is no question that parenting is the most challenging, difficult, and yet rewarding journey you will ever take. When you are secure in your moral beliefs, when you live your life in a consistently ethical way, and when you are true to your most deeply held values, you will give your child the gift of that very special road map. The one in which the main road is paved with a foundation of what's right and what's wrong. You will offer your child a smoother pathway in his life to developing an even higher EQ.

YOU ARE READY TO BEGIN THE *8 PROVEN SKILLS* TRAINING!
RELAX! HAVE FUN!

-9-

INTRODUCTION TO THE *8 PROVEN SKILLS* EQ PROGRAM

■ ■ ■

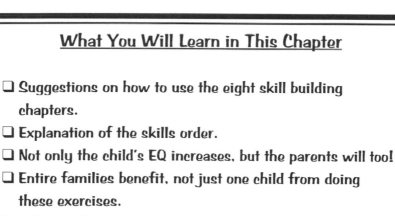

What You Will Learn in This Chapter

❑ Suggestions on how to use the eight skill building chapters.

❑ Explanation of the skills order.

❑ Not only the child's EQ increases, but the parents will too!

❑ Entire families benefit, not just one child from doing these exercises.

❑ When both parents work the skill chapters marriages improve!

❑ All eight skills interact with one another.

❑ The eight skills form the foundation to your child's healthy future.

❑ Just like any new skill you are working at, the more you practice, the better you will get.

Get Ready To Go!

The first eight chapters of this book are written to help you understand the theory and research on EQ, as well as understanding your own EQ, and lastly to understand that of your child.

If you have read the first eight chapters, and explored the questions asked, you are ready to help your child raise her own EQ. You are about to give your child a priceless gift that she will treasure and benefit from throughout her entire life.

Get Ready Go!

How To Use Part III Of This Book:

- Read each chapter all the way through.

- Read each of the exercises.

- Become familiar with the exercises so you are comfortable with presenting them to your child.

The beauty of the exercises is that even if you are not comfortable with them, but are still willing to do them, they will still work and bring benefits to both you and your child. Read and understand the explanation of each skill—you will find the explanations in the beginning of the chapter.

The Eight Steps are written in what I consider the best order to teach them to your child. The best long-term results, which I continually see among the children and adolescents I work with, are when I have followed each skill in the book's sequential order. This is because each skill builds on the previous skill and therefore continues the learning process. Every individual parent needs to choose the way that it's the most convenient and comfortable to do each chapter.

In the Personal Skills Workshops, which I offered for years to hundreds of children, I would work one skill for seventy-five minutes each week, and the children would have home assignments they would then do with their parents. The following week I would introduce the next skill while still incorporating the previous week's skill.

You, as the parent, can take a chapter a week, a chapter every two weeks, or even one chapter a month. Again, you know yourself and your family and what would work best for them and yourself. The skills you will be teaching your children they will use for a lifetime, so there doesn't need to be a rush to the end of the book. In fact, once you've completed all eight chapters of Part III, I would recommend that you continue to choose an exercise from any chapter once a week or every other week all year to revisit continually throughout your child's childhood. This way the skills become so integrated into your life you won't even notice you are doing them. They will be part of your family's way of being.

These skills are like anything you are trying to learn and become proficient at-they take time. The more you practice the skill and use the skill, the better you will become at it, and so will your child. Each chapter includes an explanation of the skill and then exercises to give you and your child the opportunity to experience and develop the skill being introduced.

**Each skill builds upon the previous skills and
continues the learning process.**

The first time you work a chapter with your child there are some exercises that are essential to lay the foundation of the learning lessons. These are marked with a ☆. The additional exercises can be done at anytime during your teaching week(s), or anytime in the following weeks and months. I hope that once you've done the essential exercises with your child you will see such improvement in that particular skill area that you are going to want to continue to do the exercise regularly.

One side benefit the parents (who have done this process) tell me is the more you practice with your child the better your skills will get. I've been told repeatedly that these exercises have helped entire families improve their communication and therefore the overall health of the family and the relationships in it. I have even had couples tell me that by working the exercises with their children the quality of their marriage increased beyond their expectations.

The Eight Steps form the foundation to your child's healthy future. Just think of a building when the foundation is solid: any type of structure can then be placed on top the foundation with no threat to the safety of the building itself.

These Eight Steps lay the foundation to your child's healthy future.

The foundation of skills, which you are building with your child, can be thought of in the shape of an octagon. Each of the sides interacts with the other, yet has its own characteristics. You can be focusing on just one skill at a time, but you will be strengthening other skills simultaneously.

The eight sides of the foundation each interact with one another consistently. For example, you now know that you have feelings going on within you every minute of everyday. Therefore, your feelings (at least four or five) are present when you:

- are communicating to anyone

- are making a decision

- are building friendships

- are trying to control your anger

- are feeling good or bad about yourself (self-acceptance)

- choose to take on a responsibility

- are using your problem-solving skills

-10-

FEELINGS

■ ■ ■

What You Will Learn in This Chapter

❑ Feelings influence our everyday decisions.

❑ How to recognize emotional reactivity.

❑ Why it's important to name our feelings.

❑ Everyone has a *feelings vocabulary*.

❑ There are no wrong feelings.

❑ We may not always agree with or like what our children tell us they are feeling.

❑ Don't assume you know what your child is feeling.

❑ *Displacement* of feelings happens when negative emotions toward a person or event are unexpressed, but later expressed toward someone else.

So What Is The Big Deal About Feelings Anyway?

We know that emotional intelligence is a person's ability to recognize and label one's own feelings and those of others, and to respond to those feelings in a healthy way. We don't think with our feelings. We don't make decisions with our feelings. So why are they so important? And why is a high EQ so essential in handling our feelings appropriately?

How Feelings Influence Our Thinking

Although the cortex area of our brain does our thinking and our feelings "whoosh" up through our amygdala, research is finding that our feelings have a powerful influence on our thinking. For example, if we are feeling content and rested and our child asks us to help him with a puzzle he's putting together, chances are we will say "Yes." If, on the other hand, we're feeling stressed and tired, we might respond in a cross voice, "No, you'll have to wait!" or "Do-it-yourself!" Another instance of influence is when our feelings overrule a more logical way of thinking about a particular situation. For example, our fear of public speaking might prevent us from giving a speech on a subject we know we're qualified to discuss. In both of these examples, our feelings dictate our behavior and prevent us from acting in our own—and our child's—best interests. How does this happen?

Our feelings have a powerful influence on our decisions.

We often do whatever it takes to avoid negative or uncomfortable feelings, whether that feeling is anger, fear, hurt, embarrassment, disappointment, or something else. Some people won't fly to California for a vacation because they want to avoid their fearful feelings: fear of flying, fear of earthquakes—even fear of Californians!

Do We Always Have Feelings?

We always have feelings present in our body, at least four or five at the same time. We are all aware of the difference between positive and negative feelings. Some feelings are more intense than others; but regardless of their intensity, feelings influence every decision we make. In the clinical world of therapy, the term emotional reactivity refers to making a decision based on the intense feelings one is experiencing at that moment. When one is emotionally reactive, feelings are as influential in the decision-making as the cognitive thinking ability. Emotional reactivity is like fusion. A person can't feel the difference between his feelings and his thoughts (cognitive process) because they are fused together. In other words, the feelings are overwhelming the person's cognitive ability. This might be okay when a person is experiencing positive feelings, but think about a situation in which the guiding emotion is anger. If we bypass our thought process and respond in anger, the potential consequences can be unfavorable.

Our feelings are wonderful in that they make the world come alive with curiosity, wonder, and passion. However, our cognitive ability is also crucial, as it allows us to make rational decisions based on current information as well as wisdom from past experiences. It also enables us to think about future consequences, to rationalize, and to hypothesize. We need to be in our cognitive mode to make the best possible decisions.

Why Is High EQ So Valuable?

The reason why having a high EQ is so valuable is because it allows us to recognize our feelings, and the feelings of others, so that those feelings don't overwhelm us into ignoring our cognitive processes. A high EQ person's feelings rarely dictate his decisions. Once a person with a high EQ recognizes his feelings and labels them, he can then access his cognitive brain to make a healthy decision. The best decisions involve a balance of emotional influence and cognitive thought process. Unfortunately, individual decisions are often made based on purely emotional responses to a given situation, which then results in discord, misunderstanding, and even violence.

The best decisions involve a balance of EQ and IQ.

Naming Your Feelings

To utilize our feelings in the healthiest way possible, we need to learn to recognize what we are feeling. That process begins by labeling our feelings. The reason this is so important is that, once we have labeled and acknowledged our feelings, we can have control over them rather than the feelings controlling us. Can you remember a time when you felt intense feelings, but didn't have the time to identify what exactly it was you were feeling? Do you recall later saying to yourself, "I don't know what came over me"? When that happens, your feelings control you by taking over your decision-making process. Learning to label what we're feeling is an important part of developing a higher EQ, and so is expanding our feelings vocabulary.

What Is A *Feelings Vocabulary?*

A *feelings vocabulary* is our accumulation of feeling words. Feelings vocabularies are unique to each individual. Some people have feelings vocabularies consisting of only ten words where others may have more than two or three hundred words in theirs. We often hear young children say, "I'm mad!", "I'm sad!", "I'm scared!", or "I'm happy!" That's because their feelings vocabulary is limited to those basic feelings. There are adults whose feelings vocabularies are also limited. Regardless of one's age, if your feelings are limited to angry, happy, sad, and a few others, then every time you become even a little annoyed, you're going to label that annoyance as anger and respond angrily. Or every time you feel a little disappointed, you'll label that feeling as sad, and perhaps sulk or cry.

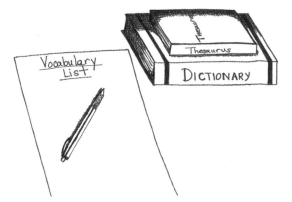

A feelings vocabulary is an accumulation of our feeling words.

What if a child had an extensive feelings vocabulary? Instead of responding in anger when his mother can't take the time to work with him on his puzzle because she's busy making dinner, he might respond with mere frustration or disappointment. His response would be more appropriate because he would have the ability to pinpoint more accurately what he was feeling. He would know that anger wasn't what he was feeling, but frustration, annoyance, or disappointment.

Again, the reason it's so important for children to learn how to accurately label their feelings is so they can respond to an event, situation, or person in a way that fits the emotions they are experiencing. Remember that our brain accepts what we send to it as truth. So if we say, "I'm angry!" we will respond in anger.

When I work with *rage-aholics*, I notice the one thing they have in common is a limited feelings vocabulary. At the top of their short list of feelings is anger. They are so used to responding in anger that almost every negative situation elicits an angry response—and they feel comfortable with this negative emotion. In other words, they are so familiar with anger that it makes them feel safe to be angry. When they begin to expand their feelings vocabulary, however, they are always amazed at how different it feels to be frustrated, annoyed, sad, or even disappointed. None of these less intense feelings have the negative impact on their bodies as anger did.

How can you help your child expand his feelings vocabulary? The more you and your child practice naming your feelings, the faster the whole process will go. Expect that at some point you will be able to go through your personal list and name what you are feeling in any given situation in fewer than thirty seconds.

I was recently on a business flight when the plane hit some turbulence. I immediately felt a "whoosh" of feelings throughout my body, and I went into "name the feelings mode." My first response was, "I'm scared!", but there was a lot more to what I was feeling than fear alone. I kept naming feelings—anxious, concerned, hopeful (the turbulence wouldn't last), and prayerful (a short prayer always feels good to me). It took me almost twenty seconds to go through the feelings-labeling process. Since I didn't want to feel anxious or scared, I told my brain to focus on feeling concerned and hopeful. Although the turbulence continued, my body became less tense. And because I didn't ultimately label my feelings as only "scared", the intensity of the fear was dramatically reduced.

The more you and your child practice naming what you both are feeling, the less overwhelmed and more in control you'll both feel. Naming your feelings more accurately will thus result in healthier responses.

When you have named what you are feeling there will be an "A-ha Moment." You will know when you have named the appropriate feeling the moment you say it. I always feel a kind of *Klunk!*, and so will your child. It is as though there is a perfect fit between the emotion in your body and the correct word that you've used to name it.

There Are No Wrong Feelings!

It's important for children to know that there's no such thing as a wrong feeling. So even as you're helping your child accurately name her feelings, be sure you don't tell her that she's wrong when she names a particular emotion.

When our child tells us she's scared or angry, our immediate reaction is often to protect her from feeling badly. We might say, "Oh honey, you don't really feel scared—you're probably just a little nervous." When we do this often enough the child begins to think," I know I feel scared because I feel it all over my body, but if my mom or dad says I don't feel scared, maybe I'm wrong—or maybe it's wrong to feel scared. I'd better not trust my own ability to name my feelings."

This leads to the child taking on the belief that, "I'd better not trust myself to make decisions." This belief can lead to the child becoming dependent, frightened, and lacking in self-confidence.

One aspect of respecting our child's feelings, regardless of how negative they might be, is to follow through with behavior that shows respect. Here's a common example: Out of respect for your grandfather, when you visit him with your children, you insist that they give him a hug and kiss. Since Grandpa has gotten older, however, his hygiene has gone downhill and his body smells. He also doesn't hear very well. One day, your seven–year-old daughter asks for permission not to hug and kiss Grandpa next time she goes with you to visit. Your first instinct is to demand that she does this or face a consequence because you don't want to hurt your grandfather's feelings. But what if you were to explore your daughter's feelings?

You might ask her why she doesn't want to hug and kiss her grandpa. She might tell you that when Grandpa talks to her it feels like he is yelling at her, and that scares her. She might also say that when he hugs her, he doesn't smell good, and that makes her feel uncomfortable, like she wants to run away.

So how do you respond? Your daughter's core beliefs about how the world works will be changed depending on how you react to the feelings she's shared with you. If you thank her for sharing her feelings, but tell her that she still has to hug and kiss Grandpa, she will learn that her feelings have no value with people in authority. She will feel devalued and disrespected, and it's likely that in the future she will keep her feelings and any requests about them to herself. This event could thus have serious consequences when she deals with teachers, authority figures, co-workers, or other important relationships.

Your alternative response to your daughter's request might be to thank her for sharing her feelings with you, to say you're sorry that you didn't realize how she was feeling, and to tell her that she doesn't have to do anything that makes her feel scared and upset. The next step is for you and your daughter to come up with a plan for the next time you go visit Grandpa. How she might feel more comfortable and still let Grandpa know that she loves him?

When you take an action that demonstrates your respect for your child's feelings, you send the message that her feelings are valuable. She thus learns that when she shares her feelings with her parents, they listen and try to understand. She also learns that when she is in an emotionally uncomfortable situation, it's okay to go to someone you trust for help and that there will be solutions to help her feel safe again.

Unfortunately, many adults don't trust their own feelings because they felt devalued or disrespected as children by their well-meaning parents. So my advice to you is to accept any emotion your child names, even if it surprises you. Then ask your child questions to explore what else he is feeling. For example, if your child tells you he's mad at his sister, even if you're thinking to yourself, "You're overreacting—there's no good reason to be angry with your sister," repeat to him what he's just said, "Oh, so you feel angry with your sister. Why?" Keep your thoughts to yourself and let your child express his own feelings. When you listen and let him know that you respect his feelings, he will feel validated. We don't need to agree with how our children are responding; we just need to let them know that we are trying to understand what they are feeling and that those feelings are valid and real.

What Happens To Unexpressed Negative Feelings?

It is important for all of us to talk to someone about our negative feelings; otherwise, those feelings become trapped inside us. Our amygdala has filed them away. When children keep their negative feelings inside, those feelings are like air being pumped into a balloon. For example, a child has his feelings hurt in the morning by a sibling and feels rejected, but doesn't express how he feels to anyone. He holds that negative feeling inside. He then goes off to school and the children at the bus stop ignore him. So he adds to that inner feeling of rejection—like more air being pumped into the balloon. He finally gets to school and runs over to play with his friends, and the bell rings to stop playing and go inside. So he might feel frustration or perhaps even anger at not being able to play with his friends. More negative buildup—more air filling in the balloon.

As soon as he enters the classroom, his teacher asks for a homework assignment he forgot to do last night. He not only feels embarrassed, he also feels a sense of fear about getting into trouble, even failing. His negative feelings continue to build up throughout the day, and because he doesn't share these with anyone, the feelings expand until there's no more room in the balloon. When his mom comes to pick him up, the boy gets in the car with his negative emotion-filled balloon at full capacity, but Mom doesn't know that.

Negative feelings can continue to build up throughout the day.

Mom mentions that she's disappointed that he forgot to take the recycling out last night. On a day when his balloon of negativity is fairly empty, he would probably apologize and say, "I'll remember next time," but because his balloon has no more space for any more negative air, he explodes. Maybe he starts yelling at Mom that his brother could have done the chore instead of him. Or maybe he shouts at her that he hates his whole family. Or he might just collapse in an emotional crying episode. What might look like a temper tantrum is actually an overload of unexpressed negative feelings.

So how should the mom handle the outpouring of negative feelings? It is important for her to understand that her son's intense emotional reaction is probably related to more than what just occurred. Understanding and dealing with a child's moodiness is one of a parent's hardest challenges because such episodes are rarely caused by just one thing. In fact, as in the above example, it's possible the accumulation of negative feelings has been going on for longer than just one day. The balloon exploding could be the result of days or weeks of people, events, or situations that produced negative feelings.

A child with a high EQ is comfortable talking about his negative feelings on a regular basis, so his balloon reaches an explosion point less often than a low EQ child. But what if your child hasn't reached that high EQ level yet?

Rudolph Driekurs said many years ago, "Children are great perceivers of feelings, but poor interpreters." This means that children pick up on most feelings, including anger, hurt, disappointment, sadness, confusion, etc. They feel these, but children especially young children don't understand why their parents are expressing those feelings. A young child rarely asks his parent, "What's wrong?" Instead, they think the worst or become upset themselves. The major source of anxiety in young children is caused by negative feelings in their home. Even when such feelings are not outwardly expressed, children pick up on the feelings, internalize them, and then are at a loss as to how to deal with them.

We don't need to give our children specific details or even the reason we are feeling the emotions we are experiencing. They simply need us to name our feelings and then to reassure them that we are okay. Children should not be burdened by being their parent's confidant.

Don't Assume You Know What Your Child Is Feeling

Another reason to talk with your child about his feelings regularly is that we are often wrong when we guess what our children are feeling. Also, our children are often wrong when they guess what our body language means.

As a Marriage Family Therapist, I would guess we misread our children's body language anywhere from 30-50% of the time. We usually think our guess is correct, and we respond to our children with the mind-set of our guess. For example, your third grader gets into the car after school and his body language seems to tell you he's exhausted. You say to him, "Boy, Nick, do you look tired. I bet you had a long day. Let's go home and have a snack and relax." Your son hears "snack" and "relax" and thinks about putting off his homework, so he agrees with you. What really happened to make him appear so beat?

Nick had the opportunity to be a hero.

At recess he was playing kickball, and the other team was up by one point. Everyone on Nick's team was cheering for him to kick the ball and run around the bases. Since two boys were on base, Nick had the opportunity to be a hero. Instead, he got up and kicked the ball right into the hands of an outfielder. His team was so disappointed they blamed him for losing. So Nick isn't simply tired—what he's feeling is sad and disappointed at not being a hero. He is angry with himself for not having made a great kick, and he's mad at his classmates for blaming him. He has had a lousy day and he wants to talk about it because he has a high EQ and has learned it's better to talk about negative feelings than to keep them inside. He knows he would feel better if he told his mom what happened, but because of her assumption that he's simply tired, as well as her offer of a snack and the chance to relax instead of doing homework, he's going to leave the negative feelings just sitting there.

Don't assume you know what your children are feeling. Explore their feelings with them and give them a chance to tell you. The exercises in this chapter were designed to establish this interaction between you and your child.

Keep in mind that children also misguess their parents' feelings and then respond to them based on those miscalculations. The most frequent error is that children often guess that their parents are angry with them when, in fact, the parent's disappointment, frustration, or fatigue has nothing to do with the child at all.

> **Check out your child's feelings—don't guess!**

Another Reason Not To Hide Your Feelings

We've talked about how feelings stay inside a person until he deals with them in someway. Think of the balloon. The negative feelings just keep filling it until it explodes, like a temper tantrum. There is something else our negative feelings do when we don't let them out. Sigmund Freud, a well-known psychiatrist from the early 1900's, identified this process and called it *displacement*.

Displacement is the process that happens when the unexpressed negative feelings you felt toward a particular person or event are then expressed towards someone else. For example, you have had a bad day at work—your boss criticized your work and you wanted to challenge his criticism. Instead, you were professionally polite and accepted his remarks, all the while thinking, "I can't believe you just said that. What a jerk you are!" You go through your day and you are not feeling any better about your boss' remarks. Finally, the workday is over and you head home. Still simmering, you pick up the children from after school day care. They are in good moods so you forget about your workday for a few minutes. After an hour, you are at home cooking dinner and your son says, "Oh, Mom, we're not having fish again for dinner, are we?" And you flip...you hear yourself saying something like, "I can't believe you just said that! I try to cook healthy meals even though it takes a lot more planning and work because I love you, and all you can do is complain! I don't know why I bother!" Your son just stands there looking at you with a puzzled look on his face. Because Mom didn't think it was appropriate to express her feelings to her boss, they spilled out at her son—which was unfair to him, and leaves him with the sense that he has done something bad.

Until the age of twelve or thirteen, children rarely understand sarcasm, and they certainly don't understand displacement. What happens when parents displace their negative feelings onto their children? The child hears the anger, criticism, or judgment, and feels his parent's negativity, and doesn't understand what he has done wrong. When displacement of negative feelings happens in a family regularly, a child's sense of safety and security is rocked to its core. He can no longer predict what type of behavior will produce what type of response from his parents. When this happens often enough, children will begin avoiding their parents for fear of upsetting them, thus initiating a behavior of "walking on eggshells." As parents, we have to make sure we don't hide our feelings from the people who make us upset only to displace them onto our children instead.

Children displace their negative feelings onto their parents as well. They do so either with their words or actions. That's why it's important for a parent not to take a child's behavior personally. More often than not, your child's negative feelings are not about you, but about something that happened during his day.

When our children displace their feelings, it's our job to help them understand what is going on within them. Children often frighten themselves with an outburst, and they appreciate it when a parent is able to help them understand what just happened.

You are about to take the first step in raising your child's EQ by doing the following exercises. Your life and your relationships will become richer as you become even more aware, and more in tune, with your own feelings.

So relax and enjoy the next couple of weeks!

EXERCISE #1 – BECOMING AWARE ☆

PURPOSE & BENEFITS:

It is time to become aware of your own feelings. At every moment of everyday, an individual experiences a minimum of four or five feelings at the same time. It is difficult to teach our children to become aware of their feelings if we are not aware of our own. The more you practice, the better you will become at recognizing and naming your feelings.

STARTING AGE: Whatever age you are today is the right age

TIME: 10-30 seconds (maybe a minute or two at first)

LOCATION: Anywhere and everywhere

MATERIALS: • the printed "Adult Feelings List" from the Appendix

INSTRUCTIONS:

1. Ask yourself right now "What am I feeling?"
2. Name as many feelings as you can think of and be aware if any of them go "Klunk!!" Do they feel right? If not, move on and name the other feelings. Look at the feelings list if you do not name at least four feelings.
3. Continue naming feelings until you have named four feelings.
4. Repeat steps #1, #2, and #3 at least five times a day.

EXERCISE #2 – TALKING ABOUT FEELINGS ☆

PURPOSE & BENEFITS:

When children hear adults talk about their feelings, they are 100% more likely to talk about their own feelings. When a child is comfortable talking about his feelings, the parents are always aware of what is happening in their child's world. Remember that your child's perceptions become his beliefs and his beliefs become reality. This allows the parent to listen for any irrational beliefs and help change them into rational beliefs before any damage is done.

STARTING AGE: Today, 0+

TIME: Ongoing, whenever the opportunity comes up

LOCATION: Anywhere and everywhere

MATERIALS: None

INSTRUCTIONS:

1. Whenever the opportunity arises name your feeling(s). Aim for a minimum of five times a day.

2. Here are some examples:

   a. I am hungry. I think I'll make us lunch.

   b. I am tired; it's been a long day. I think I'll go to bed early tonight (problem-solve).

   c. I am so excited about going to your game this afternoon.

   d. I am worried and upset because we left so late for school.

   e. I am frustrated and concerned with the instructions for this new DVD.

   f. I am so happy and thankful for your help with the . . . .

EXERCISE #3 – BUILD AN ADULT FEELINGS VOCABULARY ☆

PURPOSE & BENEFITS:

The more feeling words that you are aware of, the more feeling words you will use. The more feelings a child can name—the better her opportunity will be to face problems that come her way, understand them, and resolve them. When a person doesn't know how she feels about a problem or situation, confusion or conflicts set in and this often prevents a solution from being reached. Problems that are left unresolved usually produce stress and anxiety.

STARTING AGE: Now!

TIME: 10 to 15 minutes

LOCATION: Anywhere

MATERIALS: • the "Feelings List" in the Appendix

                • pen or pencil

INSTRUCTIONS:
1.   Read the "Feelings List" in the appendix of this book.
2.   As you read the "Feelings List," be aware of how often, if ever, you have experienced each of these feelings.
3.   Use a pen or pencil and add to the list any of feelings that I forgot!

EXERCISE #4 – BEGIN CHILD'S "FEELINGS LIST" ☆

PURPOSE & BENEFITS:

Children need their own "Feelings List" so they can begin to build their own awareness of their feelings. When your child sees the "Feelings List" in a place of importance he will be more likely to name his feelings. In the case of your child's "Feeling List" you want it to become special. As you are working with him, you can point to his list. You want the list to become part of your child's world. You are beginning your child's feelings vocabulary.

STARTING AGE: 2 years+

TIME: 10 to 20 minutes

LOCATION: Somewhere you can sit and make eye contact with your child

MATERIALS: • the age appropriate "Feelings List" in the Appendix

     • a writing instrument (pen, pencil, crayon, felt pen, etc.)

INSTRUCTIONS:
1.   Choose the appropriate "Feelings List" in the appendix.
2.   Either cut out the list or make a copy of it.
3.   Plan a time when you can sit with your child and make eye contact. You don't want your child to feel rushed. You might decide to help your child build his "Feelings List" a few words at a time.
4.   Choose your age group:

- **Between ages 2 to 4 years old:** With children as young as two, you might fill in only one or two faces with a feeling at a time and talk about them.
- **4 years old:** You can do four or five faces.
- **Starting at 5 years old:** You want to ask your child what feelings he has experienced (felt) and begin to write them on a special piece of paper with his name on the top.
- **Starting at 7 years old:** Read over the list of feelings from the appendix. Explore with your child which feelings he has felt. Ask him to tell you a time he has experienced the feeling. Then either circle, underline, or mark in someway the feeling he has named. Another alternative is to copy the identified feeling he has described on to a paper that he will keep for his "Feelings List."

5. Continue to build our child's "Feelings List" with him. Aim for at least twenty or more words. This might take days or weeks to achieve.

6. The goal is to start your child's "Feeling List" and have it continue to grow throughout his childhood.

7. It's important especially as the "Feelings List" becomes part of his life, to display the list in a location where you and your child can refer to it or add to it whenever feelings are talked about.

EXERCISE #5 – BALLOON ☆

PURPOSE & BENEFITS:

To teach your child that when she keeps her negative feelings to herself and does not share or talk to anyone about them, it's like blowing air into a balloon. The more negative feelings she holds inside, the more the balloon expands (fills up) until it is ready to explode. When the balloon explodes, it's like a person having a temper tantrum. When we talk to someone about our feelings, it's like letting the air out of the balloon so it doesn't explode.

STARTING AGE: 4 years+ (you can try it with younger children)

TIME: 10 minutes

LOCATION: Inside or outside, as long as you can make eye contact—you want your child's full attention

MATERIALS: • a balloon

INSTRUCTIONS:

1. Tell your children that a balloon is like their body.

2. Tell them: Every time you feel a negative feeling, it is like blowing air into the balloon. Give them an example: "For instance, if I bake some cookies for us and then I burn them I feel upset, angry, and disappointed." Or, "If I count on a friend going out to lunch with me and then she cancels at the last minute, I might feel disappointed, hurt, upset, or even rejected." Be creative with your examples and make them fit your life. Each time you name a negative feeling, blow some air into the balloon.

3. Ask your child for his own examples of situations, people, or things, which would make him, experience negative feelings. We let our positive feelings out so the example needs to be negative feelings: sad, mad, angry, hurt, disappointed, etc. Blow into the balloon with each example. Continue to fill the balloon until it is ready to explode.

4. Just before it is ready to pop, ask your child to whom she can talk when she feels upset so she can let out some of her negative feelings. As she names people (Mom, Dad, Grandma, Grandpa, teacher, etc.) let out air so your child can see the visible difference talking to someone can make.

5. Now have some fun and ask your child again to name some situations that cause negative feelings. This time fill the balloon until it's ready to pop. Then release the balloon and let it fly around. Your child will probably laugh and pick it up. Let her keep the balloon.

6. Repeat this exercise as often as you want.

EXERCISE #6 – FEELING-A-DAY ☆

PURPOSE & BENEFITS:

To help your child recognize what other people are feeling—both adults and children. This exercise helps your child read social cues and therefore begins the ability to be empathetic and have more friends. Socially accepted children are children who are able to pick up emotional cues from other children.

STARTING AGE: 2 years+

TIME: 10 to 20 minutes

LOCATION: Anywhere

MATERIALS: • piece of paper

   • pencil, pen, felt pen, crayon

INSTRUCTIONS:

1.   Choose a feeling and write it on a piece of paper. Each family member can take turns choosing a feeling. You can repeat the same feeling 2 or 3 days in a row. You can change the exercise to a "Feeling-A-Week."

2.   Tell everyone participating what the "Feeling-of-the-Day" is. Post it somewhere for all to see, i.e. refrigerator door, taped to the front door, etc.

3.   During the day everyone is on the lookout to recognize "the feeling" in someone else or to recognize it in themselves.

4.   Find a special time before dinner, at dinner, or before bed when each family member participating has the opportunity to share when this feeling was recognized.

EXERCISE #7 – DRAW A FEELING

PURPOSE & BENEFITS:

This exercise helps you understand how your child sees feelings in others. It also helps your child to focus on a person's face and become more aware of how a person's expression can help him recognize or guess what the person might be feeling.

STARTING AGE: 2 years+

TIME: 10 to 20 minutes

LOCATION: Anywhere

MATERIALS:
- paper
- pen, pencil, felt pen, crayon, etc.
- flat surface

INSTRUCTIONS:

1. Draw blank oval faces on a piece of paper.
2. Have your child fill in the oval face with feelings he felt yesterday, last week, anytime.
3. After your child has drawn a face, guess what feeling he has drawn.
4. Have him write the name of the feeling or you write it for him under the picture.
5. Ask him when he felt that emotion.

EXERCISE #8 – FEELINGS CHARADES

PURPOSE & BENEFITS:

The purpose of Feelings Charades is to improve your child's ability to be empathetic, and to point out how easy it can be to misguess someone's feelings.

When your child begins to realize how easy it can be to misguess someone's feelings you are helping him or her to understand why it is so important to talk about our feelings.

STARTING AGE: 4 years+ (You can include your 2- and 3-year-olds, but they will need to be assigned a partner.)

TIME: 20 minutes

LOCATION: Inside or Outside with enough room for a person to stand and act out the feeling

MATERIALS:
- small pieces of paper (Post-Its® work too)
- pen, pencil, felt pen, crayon, etc.

• a container, in which to put the pieces of paper (i.e., small basket, gift bag, box, etc.)

INSTRUCTIONS:

1. This exercise can be played with only two participants or with ten.

2. Before the game, make slips of paper, perhaps 2" x 2". Then print feelings clearly on each piece of paper. For example:

> **ANGER**

• The List: SAD, MAD, GLAD ANGRY, HAPPY, FRUSTRATED, HURT FEELINGS, DISAPPOINTED, TIRED, IRRITATED, SCARED, EMBARRASSED, JEALOUS, NERVOUS, TIRED, GUILTY, MOODY, and UPSET.

3. Put the pieces of paper into the container. I like to call the container I use the "Feelings Basket". This game can be played daily, weekly, and whenever you see a lack of empathy in your child. (Always keep it available to use at a moment's notice).

4. Each family member takes a turn picking a piece of paper from the basket with a feeling on it and acts it out.

5. All other family members guess what feeling is being acted out.

6. The person who guesses the correct feeling can go next if they want to. Otherwise a volunteer can take a turn. Make sure everyone has equal opportunities to have a turn acting out a feeling.

7. After a family member has acted out a feeling, you can put the slip of paper back in the basket. The reason for this is that everyone looks and acts just a little different from another person while they are feeling the same emotion. This also encourages family members to be more aware of each other's body language.

EXERCISE #9 – TELL A TIME ☆

PURPOSE & BENEFITS:

To have your child begin to share her feelings with you. To give you an insight into her world. To give you the opportunity to listen to your child without criticizing or judging. To provide an emotionally safe environment for your child in which to share. Your child learns that they can share their innermost feelings in a safe way without being lectured to. This feeling of emotional safety for a child with his parents is an important key to successful parenting.

STARTING AGE: 4 years+

TIME: 10 to 20 minutes

LOCATION: Anywhere

MATERIALS:
- small square of paper (Post-Its®) with names of feelings printed on them
- small basket, bag, or box to put the folded pieces of paper in

INSTRUCTIONS:

1. Prior to beginning this exercise, print on small pieces of paper names of feelings.

2. Have everyone participating sit around the basket, bag, or box with the folded pieces of paper in it.

3. Decide on first turns even if there are only two of you participating in the exercise. You are teaching good sportsmanship. The order can be determined in various ways, for example: alphabetical by first name, oldest, youngest, earliest birthday from January 1st, last in alphabet, last letter of first name, closest to beginning of alphabet...you get the idea.

4. Each member of the family chooses a piece of paper when it is her turn.

5. Each child reads the feeling on the paper and "tells a time" when she felt that feeling.

6. Rules: No one criticizes, judges, or lectures about what is said. Everyone just listens or asks questions of interest and support.

7. Decide on how many times your family will draw before you begin. (two or three turns are always good).

8. If you want to, you can use a timer for 2 minutes if you think that one of your children will constantly monopolize the time. When it's your turn, be aware that you are role-modeling how to answer the questions. So be as willing as you can be, appear thoughtful and honest as you share. If you laugh or make light of the questions, you will devalue the importance of your children being willing to share with you. You want your children to be relaxed, feel safe, and comfortable, but take their answers seriously.

EXERCISE #10 – FAMILY FEELINGS CHART ☆

PURPOSE & BENEFITS:

To help your children become aware that each member of the family has feelings. Sometimes children feel isolated with their feelings. They believe they are the only one to have certain feelings. This simple exercise is often the beginning of open communication about feelings. The lesson you want learned and practiced is to identify, label, and be able to talk about your feelings. It is only in identifying what you feel that a person can then make a good choice about what they want to do about it: let it go or take an action.

STARTING AGE: 4 years (invite younger siblings to sit with the family)

TIME: 10 minutes

LOCATION: Anywhere you can post a chart

MATERIALS:
• chart paper (it can be 8½" x 11" piece)
• pen, pencil, felt pen, crayon, etc.
• tape or magnet to hold up the paper

INSTRUCTIONS:

1. Post a chart (piece of paper) with "Family Feelings List" as the title or heading of the paper.

2. Choose someone to print all the feelings on the chart.

3. Invite all family members to call out suggestions for "The List". Accept any reasonable description for a feeling. For example: "dumped on", "left out", "outside the loop", etc.

4. Post "The List" in an obvious place where it can be referred to and added to.

EXERCISE #11 – HAVE YOU EVER FELT...?

PURPOSE & BENEFITS:

To encourage your children to share their life experiences, and the feelings which accompanied those experiences. To help you understand your child's perception of the world. To give your child an opportunity to experience emotional safety as she shares her experiences. Your child will begin to build a core belief which says, "I can talk to my parent about anything without being criticized, judged, or lectured to."

STARTING AGE: 4 years+

TIME: 15 minutes

LOCATION: Anywhere

MATERIALS:
- small basket, bag, or box
- long narrow stripes of paper (white copy paper, color paper, index cards, paper towel, etc.), which have the questions...
  - "Have you ever felt scared?" (brave?)
  - "Have you ever felt mad?" (happy?)
  - "Have you ever felt sad?" (glad?)
  - "Have you ever felt silly?" (joyful?)
  - "Have you ever felt dumb?" (smart?)
  - "Have you ever felt embarrassed?" (proud?)

• "Have you ever felt thankful?" (jealous?)

• The possibilities are endless!

INSTRUCTIONS:

1. Place the basket, bag, or box in the center of the participants with the strips of paper folded in it.

2. Decide on the order to take turns.

3. Decide how many turns each family member will have.

4. First person picks (chooses) a strip of paper, reads the question, and answers it.

5. Rules:

   • Accept any answer

   • No criticism, judgment, lecturing

   • Only comments:

      • Questions of interest

      • Support statements, such as, "I would feel the same way."

EXERCISE #12 —HOW WOULD YOU FEEL IF...?

PURPOSE & BENEFITS:

To build empathy. To help your child become aware that certain situations can produce anticipated feelings. To help your child realize while he listens to other family members that other people often feel the same way he does. When children begin to realize that other family members feel the same way they do about certain situations, a child feels a strong sense of belonging in the family. Everyone, even in a large family, feels lonely at one time or another. This lonely feeling usually occurs because the individual feels he is alone, feeling a certain way about a particular situation. This exercise helps dissipate some of the loneliness.

STARTING AGE: 4 years+

TIME: 10 to 20 minutes

LOCATION: Anywhere

MATERIALS: • small basket, bag, or box

> • the statements written below on this page copied onto stripes of paper—please add to the questions written here and write your own questions

INSTRUCTIONS:

1. Before the exercise, write the questions listened below on strips of paper, fold, and put into the basket, bag, or box.

2. Decide on the order for taking turns.

3. Each person in turn picks a folded piece of paper from the basket and reads it aloud then proceeds to answer it.

4. Rules:
    - Accept any answer
    - No criticism, judgment, lecturing

    Only comments:
    - Questions of interest (i.e., "What was that like when you were scared?")
    - Support statements, such as, "That sounds really scary."

5. Questions:
    - How would you feel if your brother/sister teased you?
    - How would you feel if your mom/dad yelled at you?
    - How would you feel if your friend hurt your feelings?
    - How would you feel if you heard a loud noise outside your bedroom window?
    - How would you feel if your mom/dad asked you to put away your toys and you weren't finished playing?
    - How would you feel if your brother/sister wouldn't let you play with them?
    - How would you feel if Mom/Dad said "no, you couldn't go to your friend's house to play"?
    - How would you feel if Mom/Dad were mad at you?
    - How would you feel if your brother/sister was mad at you?
    - How would you feel if your favorite toy broke?
    - How would you feel if your brother/sister broke your favorite toy by accident?
    - How would you feel if your mom/dad were sick?

- How would you feel if Mom/Dad asked you to help them with a chore and you were playing or watching TV?
- How would you feel if you weren't invited to a classmate's party?
- How would you feel if the clothes you wanted to wear were in the wash?
- How would you feel if you were planning on going to McDonalds and Mom/Dad said you were eating at home instead?
- How would you feel if you struck out when you got up to bat for your team?
- How would you feel if a teammate got up to bat and struck out?
- How would you feel if Mom and Dad were mad at each other?
- How would you feel if your brother/sister took your toy?
- How would you feel if you had a new baby brother or sister?

-11-

COMMUNICATION

■　■　■

What You Will Learn in This Chapter

❏ The three means of support that a parent can offer a child to meet his greatest emotional needs all involve communication.
❏ How to recognize your family of origin's pattern of communication.
❏ Most misunderstandings in relationships stem from unclear communication.
❏ How to recognize and understand your child's early communication skills.
❏ How to identify I-Statements and You-Statements.
❏ How to be aware of the two levels of communication: content level and emotional level.

Why Is Communication So Important?

Communication is the primary way relationships are developed and sustained. Lovers spend hours talking and listening to each other. Friends spend hours sharing and supporting one another. Babies coo and cry. Toddlers put together words and point. Young children spend a great deal of time laughing, crying, telling, sharing, and asking. Older children spend time explaining, demonstrating, showing, and sharing. Teenagers tell, demand, direct, question, explain, and defend.

At each stage throughout our lives, communication is the primary way we get our needs met, our strengths and talents encouraged, and our personal growth supported. Whether we are one or ninety-one years old, our communication is our lifeline to the world around us.

What Is Your Family's Communication Pattern?

The four patterns of communication described below are the most common patterns I have found in the families I've worked with during the last twenty years.

1. The Wagon Wheel

In this pattern, one central person controls the communication, similar to the cog at the center of a *wagon wheel*. All members of the family go through this person to find out what's going on and to share information. The family members talk to one another through this central person, who passes on the information given to him or her, if appropriate. One of the negatives in this pattern is the central cog has the freedom to pass or not pass on the information with whatever slant or bias he wants to add. This person can thus create hurt feelings among family members by quoting or misquoting another family member. Another negative is the "cog person" holds all the power.

It takes communication to develop a relationship. If all the members of the family are communicating through one central person, they are missing the opportunity to develop individual relationships with members of the family. Remember, strong personal relationships are built from interaction between two people, one-on-one. Group relationships are more superficial. It's nice to relate to one another in a family group, but relationships usually can't be as deep or as personal as they can when individual members relate one-on-one.

2. Linear

In the *Linear* pattern of communication, information is passed on in a similar way to the elementary school game, Telephone. For example: Dad to Mom, Mom to Son, and Son to Daughter. Since communication is one-way and not two-way, the last person to receive the information accepts it as the truth, even if it has been altered along the way and is no longer valid. The linear communication style rarely results in deep, personal relationships, which require a back-and-forth sharing and receiving of thoughts and feelings.

3. The Alliance

Another pattern of communication in families involves teams or *alliances*. For instance, Mom and Dad stand together and hold all the information. When Mom speaks, she speaks for Dad, he agrees with her, and vice versa. This encourages children to share only with one parent, expecting everything to get passed on to the other parent. In this pattern, the children usually go to the same parent regularly and miss the opportunity to develop a deeper relationship with the other parent.

The alliance pattern often makes one parent feel "out of the loop" or "disconnected" from the other members of the family. Sometimes children build their own alliances as they grow older, and thus feel like a stronger force when they go against their parents. In families where there are three or more children, children may build alliances among themselves against one another. Ultimately, this pattern of communication disconnects family members from one another emotionally and creates mistrust.

4. The Star Interactive

In the *Star Interactive* pattern, no one person or authority figure holds total control of the communication. Everyone talks with everyone. Everyone shares any information they want with whomever they want. This pattern resembles a geometric design.

The only downside that I have observed with this pattern is that it takes more time to ensure that everyone is in the loop with family information, and occasionally someone gets left out. In a high EQ family, the left out person doesn't take it personally because they are aware that family members don't align against one another, or deliberately leave people out of the loop, or pass on bad information on purpose.

Think about your family of origin's communication pattern—the one you grew up with and are most familiar with. Then take the time to decide what pattern you want to establish in your family today. If you are married, discuss the patterns with your spouse, and make the decision together.

We learned in Chapter Five the greatest emotional needs of all human beings are the need to feel a sense of belonging and the need to feel a sense of significance and self-worth. We also learned there are only three prerequisites necessary to meet these needs. Each of these three prerequisites entails healthy and positive communication.

So Let's Take A Closer Look At Communication.

Communication involves two parties: the Speaker and the Listener.

Communication always involves two parties: the Speaker and the Listener. The Listener has a more difficult role. While the Speaker is saying whatever he wants in whatever way he chooses to say it, the Listener must stay focused and listen. Often the Speaker goes on and on, or perhaps isn't clear about what he is saying. The Listener may become distracted or bored and not listen. Frequently our children are called on to be the Listeners while we speak to them about what we expect from them, what we advise, or what we want them to learn.

Children with a high EQ tell me that they will often pretend to listen to their parents. They've "zoned out," but don't want to admit it because they don't want their parents to start all over again. They even share with me that there are times they agree to do something for their parents because they want their parents to stop talking. This often lands them in trouble because they stopped listening to their parents and have no idea what they agreed to do. After working with hundreds of children, I know children often tune out what their parent is saying ten to twenty seconds after the parent has begun to speak. If the child recognizes the topic as something they've heard before or if the parent's tone of voice suggests something the child doesn't want to hear, they tune out sooner. So when you have something important to say or to teach your children, speak for only about two minutes and then check with them to find out what they've heard. You'll be training them to listen for a longer span of time.

Children and teens are not the only ones who "tune out" when they're called on to listen to what they consider "a boring speaker"—spouses, co-workers, neighbors, in-laws, and others do so as well. Part of the Speaker's job is to present what they have to say in a way that will engage the Listener, as well as, make sure the Listener has truly heard what's been said.

Often, the Speaker doesn't check out with the Listener what he has heard, or the Listener doesn't check out with the Speaker what he thinks was said. This lack of verifying what's been communicated is the source of most misunderstandings in relationships.

Even children with a high EQ can "tune out" when parents are talking.

Remember, the definition of emotional intelligence is the ability to recognize and label one's own emotions and those of others and to respond to them in a healthy way. We learned in the Feelings Chapter that parents and children misread body language approximately 30-50% of the time. One-way we can get better at reading another person's feelings is by communicating with them about feelings. In other words, checking out what they're feeling. For example, you might say to your child, "You look like you might be feeling really upset, tired, or frustrated." The more time you take to ask you child about his feelings, the more you'll encourage him child to ask about yours. When he comes to you and says, "Mom/Dad, you look really upset...tired...frustrated," you'll know you've succeeded in teaching him how to read people's feelings. The more practice he gets in reading other's people emotions, the more your child's EQ will be increased. It is important as you are teaching your child communication skills to be aware of what Cognitive Stage they are in.

What Are The Cognitive Stages?

Cognitive Stages identify developmental stages of our thinking ability. Research has consistently determined that a person cannot skip the cognitive developmental stages identified by Jean Piaget in the early 1900's.

The following is a brief summary of these stages:

AGE	STAGE	YOUR CHILD...
0-2 years	Sensorimotor	• lives in the here and now, the present • is aware of pain and pleasure • what he feels is what he thinks • thinks in terms of "black and white", either/or • believes you can read his mind
2-6 years	Preoperational	• focuses on only one idea at a time • engages in magical thinking; if I think it, it will happen • is into categorizing • is beginning to see beyond today • beginning to problem-solve
6-11 years	Concrete Operational	• can solve problems that involve concrete objects • is beginning to understand relationships • understands cause and effect
11+ years	Formal Operational	• is beginning to understand reversibility • is beginning to use logic • can hypothesize, rationalize, and engage in abstract thinking • is beginning to understand sarcasm

Communicating With Babies And Young Children

Birth To Six Months Old

Our primary way of communicating with our baby at this early stage is by mirroring back her sounds of cooing or babbling. Obviously, we don't mirror her crying—although I'm sure there are moments when parents feel like it. When we respond with like sounds to our infant, we are encouraging them to communicate. When we make eye contact, we are making an emotional connection. When we respond to our baby's cries, she is learning about communication. She is learning: if I cry, there is an action that follows that usually meets my needs. Each of these actions begins laying the foundation of communication.

These first six months are a vital time in laying a strong foundation for a child's future emotional intelligence and social attachments. During these months, an infant's brain is developing the circuitry she will use throughout her life. So our behavior toward her, and how we communicate with her, is much like programming a computer.

Six Months To One-Year-Old

It is important to talk to your infant like he understands what you are saying. When you are changing his diaper, feeding him, taking him for a walk, putting him in his car seat, or simply doing work around the house while he watches, it is important that you talk to him. Describe in detail what you are doing, how you are feeling, what you are going to do next. Talk about your feelings as you are doing this. All of these interactions role model to your child how to communicate.

One-Year-Old To Two Years Old

When you have followed all the previous suggestions, chances are that your child will try to talk in sentences and engage in conversations very early. So during her second year especially, be prepared to enjoy some nonsense conversation. Although she is making sounds and not words, your child is having a conversation with you. Your job is to talk with her. Interact as though you understand her. Laugh, smile, and enjoy the interactions. As you engage each other, you will be deepening your emotional connection. Always make sure to keep your voice calm and soothing. During this stage, notice how your child looks at you, and how she responds to different people, objects, and situations.

Two Years Old To Three Years Old

At this age, your child's vocabulary will expand daily. He will even amaze himself. Your job as parent is to continue to encourage conversations and to name feelings—yours and what you think his are. When you do this, you'll be teaching him "feeling labels" and helping him to create his feelings vocabulary. It is important to read books to your child at this stage, daily if it is possible. As you read to your child, ask him questions about what you are reading. It is important to take the time to stop and point at the illustrations and talk about them.

Three Years Old To Four Years Old

At this point in her development, your child will seem to have grown three years instead of only one. Her conversations take on an air of wisdom—and a four-year-old's wisdom is amazing. The more vocabulary she is around (through exposure to parents, siblings, TV, school, etc.) the more words she will use. It is important to remember that four-year-olds may use words without any concept of their meaning. They are masters at imitation. By four years old, they can carry on a conversation with you that may seem way beyond their years. Enjoy them and encourage them, but remember that they are still four; don't get pulled into thinking that they have the cognitive ability of a seven-year-old even if they sound like one.

Let's Take A Look At Two-Way Communication

Since communication is the primary way we deepen our relationships, it is important to remember there are two types of communication. *One-way Communication* involves one person speaking and the other person (hopefully) listening. *Two-way Communication* involves two people taking turns being the Speaker and the Listener. One-way communication between a parent and child might be when the parent gives advice, teaches a child something, lectures him, criticizes him, or judges him. Two-way communication involves conversations, discussions, negotiations, or dialogues between two people.

In two-way communication there are two types of statements people use: You-Statements and I-Statements. The most positive way of interacting with someone in a two-way communication is with an I-Statement. One of the exercises in this chapter will help you learn how to practice I-Statements with your child. Research has found that I-Statements are the most positive way of interacting with another person. When a person uses an I-Statement, the Speaker is taking responsibility for what they are saying. When a person uses a You-Statement, the Speaker is blaming the other person for how they feel or for whatever is wrong.

Let's look at a role play I use in my office to teach my clients the difference between I-Statements and You-Statements. I say to the client, "You make feel so upset when you are late for an appointment because I don't know whether or not you have been in a car accident or if something bad has happened to you and I really wish you would call me next time." What I am essentially saying to my clients is, "<u>You make me upset...</u>" In other words, I'm communicating to my client that they are to blame for how I feel. This is not the case. I am responsible for how I respond emotionally to my clients' actions.

Likewise, when you say to your child, "You make me mad," you are telling him that he is to blame for your emotions. Although a child's actions and choices contribute to how a parent responds to situations, a child is not responsible for a parent's emotions.

When you use a You-Statement with your child, you are encouraging them to take the blame for your emotions and instilling in them undeserved guilt and shame. We are pushing them toward becoming co-dependent. We don't want to do this and therefore must remember to avoid You-Statements.

When you use an I-Statement, it usually elicits a different response. For example, if I said to one of my clients, "I feel so upset when you are late for an appointment because I don't know whether or not you have been in a car accident or if something bad has happened to you and I really wish you would call me next time." What I am communicating to my client here is, "I feel upset...." I am not blaming my client for my feelings, and I am not asking my client to take responsibility for fixing "my upset." I am simply sharing my feelings and requesting the Listener to hear what I have to say.

Whenever I do this role-play, about 90% of my clients say they feel a noticeable difference in their emotional responses between the I-Statement and the You-Statement. When I use the I-Statement, the clients often say they feel bad, but not guilty or responsible, and definitely not defensive.

Words can be very powerful, and yet research on communication only attributes 7% of communication to words. Studies done in the early 70's by Dr. Richard Birdwhistle showed that 7% of communication is done with words, 23% with the tone of your voice, and 70% with body language. In the most recent research, tone of voice has been shown to be even more of a factor in communicating what we think and how we feel. The recently updated percentages are: words 7%, tone of voice 35%, and body language 58%.

I believe there are several reasons the tone of voice percentage went up. One is that more people than ever are using voicemail, message center, answering machines, and cell phones. There is no eye contact or face-to-face interaction with these machines, and therefore our voices convey more of the message.

What Damage Does A Mixed Message Do?

Another reason tone of voice is now considered more important in terms of what we communicate is because there has been more research done on the subject. As a result of the research completed over the last thirty years, we now have a better understanding of what used to be referred to as a *mixed-message*. We now know there are often two levels of communication going on simultaneously: The content or informational level and the emotional level—or what's often referred to as the underlying message or meta-message.

How do these two levels work? On the content level, a person might say, "Nice outfit!" and the words alone communicate a compliment. But on an emotional level, if the tone of voice were sarcastic, "Nice outfit!" would mean something insulting like: "How could you possibly wear an unattractive outfit like that!" And the Listener would obviously react by feeling hurt or upset. The words say one thing, but the emotional content of the person's voice sends a very different message.

When parents say one thing with their words and send a different message with their tones of voice, their children become emotionally confused. Children are not able to understand sarcasm or double meanings until they are about ten or eleven years old or later, but they feel the negative effects of a mixed message. If an adult in a child's life consistently communicates with mixed messages, by eleven years-old, the child will have developed a core belief that says, "Don't trust what people say because they say one thing and mean something different. Be careful. Be cautious. Don't trust people." It's not hard to understand why a child raised with mixed messages is likely to grow into an adult who has problems trusting people.

**A mixed message can be sent with words and
body language as well as tone of voice.**

Remember, too, that a mixed message can be sent with words and body language, as well as tone of voice. Some examples might be:

1. "Have fun when you get up to bat, it's just a game." However, the parent's serious, uptight facial expression communicates to the child: "You'd better hit a homerun or I'll be disappointed."

2. "So you really want to be a rock star when you grow up? That's terrific—I'll come to all your sold-out concerts!" However, the parent's smirking facial expression communicates to the child: "You've have to be kidding—you'll never be good enough to be successful."

3. "So you already brushed your teeth. Uh huh. Good for you," However, the parent shakes his head, meaning he doesn't believe his child for a second.

Straightforward, clear communication is a challenge for parents. The more you practice with your child when she is young, the more emotionally connected the two of you will become, and the better your child will become at communicating in a healthy way with others. This will automatically raise her EQ.

Healthy Communication Meets Our Greatest Emotional Needs

As we've mentioned earlier, a human being's greatest emotional needs are: to feel a sense of belonging and to feel a sense of significance and self-worth. There are three ways we can support our children in fulfilling those needs.

The Three Ways To Support Your Child In Meeting Her Emotional Needs:

1. Actively listen.

2. Respect your child's ideas, thoughts, and dreams.

3. Appreciate and acknowledge your child's worth as a contributor.

I believe that if all families would work on providing these three means of emotional support for their children, spouses, grandparents, aunts and uncles, cousins, and other family members, this would be a 100% better world in which to live. The rate of divorce would decrease significantly. The anger and stress, which tears families apart, would be significantly reduced. People would feel better about themselves and therefore better about the people around them.

Communication is the common denominator in each of the three means of emotional support. Let's take a closer look at each one.

1. Actively Listen

We tend to be so busy that we often listen to our child while we're on the run. We may only "half listen" because our minds are going in five or ten different directions at once. If our younger children seem to be taking a long time telling their story, we may even be aware of our self-talk saying, "Okay honey, could you just hurry your story along—I've got a lot on my mind right now."

To send the message that you are actively listening to your child, there are a few important things you need to do. First, when your child wants to talk to you and you sense that it's important to him, stop whatever else you are doing just for a few minutes, get eye level with your child, and make eye contact. This lets him know that you are interested in what he has to say. If your child comes to you and wants to talk while you are cooking, you'll send a powerful message by turning off the stove for a few minutes and giving your full attention to him. If you are busy paying bills, move away from your desk, sit down somewhere else, and make eye contact. If you are watching TV, turn it off and sit face-to-face with your child.

You get the idea. When you interrupt the activity you are involved in and sit face-to-face with your child, you are sending the message that, "I think what you have to say is important enough to focus my complete attention on it. You are significant."

When you stop the activity you are involved in to listen to your child, you send the message that she is significant.

You are obviously not going to interrupt your activities every time your child wants to share something with you. On the other hand, parents know when something is important to their children. It's normal for parents to become annoyed or frustrated when we're in the middle of something and our children pester us to pay attention to them. In reality, it actually takes less time to actively listen to them than it does to be upset with them and have them get upset back. Not only that, but when you take the time to listen attentively, children are left with the feeling that you are interested in them.

When you listen to your child, be aware of the emotions he is expressing through his words, body language, and tone of voice. Name those feelings back to him. For example, "It sounds like you are really angry." Even if you are wrong, your child will feel listened to because you are trying to understand how he feels. If you say "angry" and he's feeling sad or hurt, more than likely he will correct you. Your job is to listen and give feedback to him about what he has just said he's feeling. For instance, "So you are not angry, but you are really hurt and sad." Your child will feel so good that you got it. He will feel supported, respected, and understood. Remember, you don't have to agree with your child; you just have to respect his right to feel what he feels. This usually takes less than ten minutes.

I have to share that I recently received a phone call from a school principal the morning after she had attended one of my evening seminars. She was calling to tell me that when she got home the night before, about nine-thirty, her fourteen-year-old son asked if he could talk to her for a few minutes. Although she was tired and would have liked to go straight to bed with a good book, she thought about what I'd just talked about in the seminar. So she told herself, "This will only take a few minutes, and my son will feel like I am really listening to him."

So she put her purse down, took off her coat, made sure she made eye contact with her son, and prepared herself for about five or ten minutes of active listening. The reason for her phone call was to tell me that after forty-five min-utes of sitting and listening to her son, she felt closer to her son than she had in years. She said it was so simple, just like I'd said. She just sat and listened, and he talked and talked and talked. She didn't try to give advice, criticize, lecture, or correct him; she just listened, tried to name his emotions, and asked questions about what he was telling her. She wanted me to know that even though the time spent listening to her son was longer than she had expected, it was well worth it.

2. Respect Your Child's Ideas, Thoughts, And Dreams

We are all born with unlimited possibilities for success. Healthy children dream and fantasize about those possibilities. Visit any preschool throughout the world, and you will see the children playing out those dreams. The possibilities are endless, and the potential for success not even questioned. Children role play mommy, daddy, firefighter, doctors, astronauts, ballerinas, baseball heroes, chefs, teachers, police officer, cowboys, clowns—and the list goes on and on.

Children need to dream about what they might become. But too often we believe it is our job as parents to save our children from future hurt and disap-pointment. So instead of encouraging and enjoying our children's dreams, we discourage them with adult wisdom and knowledge. We may tell our children something we think is sensible like, "Even though you're really good at baseball, so few young men actually make it to the big leagues—I don't want you to count on it and be disappointed." Such a "sensible" message not only smashes the child's dream, but suggests to a six-, eight-, or ten-year-old: "You're not good enough so you might as well stop trying so hard because you'll never make it."

We know that chances are our sons won't make it to the big league, but there is also the reality that somebody's son does make it. Isn't it better to motivate our child to practice and work hard at something he believes in, to learn perseverance and self-discipline, than to tell him not to count on his dream? Which message is likely to help our child develop strength and competency: "I'm trying to save you from being disappointed later in your life by telling you not to count on your dream now," or "Keep dreaming. Work hard. What can I do to support you while you are following your dream?"

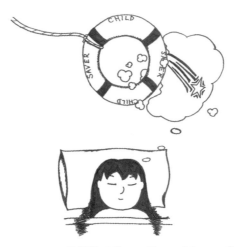

Respect your child's ideas, thoughts, and dreams.

The healthiest children have many dreams. Life usually steers them away from one into another. In the process, they learn about disappointment, frustration, and about survival. As your child develops, he begins to recognize his own strengths and talents and knows that you're going to support him as he pursues his goals, because you have always taken him seriously. As an adolescent, your child can look back and know that you have always believed in him, you have taken him seriously. What a fantastic feeling. It feels a lot like unconditional love, doesn't it?

Don't stomp on your child's dream, but keep academic expectations high. As your child enters her adolescent years and her dreams of being a model, a movie star, or a professional athlete begin to feel like they are in reach, it is important for you to continue to hold your child accountable for her grades. And if she begins to slip, you need to give encouragement and support and consequences, if needed, to keep her on track. Many parents forget that they are still the authority figure in their child's life, even when their child reaches adolescence. It is important to recognize if your child's dream has become an obsession and is controlling her world to the exclusion of everything else. If you can't get her to face reality, recruit family members and friends to point out the need of a backup career plan—"just in case"—by pointing out the statistics of successes in her dream career. If her role models have second careers, point this out. It is important for children to realize that it's always good to have a Plan A, Plan B, and even a Plan C.

To send the message that we take our children seriously, we not only need to let them know that we take their dreams seriously, but their ideas and opinions as well. This can be difficult, because sometimes their opinions are clearly wrong. But you don't have to agree with their opinion; you just need to be willing to listen to them and take them seriously when they are being serious. There will be times when you will want to laugh and say, "Are you kidding me? You really think they should lower the drinking age to sixteen, just because children are drinking anyway?"

When you listen respectfully to your child, especially when you don't agree with him, you are saying "I respect you as a person who is growing and learning. I accept you with all of your dreams and opinions. I love you unconditionally even though you and I are so different" (right now).

So practice saying statements like:

1. "That's really interesting."

2. "That's a different way to look at the situation."

3. "I never thought of it like that."

4. "Oh...that's an interesting opinion."

3. Appreciate And Acknowledge Your Child's Worth As A Contributor

When we help people out at work, in an organization we belong to, or at home, we feel good about it. We feel significant, that we have value.

It is important that we provide as many opportunities as possible for our children to feel the same way. Research has shown that children up to the age of eight need to feel this sense of what I call "worth as a contributor" at least once every twenty-four hours. Children from eight to twelve need to feel it two or three times a week. After twelve or thirteen, two to three times a month.

I know with our children, Bill and I created situations regularly so our children could feel this sense of contribution. With a two-or three-year-old, this need could be met as simply as allowing them to carry a loaf of bread from the car to the kitchen after a trip to the grocery store, and giving them a genuine expression of appreciation. For example, you might say, "Thank you for carrying in that loaf of bread. You saved Mommy an extra trip to the car."

Your child's emotional need can be met by regularly offering a genuine expression of appreciation.

With a four- or five-year-old, your expression of appreciation might sound like this: "Thank you so much for picking up your toys in the living room after I only asked you once. I really appreciate not having to nag you over and over again."

A seven- or eight-year-old needs to hear even more details when you express your gratitude, so they realize that they have contributed. For example, "Thank you so much for taking out the recycling without being told. I am so tired this evening that even taking the recycling to the garage sounded like a lot of work. You really helped me to feel better. It is wonderful to know that you are willing to be such a big help in our family."

You get the idea. Children of all ages like being thanked and appreciated. When you add specifics and make it personal, you increase their sense of value even more.

Look for opportunities to invite your children to be contributors. The earlier you begin making them feel good about what they have done to help out, the more likely they will continue to help without much resistance as they get older.

> **The earlier your child starts becoming a contributor—the better!**

If you have been running around so much during the day that you have forgotten to offer a thank you or a specific appreciation to your child and it's never too late. In fact, sometimes it even means more when you thank your child hours later. For instance, "Mike, I think I forgot to say thank you this morning when you picked up the dog's poop. I just really wanted you to know how much everyone in our family appreciates it when you do that because now we can go into the backyard and not worry about stepping on it. So again, I just wanted to make sure you know how much you contribute to our family. Thank you."

Send The Message: "You Are Significant"

The last thing I want to mention about communication is how important it is to just listen to our children without talking. All too often parents are uncomfortable with silence, and we rush to fill it. But by simply being with our children, we communicate our interest in them. Our body language speaks a million words. So become aware of your body language around your child. Begin to relax and enjoy occasional silences, and just let them happen. Your child will learn that he can be with you and feel emotionally safe without needing to talk or have any discussion. In fact, I would encourage you to deliberately be with your child from about ten years old on, especially through the teen years, without saying anything. The silence usually gets to the child after a while, and they start talking. And when they do, you'll be surprised by how much you're likely to learn about them.

I recommend to all parents of preteens to plan to just sit with your child at least two to three times a week in silence for about ten minutes. For example, when I got home from work at eight or nine in the evening, I would go into one of our children's bedrooms and just sit on the bed. The first couple of times I did this, I would always get this look, especially when they were about twelve and thirteen years old. The look sent the message, "Why are you here? What are you doing sitting on my bed?" I would ignore "the look" and hold to my spot. I had learned early on when I was teaching junior high that children at this age have 'the look' down pat by twelve, so I tried to never take it personally. I would just sit on the bed and say something like "It's been a really long day and it just feels good to be home. How was your day?" And then I'd just be quiet.

At first, they might say something like "fine" and wait for you to leave. But try to just sit there and say nothing. You'll be sending the message that, even though your life is busy, they are important enough to you that you want to take some time to just hang out with them.

If you are willing to find ten minutes two or three times a week to just be with your child, you will be letting him know that you value your relationship with him. And even better, if you can sit in his presence for ten minutes without scolding, lecturing, criticizing, or interrogating him, you will be connecting with your child or preteen in a way that says: "During this time in your life, which can be filled with conflicts and problems, you can feel emotionally safe with me without my criticizing or controlling you. You and I can just be—and it feels good."

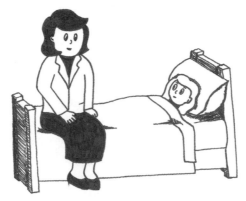

**Spending ten minutes just listening to your child
sends a powerful message.**

Over the last ten years, research has consistently shown that typical parents communicate with their child an average of fourteen and a half minutes a day. And of those fourteen and a half minutes, twelve of them are spent questioning, lecturing, directing, and criticizing: "Is your bed made?", "Did you brush your teeth?", "Have you done your homework yet?", "Who did you play with at school today?", and "Did you take out the garbage?" The remaining two and a half minutes are what the researchers refer to as quality interaction.

I find it extremely frightening to think parents spend only about two and a half minutes a day meeting their child's greatest emotional needs. This research finding may explain why more children and teens than ever before are clinically depressed and suicidal.

When you do the following exercises with your child, you will experience more ongoing communication—some silly and lighthearted, some serious. You will also find yourself becoming more and more comfortable with your two-way dialogues. You will be meeting your child's greatest emotional needs and at the same time discovering how simple the whole process is.

So relax and enjoy the exercises. Please e-mail me with some of your favorite experiences at stories@familypedia.com.

EXERCISE #1 – WHO DO YOU TALK TO EVERYDAY CHART ☆

PURPOSE & BENEFITS:

To introduce the communication exercises in a fun way.

To develop awareness for your child how many people she communicates with each day.

You will learn who your child's friends are, which teachers (preschool and up), parents, and neighbors your child talks to on a regular basis. Anyone your child talks to everyday has an influence on your child. This exercise helps your own awareness to who these people are.

STARTING AGE: 4 years+ (if your child is under 4, you can still do the exercise, but perhaps help your child draw the people she talks to everyday and help post the paper somewhere)

TIME: 10 minutes

LOCATION: Anywhere

MATERIALS:
- piece of paper (white copy paper or color paper, or you can get fancy and use chart paper)
- a writing instrument (pen, pencil, crayon, felt pen, etc.)

INSTRUCTIONS:

1. If you like, make your chart ahead of time on the computer or simply sit down with your child and make it with them as you begin this exercise.

2. Print at the top of the paper "WHO DO YOU TALK TO EVERYDAY?"

3. This exercise can be done on an individual basis or as a family. I would suggest the first time you do it, do it as a family. You can make either one general list and blend all the answers, or divide your chart for each family member. For example:

WHO DO YOU TALK TO EVERYDAY?	
Mom	Mrs. White
Dad	Mr. Jones
Kim	Chris
Mike	Caitlin
Bob	Val

WHO DO YOU TALK TO EVERYDAY?				
Mom	**Dad**	**Kim**	**Mike**	**Bob**
Dad	Mom	Chris	Caitlin	Val
Kim	Kim	Kaylee	Jessica	Abbey
Kaylee	Kaylee	Renee	Mary Beth	Jen
Pam		Mom	Dad	Dad

4.   Post the Chart somewhere for everyone to see. Invite the family to add names to the List during the week.

EXERCISE #2 – SPEAKER - LISTENER ☆

PURPOSE & BENEFITS:

After this exercise has been worked with your child, you can refer to it when you experience miscommunication. Hopefully you can refer to the drawing and laugh or at least smile as you try to figure out where the miscommunication happened.

STARTING AGE: 5 years+ (try it with 4-year-olds! ☺)

TIME: 10 minutes

LOCATION: Anywhere

MATERIALS: • piece of paper

     • a writing instrument

INSTRUCTIONS:

1. Ask your child if he knows what Communication means and how it works between people.

2. Tell him you are going to show him how communication works and you are going to practice good communication for the next couple of (days) weeks.

3. Draw two stick figures and label one Speaker and one Listener:

Speaker   Listener

4. Draw a straight line from the Speaker to the Listener. Explain that communication works well when the Speaker speaks and the Listener hears everything the Speaker says.

5. Now draw a squiggly line and explain that sometimes what the Speaker says gets mixed up between the Speaker and the Listener. The Listener doesn't hear what the Speaker says or doesn't understand what the Speaker said.

6. Give an example: Make up your own or use the following: Mom says, "John put your PJs on and get ready for bed." John hears "Go put your PJs on." Mom gets upset because John only put his PJs on. He did not brush his teeth, wash his face, put his dirty clothes in the hamper, or come out kiss her good-night. Mom gets upset with John because when she said, "get ready for bed," she meant to do all those things. There was

miscommunication.

7. Another example: Dad says, "Matt, are all of your toys picked up?" Matt says, "Yes," because all his toys in the living room are picked up. Dad gets upset with Matt because he meant Matt's toys all around the house and even in the garage and outside.

8. Ask your child if you think that you and he have ever miscommunicated and talk about the times it might have happened.

EXERCISE #3 – TELEPHONE GAME

PURPOSE & BENEFITS:

To have a practical experience of how people can hear words differently. To point out that it is harder to be the Listener than the Speaker. Your child will begin to develop an awareness of the difference between the Speaker role and the Listener role.

STARTING AGE: 4 years+

TIME: 5 minutes

LOCATION: Anywhere

MATERIALS: None, unless you choose to use the example statement as your telephone message

INSTRUCTIONS:

1. This exercise is best done with at least three or four people.

2. The first time you do this exercise, the parent starts the telephone message to be passed on.

3. The parent thinks of a statement you want your family to hear (Most children concentrate on the message because they want to pass it on correctly. No one wants to be the one who mixes up the original message. Think of a statement you really want your child to listen to).

4. The parent whispers the statement into the child's ear. That

child then whispers it to the next person, and so on. The last person to hear the message says it out loud.

5. If there are only three or four of you playing chances are the message will be intact when the last person hears it. The reason it is still important to do this exercise is because you have the opportunity to have your family members concentrate on a statement you wish they would understand.

6. Have fun with the statement. Make it as long as you want. For example, "I wish everyone in this family would do their family chores without being reminded because it would relieve stress for me and I wouldn't get so upset. I appreciate it so much when my family members do their chores without being reminded. It makes me happy, proud, helped, relaxed, supported, pleased, and I feel loved."

7. Chances are that your children, in fact not even another adult, could pass this statement on as it is, but if the message comes through, your children might actually do their chores in a different way.

8. You can also talk to your children and ask them if it is difficult sometimes for them when you give them too many directions at once to do. Talk about a better plan to give directions, i.e., one at a time and then come check in with the parent.

EXERCISE #4 – ONE-WAY COMMUNICATION ☆

PURPOSE & BENEFITS:

To give your child an opportunity to experience and talk to you about one-way communication. You will learn the importance of letting your child always ask clarification questions about something you have said. It will help you see how easy it is for two people to interrupt the same directions in a different way.

STARTING AGE: 4 years+

TIME: 10 to 15 minutes

LOCATION: Anywhere

MATERIALS: • four pictures or designs to describe (Create the picture or design yourself or find in a magazine or book)
• set of direction statements
• a piece of paper for each person participating
• a writing instrument for each person participating

INSTRUCTIONS:

1. The first time you do this exercise, a parent takes the role of the Direction Giver, Instructor, and Teacher.

2. The Direction Giver describes the picture or design, which he has on a piece of paper. He continues to describe step-by-step the picture or design. For example:

    a. Draw a long thin rectangle.

    b. Draw a circle on top of the rectangle.

    c. Draw a straight line on top of the circle.

    d. Draw 3 circles on the straight line...and so on until the Direction Giver has described everything on the paper he is holding.

3. No questions are allowed. The Direction Giver is the only person who can talk.

4. When the Direction Giver is finished giving the direction, he asks everyone to put down his or her writing instrument. He turns his picture around so everyone can see what he was describing.

5. See how different everyone's drawing are.

6. Parent, ask your children: What was it like not being able to ask any questions. Would it have helped to be able to ask questions?

7. Repeat the exercise with another person being the Direction Giver using another picture or design they are holding.

EXERCISE #5 – TWO-WAY COMMUNICATION ☆

PURPOSE & BENEFITS:

To give your child an understanding of how helpful it is to ask questions of anyone for clarification. In the future when you give directions and ask your child if she has any questions, your child will be more likely to say, "Yes" and ask for clarification. Hopefully this exercise will encourage your child to ask his teacher questions.

STARTING AGE: 4 years+

TIME: 10 to 15 minutes

LOCATION: Anywhere

MATERIALS:
- a piece of paper for everyone participating
- a writing instrument
- a picture or design to describe

INSTRUCTIONS:

1. The first time you do this exercise, a parent takes the role of Direction Giver (DG).

2. DG tells the family in this exercise anyone can ask questions to help understand the direction.

3. The DG continues to describe the picture or design until he is finished. He answers all questions along the way, except "Dad, can you show us the picture?"

4. When the DG has finished the description, everyone puts down their writing instruments and the DG shows the family the picture or design he has been describing.

5. Parent, ask your child, "What was that like to be able to ask questions? Was that helpful? Did you match the picture or design being described better by asking questions or not?"

6. Repeat the exercise in the future giving someone else the opportunity to be the Direction Giver.

EXERCISE #6 – BAG OF STUFF ☆

PURPOSE & BENEFITS:

To have your children experience talking to their family with everyone's attention on them. To encourage your child to stay focused on one topic for 30 seconds. To begin to have your children listen to constructive criticism. Your child will experience focusing on a subject for 30, 60, or 90 seconds. Your child begins to accept, or at least, tolerate constructive criticism, an important life skill.

STARTING AGE: 4 years+

TIME: 5 minutes for each participant

LOCATION: Anywhere

MATERIALS:
- bag/box of objects (random objects: a golf ball, a birthday napkin, a picture frame, a deck of cards or a single card, an envelope, a rubber band, a key, a paper clip, a toy, a bar of soap, etc.)
- a stopwatch, kitchen timer, or a watch with a second hand to count to 30 seconds, 60 seconds, or 90 seconds

INSTRUCTIONS:
1. Decide if you are going to have each person talk for 30, 60, or 90 seconds. The first time you may want to start with 30 seconds.
2. Decide in which order you will take turns.
3. When it is a family member's turn, he or she will choose one item at a time out of the bag or box and talk about it for 30, 60, or 90 seconds. It is fun to have a special chair for the Speaker to sit in during the speaking time. Begin the timer when the person begins to talk. The Speaker stops when the timer goes off.
4. Each family member then gives his or her opinion or observations of what was said, such as "interesting," "funny,"

"good," "boring," etc. I suggest the parent begin the opinion time with something positive.

 • One Rule: No put-downs, just observations.

5. After all the feedback is given, the Speaker then gives his opinion of the audience: Quiet, respectful, rude, etc.

6. Everybody in the family takes a turn. More than one person can choose the same object.

7. A fun variation is the Speaker pretends to be a T.V. commercial for the object and sell it.

EXERCISE #7 – MAILBOX

PURPOSE & BENEFITS:

To experience a different type of communication: Written Communication. To experience working together as a family to make everyone feel a sense of belonging.

STARTING AGE: 3 years

TIME: 20 minutes

LOCATION: Kitchen Table and special place to put individual mailboxes

MATERIALS:
• a writing instrument
• an envelope, paper bag, or paper to make a mailbox
• tape
• paper to write notes or draw pictures
• Optional: felt pens, stickers, glue, etc., if you choose to decorate bags

INSTRUCTIONS:

1. Meet together as a family perhaps around the kitchen table.

2. Have all the materials ready so you can enjoy decorating the mailboxes.

3. Everyone puts their names on their mailboxes and then

decorates it if they want to.

4.   Next everyone tapes their mailboxes up to their doors or the place in your home you have chosen for the mailboxes.

5.   Each day everyone writes a short note saying something nice or a happy picture to put in everyone's mailbox. The first day the parent has something prepared to put in the boxes: a note or a picture signed "love, Mom or Dad" or both.

6.   This exercise can go on for three, five, seven days, or even two weeks. You can choose to put something in the mailboxes everyday, every other day or once or twice a week. You decide which works best for your family.

7.   If you are concerned about what one child might write to a sibling, sit with them and help them write a compliment. The time you spend with each child will be worth it because of the goodwill that happens with this exercise.

EXERCISE #8 – TEACH A LESSON

PURPOSE & BENEFITS:

For your child to experience how difficult it can be to teach. She will learn to plan ahead, make decisions, and problem-solve. Your child will begin to develop an appreciation for you as you teach her about life. Your child will better appreciate you trying to help her with her homework.

STARTING AGE: 4 years+

TIME: 5 minutes to 30 minutes according to what your child decides to teach

LOCATION: Wherever the lesson needs to be taught

MATERIALS: • cards with suggestions of teaching lessons (optional)

   • materials needed to teach the lesson

INSTRUCTIONS:

1.   Suggest some ideas that your child could teach to the family.

2. Have each of your children decide from your suggestions what they want to teach their family.

3. Sit with your child and discuss what materials she will need to teach her lesson. Discuss how long it might take to teach the lesson and where she wants to do it. Then choose a time when you can gather everyone together to have her teach her lesson.

4. When she teaches her lesson, be a participant.

5. When the lesson is done, sit with her and ask her: 1) How she felt about her teaching experience, 2) Would she do anything differently next time? 3) What did she like about her experience?, and 4) What didn't she like about her experience?

6. Some teaching Suggestions:

   a. How to make cookies, peanut better and jam sandwiches, pudding, or how to decorate cookies.

   b. To draw a particular picture, paint a picture.

   c. How to paint, make certain, play dough forms

   d. How to play a card game: War, Old Maid, Go Fish, etc.

   e. How to plant a flower, seeds, bulbs, etc.

   f. How to sew, knit, cross-stitch, Lanyards, etc.

   g. How to measure something with a rule yard stick, measuring tape, etc.

   h. How to build a box, a car, a model, etc.

   i. Homemade movies.

EXERCISE #9 – I-STATEMENTS AND ACTIVE LISTENING ☆

PURPOSE & BENEFITS:

To teach your child the least defensive provoking way to communicate. I would not expect your child to use I-Statements regularly or even understand the purpose. The reason you are teaching your child now is to begin to lay the foundation of healthy communication for the rest of his life.

STARTING AGE:　5 years+

TIME:	15 minutes
LOCATION:	Anywhere
MATERIALS:	• I-Statements and Active Listening paper for children who are old enough to read
	• the "I-Statement and Active Listening" Formula – can be copied on to a poster board or a white board and posted in the kitchen or family room (the formula is on page 159)

INSTRUCTIONS:

1. Parent shows chart to family and explains that using an I-Statement is the best way to share our feelings at home, at school, anywhere.

3. The parent begins by saying each family member is going to take a turn being the Speaker and use the I-Statement formula to share how he or she feels about something in his or her life. It can be about himself or herself, school, friends, Mom, Dad, brother, sister, or whatever is important to them in the moment.

3. After the Speaker has given an I-Statement, each family member can take a turn being the Listener and repeat back what the Speaker has said using the Active Listening formula. The parent's role is to ask the speaker if the Listener heard everything the Speaker said correctly.

4. The parent might want to be the first Speaker.

5. A 5-year-old can do this exercise well: in fact, they enjoy showing off how well they listen.

6. Leave the chart on display in your house.

7. Try to practice at least one I-Statement and Active Listening statement with each family member every day. If you eat as a family, dinnertime is a wonderful time to practice this new skill. You will be amazed at how much you will learn about your children by incorporating I-Statements and Active Listening into your family. Communication will feel safer and more open.

I-Statements

I feel_____ (name the feeling) when _____

_____ (describe the situation). Because

_____

(explain why you feel the way you feel) and I wish

_____.

Active Listening

You feel_____ (name the feeling) when _____

_____ (describe the situation). Because

_____

(explain why the Speaker felt the way he felt) and and you wish

_____.

EXERCISE #10 – TV REPORTER - VIP ☆

PURPOSE & BENEFITS:

To open up communication among all family members. To help each family member become comfortable "exploring and sharing" opinions with one another. It continues to establish emotional safety in your family. It creates intimacy in communication, which some families never achieve.

STARTING AGE: 4 years+

TIME: 5 to 10 minutes

LOCATION: Anywhere

MATERIALS:
- list of questions printed on slips of papers (as you become comfortable, make up your questions)
- a container in which to put the pieces of paper (i.e., small basket, gift bag, box, etc.)
- a timer

INSTRUCTIONS:

1. Parent explains that in this exercise everyone will have an opportunity to be a TV news reporter and also a VIP (Very Important Person) being interviewed.

2. Tell the family that you have written the questions for the TV interview on slips of paper in a special basket.

3. There are two ways to do this exercise:
   a. Divide your family in half. Half the members are TV reporters, the other half VIPS. Then pair a TV reporter with a VIP.
   b. Or choose one TV reporter and one VIP to be interviewed in front of the family.

4. Have a family member pick an interview question slip out of the basket and give it to the TV reporter.

5. The TV reporter asks the VIP the question, and then listens to the answer. The TV reporter can continue to ask questions of the VIP to gather more information until the timer goes off ? 3, 4, or 5 minutes.

6. The TV reporter then reports back to the rest of the family what the VIP has shared.

7. Switch roles and repeat the exercise. The same question can be used or you can change to a new question.

8. Suggested Questions:
   a. What is your favorite activity to do with our family?
   b. Share a time when you were proud of yourself.
   c. What makes you angry (in our family)?
   d. If you could plan the perfect family vacation, where

would we go, and what would we do?

    e. If you could buy everyone in our family a special present, what would it be?

    f. If you had three wishes, what would you wish for?

    g. When do you feel the happiest and why?

    h. What do you like the most about each family member and why?

    i. What do you want to do when you grow up?

EXERCISE #11 – PASS IT ON ☆

PURPOSE & BENEFITS:

To learn and experience giving compliments and appreciation to family members. Compliments and appreciation are the doorway to intimate communication. When someone compliments and appreciates you, it is hard to be angry with them. It helps meet the Greatest Emotional Need of making a person feel a sense of worth and significance.

STARTING AGE: 4 years+

TIME: 10 minutes

LOCATION: Where your family can sit in a circle facing one another

MATERIALS: None

INSTRUCTIONS:

1.   Parent begins by giving a compliment or appreciation to someone in the family.

2.   The family member who has received the compliment or appreciation says thank you, and then gives a compliment or appreciation to another family member.

3.   This continues until everyone has given and received a compliment or an appreciation.

4.   You can do this one time around or you can have everyone give and receive two compliments and appreciations.

5.   This exercise is fun to do when your child has a friend over.

The child loves receiving a compliment and almost always goes home and says; "Guess what they do at _____'s house?" The friend's mom will probably ask you about the "thing you do at your house that made her child feel so good." Have fun!!!

ALTERNATE: Each time you do this exercise, the parent gives the direction for the compliment and appreciation to be given to the person on your right or your left. This order is followed until everyone has received a compliment or appreciation. Some families begin to do the exercise like this to eliminate a child needing to think whom they will choose to compliment. When your family has done this exercise often enough, it will be easier for each family member to choose someone to compliment without the "choosing" becoming an issue.

-12-

SELF-ACCEPTANCE

■ ■ ■

What You Will Learn in This Chapter

❑ Your child's self-acceptance is directly related to his sense of being unconditionally loved and accepted by you.

❑ Comparison with other children can lower self-acceptance.

❑ Irrational beliefs sabotage self-acceptance.

❑ There are important differences between a real self-image and an ideal self-image.

❑ How to erase "but" from the compliments you give your child.

❑ How to help your child increase his self-acceptance at various stages in his life.

❑ How to reject the behavior **NOT** the child.

What Is Self-Acceptance?

Self-acceptance is liking ourselves just for who we are. Your child's self-acceptance is directly related to his sense of being unconditionally loved and accepted by someone in his life. Hopefully that someone is you, the parent, grandparent, guardian, or caretaker.

When we like ourselves just for whom we are, we believe in ourselves. We have the self-confidence that tells us we have a good chance of succeeding in things we attempt to do. When our self-acceptance is strong, our emotional intelligence is high. We have learned not to let our emotions of the moment overwhelm us and pull us down. We can recognize our negative as well as positive emotions, and we know the negative ones are only temporary.

The Comparison Trap

As children venture out into the real world, they often fall into the common trap of comparing themselves to those around them. It can start as early as preschool. They see attributes in others that they wish they had themselves and begin to wish that they were taller, thinner, faster, smarter, prettier, and the list goes on. As they fall into this "comparison trap", they are sabotaging how they feel about themselves and lowering their self-acceptance.

You might have heard your own self-talk say:

- "I would feel so much better about myself if I were more athletic."

- "I would have so many more friends if I were prettier."

- "I would be so much happier if I were thinner."

- "People look down on me because I didn't finish college."

These are all common irrational beliefs that millions of adults hold on to and that lower their self-acceptance. Children also compare themselves to others all the time. Perhaps no one accepts themselves one hundred percent, but it is possible to like 85-90% of yourself, leaving the extra 10-15% for healthy growth.

As you continue developing your feelings and communication skills with your child, you'll want to explore on a regular basis what he thinks and how he feels about himself. The reason for doing this regularly is that our children can change how they view themselves from day-to-day, week-to-week. A new student arriving in their class, a new member on their soccer team, a new teacher, a new principal, a new kid in the neighborhood—each of these new people can temporarily upset the balance in your child's life. A new person—whether friendly, strict, talented, cool, smart, athletic, bullying, or accepting—will cause your child to have a psychological and emotional response that changes how he perceives himself and causes him to adjust his self-image accordingly. Part of your job is to be vigilant during this adjustment period and prevent your child from sabotaging his self-acceptance.

Real Self-Image Vs. Ideal Self-Image

There are two different self-images that affect our sense of self-acceptance: an *ideal self-image* and a *real self-image.* The ideal self-image often involves irrational beliefs and can set up a child (or an adult) to fail. For example, ten-year-old Katie holds an ideal self-image that demands she gets all A's in school, weigh ten pounds less, be more popular, and look more like a model for her to feel good about herself.

**Children with low EQ hold the belief that several things
have to change about themselves to be okay.**

When someone at any age holds the belief that many things have to change about themselves to feel okay, you know they have a low-level of self-acceptance. On the other hand, if your ideal self-image isn't far from your real self-image, then your self-acceptance level is high. For example, if Katie's ideal self-image leads her to say, "I wish I could get all B's and maybe branch out and make one to two new friends."

What's the general formula for high self-acceptance? **The formula is shorter the distance between your ideal self-image and your real self-image, the higher your self-acceptance.**

Another example is Austin, a four-year-old boy who may not feel good about himself because he can't ride a two-wheel bike like one of his friends or run as fast as some of the boys at preschool. He may wish he could read like his seven-year-old brother and draw like his eight-year old sister. He has tried to hit a baseball with his dad yet it seems like he always missed the ball while his brother and sister always seem to hit it.

If Austin's ideal self-image leads him to say, "I wish I could run a little faster.", "I am going to ask Dad to help me learn to ride a two-wheel bike", "I am going to keep practicing baseball because I want to get better", or "I know when I'm in school I'll learn how to read like my big brother and maybe even draw like my sister" then his self-acceptance is high.

Think of a child with high self-acceptance as a car with a full gas tank. And picture a child with low self-acceptance as a car with little gas in the tank. When the gas is low, the driver is more cautious, worried, and concerned about running out of gas. He can't take any side trips or adventures. When the gas tank is full, however, the driver has confidence. He knows that, not only can he make it to his destination, but he can also continue on even further.

When we have a full tank of gas, we are more willing to explore new places, do more errands, visit a friend, take a class—and our lives are fuller. When our tank is low, we do only what we have to do to complete our errand or reach our prescribed destination—and then go directly back home. Likewise, when children's self-acceptance is on "low":

- They don't take risks to grow and learn.

- They fear they don't have what it takes to succeed.

- They panic and blame themselves or others for their inability to succeed.

When your child believes that you love and accept him just the way he is, that core belief helps him to accept himself and also gives him confidence. In turn, that self-acceptance and confidence encourage him to take risks to grow and learn, and those experiences then increase his self-acceptance and his self-confidence. When a child feels self-confident, he automatically experiences more success in every aspect of his life. People are ultimately responsible for their own self-acceptance. But we, as parents, have a tremendous affect on our child's self-acceptance from the moment of his birth.

Accepting Your Child For Who He Really Is

Your child's future success and well-being depends on your acceptance of him—just as he is. Do you like your child's personality? Is your child different from how you dreamt he would be when you were looking forward to his birth? If you were dreaming of a star athlete and he is a whiz at computers, his future success and well-being depends on your acceptance of him. When a child feels loved and accepted for who he is at the core, he will succeed even beyond his own expectations. Let alone your expectations.

It is when we have been given an Orchid but what we really wanted was a Rose that we create problems. Then because of our disappointment we set out to turn our Orchid into a Rose. We do this by planting our Orchid in the right sunlight, exposure, and conditions that we know would help a Rosebush grow. Then we fertilize our Orchid with Rose food and vitamins we get from the local nursery. All along, we are expecting that if we ignore that our child is an Orchid and treat her like a Rose, she eventually will turn into a strong beautiful Rosebush.

No matter what you do to an Orchid—it remains an Orchid. It does not turn into a Rose. More importantly, when we put our Orchid in the wrong environment, give it the wrong fertilizer, feed it with the wrong food, it not only will not grow and flourish, but more than likely it will shrivel until you probably won't even recognize it as the beautiful Orchid it might have been. If it survives, it will be unhealthy and under nourished. How sad it is when I see this happen to children I have worked with both as a teacher and a therapist.

On the other hand, when parents accept and nourish their children for who they are and give them the guidance and encouragement they need, these children will go on to accomplish terrific things—often far beyond the parent's expectations.

Unconditional love and acceptance are the greatest motivators. We have the power to water our children with these gifts everyday, even when we are upset or disappointed with them.

**Your child's future success and well-being depends
on your acceptance of her just as she is.**

Just like adults, children have their good and bad days. But as you help them to increase their self-acceptance and raise their EQ, they will experience more good days than bad.

Success And Failure Are Important For Self-Acceptance

One of our most important jobs as parents is to teach our children that disappointment, letdowns, and failures are opportunities to learn and become stronger. No one goes through life without hardship, and if someone you know says they have, they are likely in major denial or can be labeled "a meltdown waiting to happen."

We all know someone who has fallen apart after a distressing event or situation. It could be losing a job, a divorce, the death of a loved one, or serious illness. A meltdown or, in clinical terms, depression following such an event often occurs because the person has never before had to deal with anything traumatic. They have not had to face disappointment, upheaval, or perceived failure and therefore, they never learned they will survive despite life's rocky road.

Succeeding in something they've worked hard for contributes to a child's self-acceptance, but so does experiencing failure, frustration, and rejection—and learning to survive these difficult experiences. When you nurture your child through such difficulties—showing them that they are loved and accepted, and encouraging them to thrive regardless of life's curve balls—they will grow into adolescents who are prepared to face the real world. Your child's self-acceptance will expand because she'll realize she doesn't have to be perfect to be a valuable person. She'll learn not to let life overwhelm her and not to give up. And she'll enter adult life with a high EQ.

Self-acceptance, regardless of disappointments and failures, is something we help our children develop by letting them know we accept them no matter what. When we fail to give them this foundation, they will lack the self-acceptance necessary to bounce back in the face of criticism, hardship, or failure.

Throughout my fourteen years as a classroom teacher, I noticed that children with a low-level of self-acceptance seemed to attract criticism and teasing from the other children. It was as though this happened almost from the minute they walked into the classroom. As though they wore a sign that proclaimed, "I HAVE LOW SELF-ACCEPTANCE – PICK ON ME!" So the other children did just that, and the cycle of low self-acceptance, low self-confidence, limited successes, and few friends was continued.

As a school counselor, I found that when I built a relationship with children who had low levels of self-acceptance and they began to trust me, I could help them to change their self-perception and to believe in themselves. It only takes one person who believes a child is genuinely capable of success to help that child change his perception of himself. Once a child has someone he can count on to unconditionally accept him, encourage him to try new things, celebrate his successes with him, and be with him through his failures, he will begin to value and believe in himself.

We know that to achieve we must believe that we can. Remember the story of the little engine that said, "I think I can, I think I can"? Well that little train had high self-acceptance and self-confidence. We want our children to have that faith in themselves, and we can help them by encouraging their self-acceptance every day.

When a child knows that he won't be overwhelmed by his emotions, even in the face of adversity, his self-acceptance will expand and his emotional intelligence will soar. He will make healthy decisions, and he'll know that not only will he survive, but he will grow and succeed as well.

Skill Development Contributes To High Self-Acceptance

It is our job to discover our child's unique interests and talents, and to support and encourage him to develop those pursuits. Regardless of their age, we need to offer our children opportunities to explore and discover their strengths so they can feel a sense of accomplishment and feel good about themselves.

Be aware that your child might have a skill or talent you're unfamiliar with or disinterested in. Such was the case with the father of a twelve-year-old client of mine. The young man's mother loves and accepts him unconditionally, but his father has struggled to accept the path this boy has chosen. The son is not what the father expected him to be. Whereas, the father is a very athletic man who loves sports, the son is a gifted musician with no interest in sports. It has taken awhile for the dad to accept this important aspect of his son because being a musician is something the dad has little understanding of. Still, the dad recognizes his son's need for acceptance from him. He is beginning to realize that showing unconditional love for, and acceptance of, his son as a person must include his musical talent, which is part of who the boy is and who he will become as an adult. The father must also accept that his own future will include attending his son's musical recitals rather than attending his son's baseball, basketball, or football games.

There is a strong correlation between self-acceptance and personal skills development. It appears that when one part of this equation increases, the other part increases at similar rates. As a child's self-acceptance increases, his competence in all areas of his life increases, and the more positive his core beliefs about himself become.

Being motivated at any age always stems from the belief, "I have a good chance of succeeding in this goal I have set!!!"

Don't Rescue Your Child

Unless your child is in physical danger, attempting to rescue him will likely inhibit his self-acceptance and self-confidence. When you rescue a young child, you send the message that you don't believe he's capable of doing the task himself. When we send this message often enough, our children begin to believe that they are not capable of succeeding on their own, and that it's better to wait for Mom or Dad to help them.

Rescuing can be as simple as building a tower of blocks for your toddler because his tower keeps falling down. Rather than doing the job for him, it is important to encourage him to continue to try, because that's how he will eventually succeed. In the process of striving to succeed, he will develop his patience and perseverance.

A common rescue scenario involves being responsible on behalf of your child—rather than leaving the responsibility up to him and letting the cards fall where they may. For example, if your school-age child forgets his lunch or homework, don't rush to school and bring the forgotten item. You'll be teaching him this life lesson: "If I can get somebody else to remember for me, why remember it myself." On the other hand, it usually takes only one or two days of forgetting his lunch for your child to develop a plan to not forget it.

It is important to let our children learn from the consequences of their actions. If you forget your homework and you get in trouble from your teacher, hopefully you will learn to come up with a plan to prevent this from happening the next time. For example, you might put your homework in your backpack the night before.

Our job is to check out with our children what caused the problem. Then to ask them what they would do differently next time. Sending the message that we believe they are capable of growing, changing, and learning empowers our children to believe in themselves.

All too often in today's busy world, parents rescue their children simply to save time. A common example of this is a mom or dad tying their child's shoelaces or helping them get dressed when the children are capable of doing it themselves. Remember the message we send to our child when we step in too soon and don't allow them to succeed on their own: "I don't think you're capable of succeeding in this task now or in your future, so I am rescuing you." The child then believes they're incapable, they have little motivation to try, and their self-acceptance declines.

Another reason a mom or dad rescues a child is to make themselves feel better. Perhaps a parent works long hours and doesn't get to spend much time with his child. So to make himself feel more involved in his child's life, he ties his son's shoes or brings his daughter's forgotten homework to school. The parent feels better about himself for having helped his child, but the child still receives the same message from the parent: "You're not capable of doing this on your own, so I'll do it for you." It's no wonder that a child's self-acceptance would suffer if this happened too often. Such rescuing could even teach the child to manipulate other people into doing what he doesn't believe he can do himself.

Parents often rescue children simply to save time.

Don't Let "But" Trap Erase Your Compliment

Sometimes we unintentionally send messages to our children that damage their sense of self-acceptance. It's as if we're telling them that, no matter how well they've done, it isn't good enough. You might be thinking to yourself, "I never do that," yet too often our negative statements about our children are camouflaged within a supposedly positive one. For instance you might say...

- to your three-year-old, "You must be so proud of yourself for getting dressed all by yourself, honey, <u>but</u> you need to change out of your sandals into your tennis shoes because it's cold outside."

- to your four-year-old, "You're getting so good at making your own bed, <u>but</u> could you just tuck in the blanket that's dragging on the floor?"

- to your eight-year-old, "You did a great job cleaning your room, <u>but</u> could you also empty your wastebasket?"

• to your school aged child, "Wow—you raised almost all your grades on this report card, <u>but</u> tell me what happened in science."

When you hear yourself tack on a "but" to your compliment, realize that you're telling your child they may have done a good job..."but" it wasn't good enough. When a child hears the "but" often enough, they begin to hold onto the following as a core belief: "No matter what I do, it's not good enough so why bother to try at all?" When I work with a child who is obviously bright enough to succeed, but isn't doing well, I always begin by exploring his belief about success. If he tells me he's never good enough, I bring the parents in and teach them about the "but" trap. It is amazing how many children begin succeeding when the parents drop the "but" from their compliments.

So what can parents do to help children improve their skills—without raining on their parades by using the "but" phrase? First, it's important to let children celebrate and enjoy their successes before you talk to them about how to do even better. Then, at a later time, talk about how they can plan to succeed even more next time. For instance, in the case of the inappropriate shoes, explore with your young child what they might think about before they decide what shoes to wear. Perhaps talk about the weather and then let them be. In the case of the report card, if your child improved in several subjects, celebrate the success for several days before you begin discussing what she could do differently this semester in science.

Children (and adults) who feel successful on a regular basis will take more risks to succeed in the future because they believe they can succeed. It is always easy to point out what's wrong. Instead, be on the look out for what's good about your child's behavior or accomplishments and point that out to her. Celebrate her successes with her, and she will enjoy a high-level of self-acceptance.

Avoid *Grading* Statements

One last thing you can do to prevent low self-acceptance in your child is to avoid what I call grading statements. These are any statements that include judgmental words. For example:

- "You did a <u>great</u> job."

- "You are <u>terrific</u>."

- "You are a <u>good/bad</u> girl."

- "You <u>are one of the best....</u>"

All of these statements are grading statements because they reflect the parent's judgment of the child. Our goal when we make such statements is usually to make children feel good about themselves. What often happens instead is that children become dependent on our (or other people's) approval. What we want to do is empower our children to feel good about themselves intrinsically. That is, we want them to feel good about themselves because they are proud of themselves for having accomplished something they set out to do. We want them to feel great or terrific because they recognize <u>they</u> have succeeded in something, not because someone else has passed judgment on them.

When our children are dependent on other people's opinions of themselves to feel good, they are vulnerable to peer pressure, gangs, or cults. High self-acceptance means, "I like myself not because of what you tell me, but because I have the core belief that I am a valuable and capable person. "

So parents will want to make statements like the following:

- "I would be so proud of myself if I were you."

- "I hope you're proud of yourself."

- "Wow, I bet you feel terrific about what you just accomplished."

- "How great you must be feeling about your success."

Each of these statements encourages your child to feel the sense of pride from within.

Enhancing Your Child's Self-Acceptance—Stage By Stage

Let's take a look at what you can do at each stage of your child's development to help him to like and accept himself and thus raise his EQ.

Birth To Six Months: Time Of Reacting

- Smile at your infant while making eye contact.

- Talk to him in a positive soothing voice.

- Hug and hold your infant and discover soothing actions—for example, rub his back in a circular motion or gently pat his back.

- Take him for walks in the stroller, and point out things of interest along the way—for example, trees, flowers, and birds.

- Sit and play with him with his toys. (Smile and laugh while you are doing this.) Include books, and primary color toys.

- Sing to him.

Six Months To One-Year-Old: Time Of Responding

- Play peek-a-boo and pat-a-cake.

- Continue all of birth to six months interactions.

- Offer new opportunities to explore and stay in emotional contact. For example, give your child a small plastic bowl with a lid on it and sit with him and smile while he explores it.

- Talk with him while he explores his toys.

- Give him a piece of paper, a letter, or a book and talk with him as he explores it. He will probably feel it, bite it, turn it over, and try to rip it. The possibilities are endless. The emotional payoff is tremendous; he feels good about himself.

- While you are taking him for a walk, continue to point things out at which to look at. If your infant points to something, stop walking and point with him, talk to him about what he pointed out.

One-Year-Old: Year Of Exploring

- She is starting to walk, talk, and explore. When you have the time, just sit and be present as she explores. Let her show you her discoveries. Show interest and talk to her about her discoveries.

- She will begin to talk with you using sounds. Engage with her. You can either use real words or mirror back her sounds and facial expressions.

- Continue to point out things around you, and talk about them.

- Introduce new objects. Let her explore in her own way. If she starts by biting her new book instead of looking at the pictures, let her be.

- By now, you have introduced no. Say it firmly and mean it. Otherwise don't waste your time to say it. Your child is beginning to connect words and actions. You want her to learn that no means to stop the action. If you say no and she continues—say "No" firmly, pick her up, and move her to another activity. The no doesn't have to be scary; it just has to be firm. If you say no at this age and don't follow through, she is learning that no means nothing.

Two Years Old: Year Of Separation From Mom

- Be aware that during this year your child begins to understand that he is separate from his mom. This year lays the foundation for being able to value himself as a separate human being.

- Understand that during this year, your child continues to develop his physical abilities, as well as his vocabulary. His challenge is to assert his individuality. This may come across as demanding and negative. His two favorite words, which you may hear a great deal, are no and mine. Be patient—these are normal expressions.

- Teach him acceptable ways of being assertive, such as asking rather than grabbing.

- As often as possible—perhaps two or three times a day—give your two-year-old choices with which you can live. This helps him to feel an assertive sense of being in control of himself and builds his belief that he is capable.

As often as possible, give your child choices you can live with.

- Remember that your two-year-old is being stubborn or defiant; he is trying to discover his power, and your job is teaching him how to assert it safely.

- Continue to set boundaries and follow through with a firm NO when the boundaries are disregarded. Your consistency will pay off later.

Three Years Old: Year Of Autonomy And Competence

- Understand that a three-year-old's challenge is to discover her sense of competence and value, and to recognize and accept her separation from Mom.

- Allow your child to experience successes in all aspects of her life. Success at this stage plays an important role in her self-acceptance.

- Recognize her achievements with specific acknowledgment and celebrate. If she has drawn a picture, put it up somewhere where the family can see it.

- A three-year-old thrives on success, but she may take awhile getting there. So be patient, even if it seems like she's taking forever.

- Actively listen when she's sharing with you. Make eye contact and ask questions about what she is saying, and repeat back what she has said.

- Be aware that your child is looking for your acknowledgment and feedback, which she needs to feel successful. Your clue that she's seeking your acknowledgment will be something like, "Mommy, Daddy, watch me, watch me!"

- Let her have play dates whenever possible. This is a year of sociability and learning to play with friends.

- She may have moments or days of insecurity, so practice your communication skills, and check out how she is feeling and what she is thinking.

- Let her know that she is unconditionally loved and accepted.

- When you have had a conflict with your three-year-old, always follow it up by hugging her and saying, "I love you." This is a reminder that you are unhappy or disappointed with the behavior, but not with who she is.

Four Years Old: Year Of Independence And Motivation

- Be aware that a four-year-old's challenge is one of independence. Success during this year lays the foundation for his ability to be motivated in his future.

- Let your child take on new challanges (as long as they are safe) even if you know he won't succeed, and then compliment him for his willingness to help. He is looking for ways to take on more responsibility in the family and to show he is capable, such as making his bed, cleaning his room, dressing himself for school, or helping you make dinner.

- Don't redo an imperfect job (i.e. remake the bed or reset the table) or you will discourage him from wanting to try again.

- If you want your child to improve the way he does a particular job, show him by doing it with him—rather than for him.

Five Years Old: Year Of Reaching Out And Running Back

- Understand that this is often a mellow year for your child. A five-year-old feels like they are reconnecting with Mom and Dad after a year of pulling away.

- Separation anxiety can creep into some five-year-old's sense of safety and security. If this happens to your child, understand that it is real for him. You can ease his discomfort and reinforce your unconditional love and acceptance by respecting your child's fears and concerns. When you are going out, let him know where you are going, that you will be safe, and how the baby-sitter can reach you.

- If you go away on a long business trip or vacation, call and talk to her. Tell her when you will return and that you love and miss her.

When you are away overnight, call and talk to your child.

- Celebrate with your child for making good choices.
- Continue to explore his strengths and talents and find ways to begin to improve his ability in these areas.
- Begin keeping a box or file of your child's work to show him his growth.

Six Years Old: Year Of Exploring New Skills

- Be aware there is a normal self-centeredness at this age.

- Understand the six-year-old's challenge is to begin to understand herself, what she likes and doesn't like about herself and others. She is opinionated and likes to have her own way.

- This is a year to continue to encourage your child to explore new skills. Expose her to more interests. Sign her up for classes at the park or playground. Create situations that will encourage new learning experiences, such as helping your child make or build something, playing board games, etc.

- You will be constantly setting healthy boundaries and limits this year. Show empathy and acceptance as you enforce these.

- Even if you feel your buttons pushed, avoid sarcasm.

- Be aware of any comparison you make to siblings, classmates, teammates, friends, or neighbors.

- Again, give your child choices with which you can live.

- If you have more than one child, plan to spend time separately with each one, doing what interests them individually.

Seven Years Old And Eight Years Old: Year Of Exploring Social Skills

- Be aware that your child is shifting from the self-centeredness of the six-year-old to the sociability of this stage. Relationships with friends are important, as is their influence on your child's life. Being accepted by friends will impact your child's sense of self-acceptance.

- Help your child to avoid comparing themselves to friends by making her aware of her unique qualities and strengths.

- Continue to provide opportunities to develop skills in a variety of areas.

- Continue to encourage play dates.

- Encourage your child to join same-age groups, sports teams, girl or boy scouts, etc.

- This is an important time to reinforce what you have taught in your family about cooperation and fairness.

• Continue to communicate and explore with your child how she feels about herself.

Nine Years Old And Ten Years Old: Year Of Confidence

• Be aware that this is a confident time in your child's life, during which he usually enjoys and takes pride in his family. There is a new sense of cooperation, and he feels especially good about himself. His self-acceptance is usually at a high.

• Your child's personal challenge during these years is to explore his sexual identity. He needs to imitate the same sex parent, so make sure you role model behavior you want your same sex child to develop.

• It is also important to help your child develop a positive relationship with the opposite sex parent.

• Continue to set up play dates.

• Allow your child to follow fun fads (if they are within your budget and value system) so he will feel part of the general school community.

• Continue to verbally communicate your love and acceptance of him. Convey your confidence in your child and in his future.

• Encourage development of new skills, at which your child could become the family expert; for example, cooking, sports, etc.

It is important to expose children to as many experiences as possible.

New Experiences = New Opportunities To Develop Self-Acceptance

As we've learned throughout this chapter, it is important for our children's self-acceptance to expose them to as many experiences as possible. Some children are resistant to trying new things, but also be aware that some may say "No" just to say "No." They may like their parent to work at talking them into yes, so don't become discouraged. Be open to their opinions, and be willing to address their skepticism about whatever it is you're suggesting they try—whether it's an art museum or kayaking. It always amazed me to hear back from a friend or a teacher that one of our children had talked about how much he liked an experience that he had been resistant to with us. So even if your children seem less-than-enthusiastic about a new family activity, be alert to the signs that they are actually enjoying it!

Here's a list of places, events, and activities that can provide your children with inspiring new experiences. Use this as a jumping-off point to brainstorm further possibilities with your family:

Places:

- Science museum
- National park
- Art museum
- Aquarium
- Zoo
- Historical monuments
- Another neighborhood, city, state, or country

Events:

- Play
- Concert
- Opera
- Ballet or other dance performance
- Lecture
- Political rally
- Local college football or basketball game
- County fair
- Neighborhood street fair

Activities:

- Volunteering (at a food bank, homeless shelter, hospital, Special Olympics...)
- Scouting
- Sports (swimming, tennis, boating, volleyball, golf, baseball, basketball...)
- Walk-a-thon, Marathon, Junior Tri-Athlete
- Organized hikes (Sierra Club, etc.)
- Cooking classes
- Art classes
- Music classes
- Board and card games

Reject The Behavior, Not The Child

In considering how to best encourage your child's self-acceptance, be aware of another important guideline: Avoid yelling and name-calling. Children are hypersensitive to a parent's yelling. Almost all children I've worked with interpret their parent's yelling as disapproval of <u>who they are</u>. In other words, when a parent yells on a regular basis, a child believes they are being yelled at because the parent doesn't like them, or worse, doesn't love them.

When you need to scold your child, be clear that it is his <u>behavior</u> you are unhappy or disappointed with, <u>not him</u>. Let him know that you are upset with his bad choice, but that he has the power to change bad choices by learning how to act differently next time.

When you reprimand your child, never use any devaluing names, like "stupid" or "idiot" because that is all your child will hear. They will believe that you think they are stupid or an idiot.

A child can be devestated by a parent's tone of voice.

Remember that your child is extremely sensitive to the way you address him. Although children can ignore a sibling's yelling or taunting, they can be instantly devastated by a parent's critical tone of voice. I am not sure where this hypersensitivity comes from, but it is certainly present until at least age twelve or thirteen, when it doesn't so much disappear as it transforms into defensiveness and anger. Adolescents and teens take on the attitude that, "If you don't like me for who I am, then I will find peers who do. They'll accept me as I am and won't constantly criticize me like you do."

When parents' relationships with their children are built on a strong foundation of unconditional love and acceptance—as well as communication, boundaries, and rules—the children will not depend solely on their peers for their sense of self-acceptance. A child with such solid parental support knows that she always has a safe place to go where she is loved and accepted. It doesn't get any better than that. (Not even for adults!!!)

Celebrate Your Child!

Our job as parents is to encourage, support, celebrate, love, and accept our children's individuality and uniqueness.

The following exercises are designed to help you help your child to develop his self-acceptance and self-confidence. I hope that you are open to the changes that I may ask you to make, as they will benefit not only your child, but all of your relationships as well.

So get ready to have fun and feel good about your child and yourself. When our children's self-acceptance is high, their EQ soars.

EXERCISE #1 - THINGS I LIKE ABOUT ME ☆

PURPOSE & BENEFITS:

To encourage your children to value and appreciate their strengths. To build their core belief: "I am a capable person. I have worth and value." When people of any age feel good about who they are, they live their days with a more positive outlook.

STARTING AGE: 4 years (you can help your 3-year-old do these exercises)

TIME: 10 to 20 minutes

LOCATION: Anywhere

MATERIALS:
- piece of paper per person participating (plain or decorated)
- pens, pencils, crayons, or felt pens
- put the heading on each piece of paper "Things I Like About Me"

INSTRUCTIONS:

1. Sit with your child (or children) and tell him you are each going to list twenty-five things you like about yourselves.

2. Give your child some suggestions to begin his list: smart, funny, brown eyes, black hair, runs fast, is nice. You want to encourage him to list physical features, personality strengths, talents, and abilities.

3. Ask your child to tell you things they like about you to begin your list.

4. When your lists are completed, put them somewhere where you will see them each day: the refrigerator in the kitchen, a bulletin board in the family room, etc.

NOTE: If you have a 2-year-old, sit and tell your child things you like about them. Then print ten things on a list and post it. Tell your child what you have written on the list.

EXERCISE #2 - THINGS OTHERS LIKE ABOUT ME ☆

PURPOSE & BENEFITS:

To have your child feel loved and valued by his family and others. To continue to build their core belief "I am a capable person. I have worth and value." Your child will feel a sense of belonging and significance.

STARTING AGE: 4 years (you can help your 3-year-old)

TIME: 5 to 10 minutes to begin—it may take a few days to complete if you want grandparents, friends, and neighbors to contribute to the list

LOCATION: Anywhere

MATERIALS:
- piece of paper per person participating (plain or decorated)
- pens, pencils, crayons, or felt pens
- put the heading on each piece of paper "Things Other People Like About Me"

INSTRUCTIONS:

1. Sit with your child (children) and tell him that he is to ask other people what they like about him and list their answers on the piece of paper.

2. Each person participating is to list twenty-five things that other people like about him.

3. You, the parent should start this exercise by telling each child some things you like about them and begin their lists.

4. When the list of twenty-five is completed, the family will meet together and share their lists.

5. The parent also asks the children to help begin the parents' list by telling the parent some things they like about them.

EXERCISE #3 - BE AWARE! ☆

PURPOSE & BENEFITS:

To become aware of your child's body language about themselves – when they feel good and when they feel bad. A child's self-acceptance can change at any time and when we are aware of a change, we can help our children grow through difficult times rather than being pulled down and getting stuck. Often children feel bad and they don't know how to ask for help. When we, as parents, know how to read our children's body language (even if we read it incorrectly 30% of the time), we can offer our child the opportunity to explore how they are feeling about themselves and formulate a plan to change the feeling if they want to.

STARTING AGE: 3 years

TIME: seconds to minutes

LOCATION: Everywhere

MATERIALS: None

INSTRUCTIONS:

1. Begin to notice your child's body language when he is relaxed, comfortable, upset, assertive, reluctant, happy, etc.

2. Begin to notice your child's body language when he interacts with you (Mom, Dad), siblings, neighbors, Grandma, Grandpa, friends, classmates, sports, team members, teachers, coaches, etc.

3. You are looking for a change in your child's body language at difficult times in your child's interactions with individuals and groups.

4. If you notice that your child's body language changes with different people he interacts with, you want to explore what causes your child to feel uncomfortable, unhappy, upset or even intimidated in particular situations or with certain individuals. The goal is to help empower him to feel better.

5. The next exercise will help you to learn to explore with your child what and how he is feeling.

EXERCISE #4 -EXPLORE ☆

PURPOSE & BENEFITS:

To begin the process of teaching your child how to discover the source of his negative feelings and then empower him to move beyond them with some type of plan. Your child begins to learn he can empower himself to feel better in life when he is willing to explore for the source of the negative feeling.

STARTING AGE: 4 years

TIME: 5 minutes + (when your child is showing signs of negative feelings)

LOCATION: Anywhere

MATERIALS: None

INSTRUCTIONS:

1.   Parent sits with the child anywhere they can find with the least amount of distraction. Parent is able to make eye contact.

2.   Parent tells the child "We're going to **EXPLORE** just like a scientist looking for an answer, or an astronaut exploring space, or a pioneer looking for a new land in which to settle in. You can use any example that you know your child would understand.

3.   Explorers always begin with questions. So does the parent. The parent tells the child, "I am going to ask exploring questions to see if I can help you discover what is making you feel badly."

4.   "Let's explore what you are feeling <u>right now</u>. Let's see if you can name at least four of five <u>feelings</u>." If you have worked the exercises in the Feelings chapter, your child will be used to recognizing and naming at least four or five feelings. Listen to all the feelings your child names. The more you do this exercise with your child, the easier the process will go.

5.   When your child has listed all of her feelings, begin to explore each of them individually until you have figured out what is upsetting your child. For example, "<u>Tell me more</u> about feeling scared (etc.)." "<u>What does it feel like</u> to be angry (etc.)?" "<u>How does it feel</u> to be sad (etc.)?" Avoid asking "Why" questions

because often your child doesn't know the why and they might shut down.

6.   When you have explored your child's listed feelings, you will have enough information to help him develop a plan to feel better.

- All the parents I have ever worked with have a creative streak when it comes to helping their children, but if you get stuck at this step, your child can help come up with a plan.

7.   Plans can be simple. For example, if a child is feeling like they have no friends:

- Mom might set up a play date.
- Mom might sign her child up 1) to take a class at the Park and Recreation Department: 2) for a soccer team, T-ball team, etc.
- Plan a family "feel good" party.
- Plan to talk and come up with an idea everyday for the child to try at preschool or school the next day.

8.   Tell your child you will talk and reevaluate the plan in two or three days.

9.   The empowering has begun. Your child has begun to feel a little more control in her life.

10.   Let's Review:

- Explore with your child how she feels.
- Make a plan to feel better.
- Reevaluate the plan.

EXERCISE #5 - NAME PAGE ☆

PURPOSE & BENEFITS:

To feel a sense of belonging and acceptance in the family. Meets one of your child's greatest emotional needs.

STARTING AGE: 4 years (you can help your 3-year-old)

TIME: 20 minutes

LOCATION: Somewhere with a flat surface: kitchen table, family room, living room coffee table, outdoor table, etc.

MATERIALS:
- 8½" x 11" paper (or be creative)
- pens, pencils, crayons, or felt pens

INSTRUCTIONS:
1. Have everyone sit around the table.
2. Give each family member a piece of paper.
3. Everyone prints or writes their names in the center of their paper (fancy or simple).
4. Then everyone passes their paper to the family member on their left (or right) to write a note on it.

Caitlin

---

5. All family members are to write a note naming at least two things they like about the person whose name is in the center of the paper.
6. The papers are passed around the table until everyone has their own paper back. Then everyone reads and enjoys what's been said about them.
7. Everyone posts their own paper somewhere in sight so they are able to look at it each day and feel good.

NOTE: A 3-year-old can draw a picture of something they like on each paper.

EXERCISE #6 - OPINIONS ☆

PURPOSE & BENEFITS:

To send the message to your child that you value him. You will learn how your child thinks and feels about various things. Your child's sense of significance and worth will increase.

STARTING AGE: 3 years

TIME:	5 to 10 minutes
LOCATION:	Anywhere
MATERIALS:	None

INSTRUCTIONS:

1. Ask your child for his opinion as often as your can. For example: what you are wearing, what to make for lunch, cook for dinner, a TV show, a movie, something on the news, decorating his room or the house, planting in the garden, planning a dinner party, family or birthday party, a game to play, a present to buy, your baseball, football, basketball, soccer, high school, college teams, plan a picnic, a vacation, a special family night, family outing, setting the table, the list is endless.

2. When your child has shared his opinion, always acknowledge it.

3. Whenever possible, use your child's suggestion whether it's his whole idea or even part of it. Make sure you acknowledge it and give credit to your child in front of the rest of your family.

4. The goal is to have your child feel a sense of value and significance.

EXERCISE #7 - SELF-PRAISE ☆

PURPOSE & BENEFITS:

Children need to be able to praise themselves. This helps them to see themselves as capable human beings. There is a difference between self-praise (I feel good about what I have accomplished) and bragging (Look at me, I am better than everyone else). This exercise helps children to see the difference between self-praise and bragging. It helps to build positive self-talk.

STARTING AGE:	3 years
TIME:	2 to 3 minutes per family member
LOCATION:	Anywhere
MATERIALS:	None

INSTRUCTIONS:
1.   Parent chooses a time when the family is all together. Dinner-time is a wonderful time to do this exercise.
2.   When you are just beginning to do this exercise the parent begins it.
3.   Everyone thinks of a success they have had that day or the day before and shares it with the family. They share what effort went into the success.
4.   Everyone takes a turn and shares for about 2-3 minutes. A 3-year-old can share that they dressed themselves or brushed their teeth.
5.   The parent role models celebrating individual success and support. You want the expectation to be each family member supports the others' successes. This exercise can diffuse sibling envy.

EXERCISE #8 - SET A GOAL ☆

PURPOSE & BENEFITS:

To begin teaching our children to set goals. Setting goals is the key to motivation. Motivation only exists when there is somewhere to go. Your child begins to feel the satisfaction and often the sense of accomplishment when he has succeeded in meeting his goal. Your child learns that even if his goal isn't met, life goes on, and he learns that sometimes a goal has to be reevaluated.

STARTING AGE: 4 years
TIME: Variable, depending on the goal
LOCATION: Depends on goal set
MATERIALS: Depends on goal set

INSTRUCTIONS:
1.   The parent helps the child to set a goal. Talk to your child about what he wants to do. Help him to clarify his goal. For example: brushing his teeth by himself, picking up his toys without being reminded, helping Mom make his bed, setting the table, drawing a picture for Grandpa or Grandma, dressing

himself, cooking a meal for the family, or making cookies with Mom's help, planning a party or a family night, completing homework by a certain time, getting up in the morning right away, writing a thank you note, reading a book, or inviting a new friend over. The possibilities are endless. This exercise could be done everyday.

2. When the goal has been achieved, share it with the family. Celebrate the feeling of success.

3. If it turns out the goal cannot be achieved, help your child reevaluate the goal, identify the problems, and restate a new goal.

EXERCISE #9 - PLAN A PROJECT

PURPOSE & BENEFITS:

To help your child learn the steps necessary in planning a project. To build your child's self-confidence by expanding his life experience. To spend special one-on-one time with your child; to build special memories.

STARTING AGE: 3 years

TIME: Depends on the project

LOCATION: Depends on the project

MATERIALS: Depends on the project

INSTRUCTIONS:

1. The first time this exercise is done, the parent chooses a project she would like to do with her child.

2. Talk to your child about the project:

    a. How do you think we can do this?

    b. What do you think we need to do this?

    c. When should we do the project?

3. Choose a time to do the project when you know you'll be available.

4. Do the project.

5. Reevaluate the project with your child.

        a. How do you think we did?

        b. Would you do anything different next time?

        c. What did you and I learn?

6.   If it turns out the goal cannot be achieved, help your child reevaluate the goal, identify the problems, and restate a new goal.

7.   Suggestions:

        a. Plan and cook a meal together.

        b. Rearrange the child's bedroom.

        c. Paint a room, a dresser, etc.

        d. Plant a garden.

        e. Build a model airplane.

        f. Make a scrapbook or family photo album.

EXERCISE #10 - Q&A BASKET ☆

PURPOSE & BENEFITS:

To encourage your child to share situations which could negatively affect his self-acceptance. To help your child realize he doesn't have to feel alone in his negativity, that he can always talk to Mom or Dad. Your child will become even more comfortable sharing his negative feelings, which can lead to empowering him with a plan.

STARTING AGE: 4 years

TIME: 15 to 20 minutes

LOCATION: Anywhere

MATERIALS: • basket, box, or bag

                   • strips of paper with questions written on them

INSTRUCTIONS:

1.   Parent copies the following questions onto strips of paper. Fold the paper in half and put into the special "Q&A Basket" (box, bag).

2.   Each family member takes a turn–including Mom and

Dad—drawing a slip of paper, reading, and answering it. Mom, Dad, or an older sibling can read the question for a younger child.

3. Make up your own questions and add or replace the ones listed below.

4. Suggested Questions:

   a. When was the last time you wanted to cry or you did cry? What would make you feel better?

   b. Is there someone who always makes you feel badly? Who? Why? What could you do to feel better?

   c. When do you feel like you are going to fail or goof up? What would it take to make you know you would succeed?

   d. When do you feel afraid to try something? What would make it better? What could you do to make it better?

   e. Does anyone ever tease you? Who? What do they say? What would you like to say to them? What would make you feel better?

   f. When do you feel sad? What would make you feel better?

EXERCISE #11 - BE A FINDER ☆

PURPOSE & BENEFITS:

To let your child know that you think he is capable. Children need acknowledgment when they do things well. When a child realizes you notice when he does things well, he will begin to do more things well because it feels good.

STARTING AGE: 3 years
TIME: 2 to 3 minutes
LOCATION: Anywhere
MATERIALS: None
INSTRUCTIONS:

1. Parents notice when a child is doing something well and takes

the time to acknowledge it to the child, either right at the moment or at a later time.

EXERCISE #12 - FAMILY FEEL GOOD BOOK

PURPOSE & BENEFITS:

To give a sense of belonging and connection for everyone in your family. You will end up with a wonderful memory book when your child is grown.

STARTING AGE: 3 years

TIME: 5 minutes + (Long to initially set it up)

LOCATION: The book is to be left in a general location in your house

MATERIALS:
- a scrapbook or large size photo album
- glue or paste
- scissors
- pens, pencils, crayons, or felt pens
- Extra: stickers, colored paper, fancy scrap booking scissors, decorations, etc.

INSTRUCTIONS:

1. Parent shows the "Family Feel Good Book" to the family and explains the purpose of the book is to put into it things such as special photos, drawings, poems, short stories, cartoons, jokes, songs, letters, cards, etc. that make individual family members feel good.

2. The purpose of the book is to make everyone in the family feel good if they need a "pick-me-up."

3. The parent invites anyone to contribute to the book whenever they want to.

4. The parent wants to contribute to the book regularly and remind the others. The parent also wants to role model taking it out and looking through it.

Variation: A Family Journal, which is left in a convenient place with a pen or pencil with it. The family members are invited and encouraged to write positive thoughts they want to share in it. Unlike a private journal, a Family Journal is to be read by all.

EXERCISE #13 - IALAC BOOK

PURPOSE & BENEFITS:

To remind our children that we all have bad days, but that tomorrow is always a brand-new day and that no matter how bad a day they've had, they are still loveable and capable of learning from the "Bad Stuff" and "Hurtful Stuff." One bad day, event, or situation doesn't determine one's future. After reading this book to your child, you will be able to reference back to it when your child is having a bad day.

STARTING AGE: 5 years (maybe 4 depending on the child)

TIME: 10 to 15 minutes

LOCATION: Anywhere

MATERIALS: Book: I Am Loveable and Capable by Sidney Simon. You can purchase this book from Dr. Simon's website: www.simonworkshops.com/books.html

INSTRUCTIONS:

1. Make a sign with "IALAC" on it for each child before you read the story to give out at the end of your reading. Make one sign to have available to rip during the story.

2. As you begin to read the story, take out your sign and put it on so you or your child can rip off parts of it as you read.

3. Read the story by yourself before you do this exercise. I have never read the story word-for-word or even page-by-page for young children because it would take too long. When you read it ahead choose the thumbs-up and thumbs-down situations that you would like to incorporate into your telling of the IALAC story.

4. As you turn the pages, show them the thumbs-up and thumbs-

down so they can look at the kind of day Randy is having. Begin the story by taking out your sign and saying:

- "Everyone I know wears one of these signs everyday. Oh, I know you can't see it, but it's there and there's no way that I know of that you can go through a day without it. Every morning as we start our day, the first thing we do when we wake up is put on your IALAC sign."

5.   As you read or tell the story, every age group enjoys ripping off pieces of the sign when Randy experiences a thumbs-down. Dr. Simon suggests that you may want to let the children tape a piece of the sign back when there is a thumbs-up situation. I don't normally do this because it takes more time and, for me, it slows down the story.

6.   At the end of the story, it is important to say:

- "As Randy gets ready for bed and turns off the light, he takes off is IALAC sign and hangs it by the bed. And, every morning when he wakes up and puts on his sign on, he has a whole new sign to begin the day with. So don't ever give up when you've had a terrible day, because tomorrow is a brand-new beginning with a brand-new IALAC sign and it might turn out to be a good day."

7.   At this point, give each child a sign.

8.   While you are still sitting down from the story, go around the family and ask each family member to take a turn filling in the blank of the following statement:

"What I like about myself is: _____"

-13-

PROBLEM-SOLVING

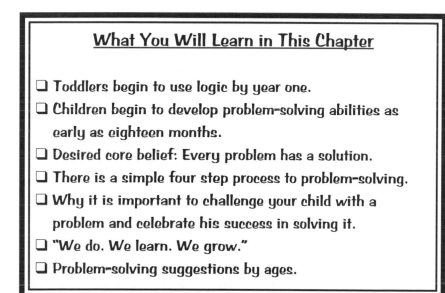

What You Will Learn in This Chapter

❑ Toddlers begin to use logic by year one.
❑ Children begin to develop problem-solving abilities as early as eighteen months.
❑ Desired core belief: Every problem has a solution.
❑ There is a simple four step process to problem-solving.
❑ Why it is important to challenge your child with a problem and celebrate his success in solving it.
❑ "We do. We learn. We grow."
❑ Problem-solving suggestions by ages.

Problem-Solving Is Easy With High EQ

A person's ability to problem-solve is an indicator of future success, mental health, good relationships, and a satisfying quality of life. When a person has a high emotional intelligence, he has learned not to let his emotions overwhelm him. He is able to identify and label his emotions and then access his cognitive ability to problem-solve whatever difficulties come his way.

Unfortunately, we have become a nation of problem-identifiers rather than problem-solvers. From a young age, our children are great at identifying problems:

- "I'm hungry."
- "I'm cold."
- "I'm tired!"
- "I can't find my homework, backpack, sweatshirt, etc."

In the above examples, children identify and state a problem, but it's as though they're waiting for someone else to solve them. For example: Go get something to eat, put on a jacket, take a nap, or go look for your homework. Too often, children forget that they have the power to solve problems. They've either forgotten or have never experienced a tremendous sense of accomplishment that comes from solving even the smallest of predicaments.

It's not just our children: all over America conversations take place in which someone is blaming someone else for his problems. In my office, I hear clients say, "It's his fault", "If he would just change", "She's to blame", or "If only X would happen: then I'd feel better." We spend so much time and energy putting the blame on someone—or something else—for what's wrong in our lives. We have forgotten that we have the ability to solve our problems ourselves. So let's get our children off on the right track by teaching them to become their own problem-solvers.

Problem-Solving Begins Early

Children begin to learn how the world works from the first day of their lives. During the first few months, they are learning how to fine-tune their senses. They are looking, smelling, hearing, tasting, and touching—and imputing each of their experiences, which lay the foundation of their beliefs about reality.

The exchange of looks and smiles between parents and their two- to four-month-old baby helps to develop an emotional connection. When a child is five- or six-months-old, we find ourselves playing simple games with him. Whether it is peek-a-boo or hiding a toy and having him respond with concern (and then smiles when we uncover it), such interaction not only teaches our infant about two-way communication and emotional intimacy, it also teaches him beginning logic. He is beginning to connect our actions and his reactions. Such simple interactions are vital for infants to learn about cause and effect. If this type of exchange continues regularly, by thirteen months your child will begin to look for the hidden toy and experience delight when he discovers it.

Although still lacking the vocabulary to communicate his needs, a baby or young child will begin to communicate non-verbally. A toddler might take his mom's hand and lead her to the refrigerator because he has learned that when Mom goes to this big white box, he always gets something to eat. By fourteen months, he might also bring you his bottle when he is thirsty because he has connected his mom, his bottle, and his thirst. Or he might go and look for his bottle in the diaper bag you brought with you when you went to visit friends. In other words: <u>He has begun to problem-solve</u>.

Your child will feel a sense of pride and joy when he has solved the smallest problem, because for him it is a huge accomplishment. The parent's responsibility is to be aware of these successes. It is important to notice and encourage them.

When you engage in play with your children, remember to be aware of creating play problems to solve. For example if you are playing house with your son or daughter and it's time to change the baby doll's diaper, you might say, "Oh no, we're out of diapers – what should we do?" Your child might come up with a dozen solutions, ranging from "We can use paper towels!" to asking you to drive to the store and buy some new ones. If you are pretending to make dinner, you might pretend to burn your finger and ask your child to help you. I think you get the idea.

Research has shown that children begin to develop problem-solving abilities as early as eighteen months. But why shouldn't your child start even earlier and have fun while he is learning?

Your fourteen-month-old brings you her bottle when she is thirsty because she has connected her mom, her bottle, and her thirst.

Believing That Every Problem Has A Solution

One of my favorite TV shows of all times was <u>MacGyver</u>. Every week the hero would be caught in the middle of any number of problems that he would then have to solve in order to save the day. I loved watching him figure out week after week the solution to the latest problem the writers had dreamed up for him. The show was empowering; it taught the viewers that whatever problem is thrown at you in life, you have the intelligence, resourcefulness, and ability to figure out solutions.

The belief that every problem has a solution prevents you from getting stuck. It empowers you to always have hope. People who know that "every problem has a solution" rarely let the problem overtake them or waste time blaming others. They persist despite frustration, challenges, and fear. They don't give up.

As you teach your child about problem-solving, remember there is not just one right solution: there are always several. If you know your solution is better than your child's, keep it to yourself and allow your child to learn that he has the ability to problem-solve on his own. If his solution has any chance of succeeding, let him go with it. He will get better at considering more solutions if he learns early in life that he is a problem-solver—that he can do it!

People who don't believe that every problem has a solution often become overwhelmed with life's difficulties and experience depression. Or worse, they begin to *ruminate*. *Ruminating* is the act of thinking about the same thing over and over. In other words, when people don't believe they have the ability to solve a problem, they can get stuck in it. When adults or children get stuck in a problem, it overtakes them.

For instance, an adult may realize he is in a job he doesn't like. The job might even make him physically sick. This person may stay at that job his entire career, never feeling any better—OR if he is a problem-solver, the person who is dissatisfied with his job will follow these four simple problem-solving steps.

The Four Simple Problem-Solving Steps

Step #1: What is my problem? (Name it)

1. I hate the work I do.

2. I don't like my co-workers.

3. I hate my commute.

4. I feel like I'm at a dead end with no possibility of moving up.

Step #2: What can I do to solve my problem? (Come up with at least 5 possible solutions)

1. I could look for a new job that I think I would like.

2. I could consider another way to do my job.

3. I will list the positives and negatives about my job and see if I can focus on the positives.

4. I could consider creating another job in the company that I might like better and that might benefit the company.

5. I might keep my job while I train for another job after work or on the weekends.

6. I could see if there is another department in my company with more opportunity.

7. Maybe I can telecommute my job from home a few days a week.

Step #3: Choose a solution and put it into action.

Step #4: Reevaluate your solution.

If it's working, keep at it; otherwise, try another solution.

Problem-solvers only get stuck temporarily and then they move on. They are not done in by frustration or disappointment. If we want our children to become problem-solvers, we need to encourage them to follow the simple four problem-solving steps as well. For example, if your child doesn't like his teacher, help him to go through the Problem-Solving Steps:

Step #1 – What is my problem? (Name it)

"I don't like my teacher—she's mean! I don't think my teacher likes me."

Step #2 – What can I do to solve my problem? (Come up with 5 possible solutions)

1. Make a list of things you like and don't like about her and then focus on the positive things.

2. Make an appointment with the teacher and go with Mom or Dad and talk to her.

3. Ask your classmates what they like about her.

4. Share your feelings with Mom or Dad each day to help vent.

5. Write her a letter with Mom or Dad's help asking her to your house to get to know her better.

Step #3 – Choose a solution and put it into action.
Step #4 – Reevaluate your solution. If it's working, keep at it; otherwise, choose another solution.

The bottom line is this: A problem-solving parent and child will say, "I know we can come up with a plan together that will make the situation better."

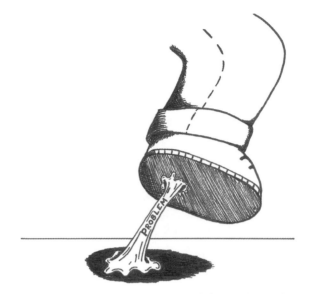

High EQ children do not get stuck in their problems.

As you help your child come up with solutions to his problem, suggest a few choices that will help him feel like he has some control. Then let him brainstorm on his own. You are teaching him the value of independent problem-solving and resourcefulness.

We Problem-Solve, We Learn, We Grow

Until the age of about fourteen, children may need you to help them come up with possible solutions to their problems. As they gain more experience problem-solving, they'll become more proficient at it. For them to believe that "every problem has a solution," they need to practice solving problems regularly. Help them by offering simple problems and allowing them to solve these every day. For instance, if your three-year-old is helping you put the groceries away; ask her, "How can we fit all the groceries into the cupboard?" Or if your five-year-old is helping you make cookies, and the recipe calls for a cup of milk, hand him a measuring cup and ask, "How do we measure exactly a cup?" If your ten-year-old is frustrated by the mess on her desk, you might ask her, "How could you organize the things on your desk so you can keep track of your books, paper, pencils, etc.?" Your goal is to make sure that your child believes the following statement to her core.

EVERY PROBLEM HAS A SOLUTION!

Throughout the fourteen years I taught elementary school and junior high, every child who walked into my classroom soon learned that Mrs. Healy wasn't going to solve any of their problems. She was going to help them learn to solve their own problems. In every classroom I've been in over the last thirty years—whether I was the teacher, the school counselor, or the invited guest speaker—my goal was always to empower the children I was working with, so they believed they had the ability to overcome whatever trouble came their way.

Similarly, when my husband and I helped to plan events with our children's scout troops, we were successful because we didn't DIRECT the children what to do and how to do it. Rather, we explored with them the various options and then let them walk through the necessary steps as they planned the events. Sometimes they were successful, and other times they learned from the events what they would do differently next time. What a great learning experience for eight-, nine-, and ten-year-olds. They could say to themselves, "We chose it. We planned it. We accomplished it. We learned from it. And we grew."

Isn't that what life is all about? WE DO SOMETHING NEW, WE LEARN, AND WE GROW.... When we live fulfilled, satisfying lives we never stop doing, learning, and growing. Think about the seventy-year-old who signs up for a computer class, or leaves the golf course and tells his friends, "It's time for me to take lessons."

When we know inside that we are capable of solving any problem that comes our way, our life is filled with possibilities. Sometimes the solution to a problem is not to do anything differently, but rather to change our attitude toward the problem!

**Parents strengthen a child's positive outlook towards life
by teaching him to be a problem-solver.**

When we teach our children to not only be problem identifiers, but problem-solvers, we empower them with the self-confidence to meet any challenge in their lives head on and to do something about it. We strengthen them with the belief that they can come up with possible solutions to any problem that arises. We arm them with the knowledge and experience that they will always have choices; even if the choice is to ask for help or choose to accept that "this is how it is." Even when they choose to accept things as they are, children are empowered—because they've made a choice and thus have a sense of control over their lives.

We all know children (and adults) who spend their lives complaining about everything and everyone else. These are usually individuals with low EQ. When we teach our children to be problem-solvers, we open a whole new world for them—a world in which they take responsibility for their actions and their choices. These children grow into healthy teenagers and resourceful, resilient adults with high EQ.

The skills you are about to teach your child in this chapter are linked into every other skill in this book: Feelings, Communication, Self-Acceptance, Decision-Making, Responsibility, Anger Management, and Friendship. So buckle your seat belts and get ready to do the Problem-Solving exercises!

Here is a short list of suggested "problems to solve." Challenge your children with any or all of them. Remember that children learn from repetition. So don't hesitate to repeat a particular activity several times at various ages. You do not need to spend a lot of money to challenge your child.

Six Months To One-Year-Old

Hand your child a variety of safe objects one at a time to examine. Don't rush her. A single plastic cup might be examined for ten minutes. Let her feel, touch, bite, and drop the objects. This develops and supports curiosity, which is a sign of intelligence. Laugh, talk, and sing as you share each new object with your infant. At this age they are responding to each of their senses: taste, sight, sound, texture, and smell.

Some sample objects for your child to explore:
- Age appropriate toys, including toys that rattle or make noise
- Bright colored objects, including toys, boxes, books, and birthday cards
- Plastic containers with tops, in a variety of sizes, measuring cups, or measuring spoons

One-Year-Old To Two Years Old

Continue to encourage your child to explore objects. Talk to him about the objects and demonstrate tasks that can be done with them. i.e., stacking the measuring cups. Just sit and play with the objects with your child. This role modeling alone will challenge him to imitate your actions. If you have stacked the blocks, deliberately knock them down and role model an attitude of "Oh well, they fell down. Now I'll stack them up again." You will be teaching him that life has frustrations and disappointments. Upsets happen, we accept them, we adjust to them, and we move on without anger or stress. Laugh and talk with him as he is playing. Remember: the circuitry in his brain is still developing. Every time he explores a new object and has an emotional response, such as "Wow, this is fun! This is soft, smooth, feels good," he is connecting more of that circuitry in his brain. Play is necessary and powerful for the healthy development of our children's emotional intelligence.

Some sample objects:
- Building blocks, or any safe objects (and let them crash)
- Cups and containers that fit inside one another
- Bright colored, age appropriate toys—show how to use them and then let your child use in any way he wants
- Toys that challenge with sizes and shapes fitting inside one another
- Discovery Toys®, Leap Frog®, Sassy®, Baby Einstein®, Tiny Love®, Lamaze®, and Fischer-Price® have lines of toys designed for each age ability challenge
- Talk to your child and explain things as though she can understand every word you say. Although she won't understand all of your words, she will learn to feel comfortable with your "explanation voice." This will lay the groundwork for communicating around problem issues to come
- Especially important during this year are physical challenges with as many successes as possible. Your child is discovering the independence of walking and is feeling proud of herself. Look for toys which she can test her hand-eye coordination. Pounding, building, and stacking are all challenging, as is using her sense of touch with various textures
- Continue to read colorful books to your child. Point at the pictures and engage him with descriptions of what he sees. You will be connecting him to books by doing this. This comfortable connection will pay off when your child is ready to read
  NOTE: If your house isn't child proofed yet, don't wait any longer! Your home should be a place of safety for your child.

Two Years Old To Three Years Old

During this time, your child's vocabulary is exploding, and you can now ask him questions and receive a clear answer. Accept any answer he gives you at this time. When you are making his bed or picking up his toys, ask him to join in and thank him. Begin to teach him where things go. You can explore with him new ways to keep his toys stored. Let him give suggestions for how to put toys away. Ask your child to help carry things, to bring in groceries from the car to the house, linens to the linen closet. He will be watching and learning from you how such things are done, role modeling is the most powerful teacher.

Purchase or make toys that fit together and pull apart:
- Age appropriate puzzles
- Magnetized trains and cars
- Pull apart beads (Show him how to put them back together).
- Stacking blocks
- Toys with safe pieces to take apart and put back together
- Shape toys (So toddlers can figure out how to put certain shapes through matching holes. Tupperware® makes a red and blue shape ball. And again, Discovery Toys®, Leap Frog®, Sassy®, Baby Einstein®, Tiny Love®, Lamaze®, and Fischer-Price® have fit together; take apart safe toys designed in primary colors
- Dolls or stuffed animals that allow you to take clothes on and off, or have clothes with zippers, snaps, etc

  NOTE: Remember to take the time to sit with your child, laugh, and enjoy playing. Play is important in your child's life, so schedule the time. The rewards down the road are incredible for the time spent now. Your child doesn't need a hundred toys. He needs you to show interest and excitement about the ones he has—and to interact and teach him what is possible with these toys. When parents buy too many toys for their children, children don't value and appreciate, or learn to be creative, with the toys they have. Instead, they learn, "When I 'm bored I need a new toy to be happy." What you want your child to do is be inventive and creative in play with the toys or objects around him. A big empty cardboard box can become a wonderful creative opportunity for a resourceful child. Teaching your child problem-solving, resiliency, and resourcefulness doesn't require that you break the bank.

Three Years Old To Four Years Old

Inspiring creative play is your goal for this year. This age group loves to dress up and act out their idea of real life, whether it's having a tea party with a friend, being a fairy princess, a super hero, a firefighter, a mom or a dad. Encourage your child to expand his imagination. Sit down with your child and have an empty cup of tea. Help your little firefighter to build a pretend fire truck from chairs or boxes, or sit on the floor and move the toy fire truck and emergency vehicles to a successful rescue.

- Keep a box of dress up clothes available to be pulled out at a moment's notice.
- Be tolerant if your super hero wants to wear his cape to the grocery store with you—why not? It's fun, and the message you are sending is "Playing is a good thing."
- Puppet shows are exciting at four years old, whether it's hand drawn paper puppets, finger puppets, or store-bought fancy puppets. The stage can be a box your child can hide behind or a blanket hung over two chairs. Be creative yourself!!
- Let them play with any toys or containers that allow your child to begin to sort and categorize.
- Also encourage them to use blocks and bricks that allow your child to build and create. Legos® are wonderful!
- Begin to play board games, such as Candyland®, Chutes and Ladders®, etc.
- Begin to ask your child's opinion about various things, and listen seriously to their answers.
- Allow your child to problem-solve real life problems by giving him chores, such as:
  - Helping you match the socks when you're folding the laundry.
  - Helping you set the table and figuring out how many plates, how much silverware, etc.
  - Helping to put his toys away so they all fit on a particular shelf or box.

Four Years Old To Five Years Old

From four to five, your child's cognitive ability is continuing to develop. He is beginning to draw from a wider arena of life to incorporate into his play. Instead of playing with just a car or truck, he can put them into a gas station, on a freeway, on a racetrack, in a city, or in the country.

Continue to keep the dress up box readily available because their playing also includes more details. They bring more of real life into their make-believe. If you are willing to dress up with your child, relax and have fun being a child again. But if this is uncomfortable for you, don't do it; instead just be willing to listen as your child explains to you who she is, what she's doing, what the crisis is, who she is saving.

As your child grows, continue to keep the dress up box available because his playing includes more details.

A child's world is fascinating; be willing to listen to it. You will be amazed!
- Ask your child for his opinion, and then attentively listen to the response. Ask about a problem and what he would do about it. For example, a problem:
    - at preschool
    - with a sibling
    - with a neighbor
    - about what to have for dinner, lunch, etc.
    - about cleaning his room
    - about something he saw on TV
- Read to your child as often as you can. Choose books with colorful illustrations and story plots which present problems to be solved. Ask him questions about the illustrations. Convey a sense of enjoyment when you read to him. This will send the message that you love reading and that it is something you look forward to. These simple actions will encourage your child to want to read as soon as he can.

Five Years Old And Six Years Old

Your child has started kindergarten by this time and is becoming more independent in his play and in his life. After school he probably would like to have play dates. I would recommend that you set these up whenever possible. The play dates can be for just one or two hours. Do not feel like they have to be all afternoon until dinnertime. If you are able to have play dates, talk with him ahead of time about potential problems, rules for when friends are over, possible games to play, and your expectation that he help clean up with or without the friend's help. When planning fo a playdate, encourage him to:

- Choose toys, which your child can complete in one sitting. It will give him a sense of satisfaction and success. This could be Play Dough®, Legos®, painting or drawing, blocks, craft projects, board games, etc.

Continue to ask his opinion about a problem you're trying to solve:

- Where do you think I should plant these flowers?
- Where do you think I should hang these pictures?
- I'm having a hard time deciding between two things for dinner? What do you think we should have?
- Let your child hear you talk aloud about problem-solving.

Seven Years Old And Eight Years Old

Once again, your child is moving into a new stage cognitively. Your job is to challenge his problem-solving skills at a deeper level. He is now moving from the Preoperational Cognitive Stage into the Concrete Operational Stage. This means that his reasoning process has become more logical. He learns the most through further exploration of his environment. He is able to understand the use of symbols, such as numbers, letters, and codes. He has a conceptual knowledge of space and time and begins to understand distance in time and space. Children at this age are more social in their play. The challenge for the parent is exciting because of the child's increased cognitive ability.

- Continue to ask your child's opinion about life, school, movies, TV, sports, events, etc.
- Continue to point out problems around the house and ask his opinion about how to solve them:
  - how to rearrange furniture
  - how to hang a picture
  - how to clean and organize the garage
  - how to fit ten guests around the dining room table
  - what is the best room is to put the family scale

- • how we can plan a healthy meal
- • how we can plan our family evening
- • It is important to begin to play games with your children if you haven't done so in the past. Here are some possibilities:
    - • <u>Card Games:</u>   Old Maid, Gin Rummy, War, Twenty-One, Go Fish
    - • <u>Board Games:</u> Candyland®, Chutes and Ladders®, Junior Scrabble®, Sorry®, and Life®
    - • <u>Active Games:</u> Boggle®, Yahtzee®, Hungry Hippo®, Cherries in a Basket®, Kerplunk®, Jenga®, Connect Four®
- • Choose games that you like and enjoy playing. Every game has problems to solve. Games also teach children good sportsmanship when role-modeled by the parent.
    - • When you play games with your children and the experience is enjoyable and emotionally safe ("It feels okay to lose, because I'm not laughed at or teased,") you'll establish an intimate bond.

At seven and eight years old, your child is able to understand the use of symbols, such as numbers, letters, and codes.

Nine Years Old And Ten Years Old

This age is challenging because it seems like our children are smarter every day. Their ability to reason in a logical way grows stronger all the time; however, their life experiences still limit their thinking. So your child might ask you for a new pair of hundred dollar Nikes® and not understand why you have to say no. Their focus is on the positive reasoning, which works for them. Rarely does a child bring in negative reasoning. Your challenge is not to discourage his developing reasoning abilities, but to frame the situation as a solvable problem, which will help him understand real life pros and cons.

- Continue to play games. Don't let your children win, but make sure when you win or lose that you role model good sportsmanship. If you haven't included the following games yet, this is a good time to add:
  - Tic-tac-toe
  - Connect Four®
  - Hangman
  - Checkers
  - Chess
  - Cribbage
  - UNO®
  - Mancala®
- When appropriate, involve your children in real life problems around the house, and work together to solve:
  - Laying out and planting a garden
  - Building a hutch for a pet rabbit
  - Putting up shelves in the garage, workroom
  - Reading a recipe and making what is says
  - Building a wooden race car
  - Taking apart an old vacuum cleaner, clock, radio, or computer and trying to put it back together
  - Building a model car, plane, or boat from a hobby store
- Family problems, school problems, friend problems, sibling problems— which everyone in the family can discuss at regular family meetings. Come up with solutions and celebrate.

Your goal is to empower your child with the belief that "Every problem has a solution." Also to give him the life experience that teaches him, "If I need help figuring out a solution, I can go to my mom or dad and they will help me, because they always have. And it feels safe to problem-solve with them".

So once again relax and enjoy the following exercises. You are not only helping your child to enjoy life more today, but you are giving him skills he will use to create a fulfilling adult life.

EXERCISE # 1 - EVERY PROBLEM HAS A SOLUTION ☆

PURPOSE & BENEFITS:

To begin laying the foundation in your children's belief systems that they can overcome every problem that life sends their way. Your child's attitude toward life will begin to shift in a dramatic way. Someone who believes life has problems and the problems are solvable lives in a much more positive and confident way.

STARTING AGE: 4 years (3 years depending on your child)
TIME: 5 minutes
LOCATION: Anywhere
MATERIALS: • chart with the statement "Every Problem Has a Solution"—your chart can be as plain or fancy as you want and any size

INSTRUCTIONS:
1.   Parent shows and reads chart to the family, then leads a discussion about the statement.
2.   Post the chart somewhere in the house where everyone can see it.
3.   Parent takes time to discuss the statement with family, both individually with each child and again as a family, perhaps at dinner or at a family meeting.

EXERCISE # 2 - Q&A BASKET ☆

PURPOSE & BENEFITS:

To encourage your child to begin to think about problem-solving. To teach your child about solutions. Your child will become more comfortable identifying and discussing problems aloud. Children often internalize their problems, which can produce anxiety.

STARTING AGE: 4 years

TIME: 15 to 20 minutes

LOCATION: A place where family members can sit around in a circle with a basket in the center

MATERIALS:
- a special basket, box, or bag
- slips of paper folded in half with a problem printed on each paper–make up your own problems or copy the problems listed below

INSTRUCTIONS:

1. Parent and child sit and place basket with slips of paper in the middle of them.

2. Each family member takes a turn picking a slip of paper and reading the problem written on it. If a child needs help reading it, someone can read it for them.

3. The person who has drawn the problem then offers a solution to the problem. Offer this definition of solution: "A solution is something you can do to make yourself feel better about a problem."

4. Rules:
   - No put-downs or criticisms about the solution given.
   - If you need a time limit, use a timer for 60 or 90 seconds.
   - If the person needs help they can choose a family member to ask for help with a solution. As you repeat this exercise, notice if this becomes a pattern. It is better for a child to offer a weak solution of her own than to believe they can't think of one, and that they always need help.

PROBLEMS TO SOLVE (write on slip of paper)
- You cut your finger.
- You are bored.
- You are scared.
- You feel sad.
- You threw a ball and broke a lamp.
- Your friend fell off his bike and is hurt.
- Your friend called to say he couldn't come over and play.
- You don't know how to do your homework assignment.

- You smell smoke in your house.
- Your little sister/brother is crying.
- You are hungry.
- You are mad at your brother/sister.
- You accidentally spilled milk on your homework paper.
- You wet your pants/bed.
- You lost your new sweatshirt.
- You broke a glass.
- You made a mess in the kitchen fixing a snack.
- Your shoes had mud on them and you walked on the living room rug.
- Mom/Dad yelled at you and you feel bad.
- You yelled at your mom/dad and you feel badly.

EXERCISE # 3 - EVERY PROBLEM HAS AT LEAST FIVE SOLUTIONS ☆

PURPOSE & BENEFITS:

To teach your child there are always several solutions to every problem. To empower your child not to get overwhelmed with life's problems.

STARTING AGE: 4 years

TIME: 10 to 15 minutes

LOCATION: Anywhere (even in the car)

MATERIALS: • index cards or pieces of paper with problems written on them (This exercise can be done without any props. Simply come up with problems and state them one at a time to your child.)

INSTRUCTIONS:

1. Parent names a problem or has a child choose an index card or piece of paper with a problem written on it.
2. The family then offers as many possible solutions as possible.
3. The goal is to name at least five solutions. Challenge your

family to come up with more.

4.   It is important that every solution is acknowledged and validated for its possibilities.

5.   Do not allow put-downs for weak solutions; role model support for any idea.

SUGGESTED PROBLEMS:

- Your friend is over to play with you and he cuts his hand and it is bleeding. What do you do?
- It's a windy night and you hear a lot of noise outside your window. You are scared. What do you do?
- You are bored. Mom is busy in the kitchen. Dad is busy on the phone. Your brother/sister is doing homework. What do you do?
- Your family is cooking Thanksgiving Dinner for your relatives. What has to be done to get ready?
- Your family is going away for the weekend. What needs to be done to get ready for the trip?
- You have a project to do for school. What do you need do get it done?
- You are at the playground and a stranger comes up and starts talking to you. What do you do?
- You feel sad. You don't know why. What do you do?
- You are staying with your grandma and she faints. What do you do?
- You are angry with your brother/sister for taking your toy from your room without asking. What do you do?

EXERCISE # 4 - REFRAME

PURPOSE & BENEFITS:

To teach your child one of the most empowering techniques known to help a person not become overwhelmed with life's problems. Your child will begin practicing a technique he will use throughout his life.

STARTING AGE: 5 years (perhaps 4 years, depending on your

	child)
TIME:	5 to 10 minutes
LOCATION:	Anywhere
MATERIALS:	• a color picture with a frame—it can be a print, photograph, watercolor, or oil painting
	• a copy of the frame on the next page with the information inside in this exercise

INSTRUCTIONS:

1. Parent shows the framed picture to child. Ask them what stands out to them. The trees, the water, the sky, etc.

2. Now ask your child if the color of the frame were different, would the picture look different. For example, if you are showing your child a picture of the ocean with a white frame, the blue of the ocean, the white foam of the wave, and the white clouds in a blue sky might stand out. If the same picture had an oak wood frame, then any brown weeds or grass would catch your eye. Perhaps if there were a fence along the sand it would stand out more because of a different frame.

   The picture would be the identical picture, but it would present differently to the viewer's eye. When a life event or situation happens, we immediately put an emotional frame around it. We may feel happy, upset, or even angry. Reframing is a technique by which we look at the same life event or situation in a different way, which produces a different emotional response. We know that our emotional response to life influences our decisions of how to respond to life. Therefore, when we are able to reframe the way we look at life in a more positive way, we are much more open to seeing solutions to the problems that come our way.

   For example:
   - It is a windy night and you hear noises. You are scared.
     One Frame: There is someone outside my window trying to break in and hurt me. I'm going to hide under my bed until morning. I'm going to scream.
     Reframe: The wind is causing my house to make

weird noises. I'm going to go ask Mom or Dad for a hug and reassurance.

- My brother took a toy from my room and I'm mad.

    One Frame: My brother always takes my toys. I hate him.

    Reframe: I hate it when my brother takes my toys. I'm going to ask Mom and Dad to get him to stop taking my things. I know they will help.

3. Practice with your child, reframing things that bother him.

4. Practice a little every day as life situations come up.

5. Copy and post the chart below:

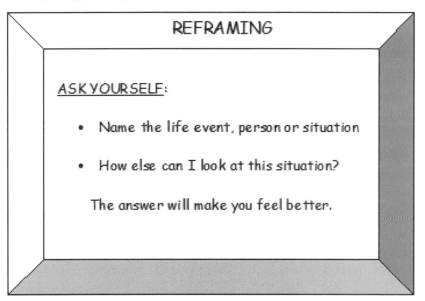

REFRAMING

ASK YOURSELF:

- Name the life event, person or situation

- How else can I look at this situation?

The answer will make you feel better.

EXERCISE # 5 - SOLVE A PROBLEM ☆

PURPOSE & BENEFITS:

To become aware that everyone has problems. To experience that family members can offer support to one another in solving problems. Your child will realize that problems are a normal part of life. Everyone has them. Your child will learn that there are always at least four or five solutions for every problem.

STARTING AGE: 5 years (4 years, depending on your child)

TIME: 20 minutes

LOCATION: An area where you can put up a large piece of paper

MATERIALS: • a large piece of paper (11" x 18" or larger)
             • pens, pencils, crayons, felt pens
             • Post-Its® or small pieces of paper
             • tape if you are not using Post-Its®

INSTRUCTIONS:

1. Parents draw an outline of a figure, such as a heart, circle, vase, picture frame, computer screen, a box, a fishbowl, etc.

2. Have each family member write a problem they have on one side of the Post-It®. Have them list the feelings they experience because of this problem on the other side of the Post-It®.

3. After everyone has written their problems and feelings on the Post-It®, put them in the figure drawn on the large paper.

4. Each family member can write more than one problem. Set a timer for five or ten minutes to write the problems.

5. Each family member then takes a turn choosing a Post-It® problem, reading it, and offering solutions.

6. When the reader is finished offering solutions, anyone else can join in with additional solutions.

7. The parent decides ahead of time how many turns each person will take.

8. If there are leftover problems on the poster, keep the poster in a safe place to repeat the exercise at a later date.

EXERCISE # 6 - TEACH PROBLEM-SOLVING TECHNIQUES ☆

PURPOSE & BENEFITS:

To teach a problem-solving technique which can be used throughout your child's life. Your child will realize that problems have solutions and do not need to overwhelm him.

STARTING AGE: 5 years

TIME: 20 minutes

LOCATION: Anywhere

MATERIALS: • piece of paper or a white board on which to
take notes.

INSTRUCTIONS:

1. Parent tells the family they are going to learn and practice a
well-known problem-solving technique. The technique has
four steps:

   STEP #1: Name the problem (choose a real family
   problem):
   - As simple as possible.
   - In one sentence, "Mom and Dad don't like it
   when the kids yell and scream in the house."

   STEP #2: Brainstorm solutions

   Everyone makes suggestions and someone lists all of them
   on a paper or white board. For example:
   - Whoever yells and screams gets a 20-minute
   time-out on a chair in the living room.
   - Whoever yells and screams can't have a play date
   for a month.
   - Whoever yells and screams doesn't get dessert for
   a week.

   Don't judge, criticize, or discuss any suggestions.

   STEP #3: Then read the listed suggestions one at a time:
   (do not discuss suggestions—simply read them.)
   - Each family member involved gets to say "Yes" or
   "No" to each suggestion.
   - If anyone says No, draw a line through the
   suggestion. Otherwise leave the possible solution.
   - When you have done this with the whole list of
   suggested solutions, go back and circle the ones
   that were responded to with a "Yes."
   - The "Yes" suggestions are the ones you will try
   out for a couple of days, up to a week, depending
   on your family.

STEP#4: Set a time to evaluate how solutions are working or not working.

2.   If none of the solutions are working, begin the process over again. You haven't wasted any time because: a) you have been exploring and testing possible solutions, b) you have role modeled to your child that sometimes you need to try various solutions to find the best one.

3.   Summary:

1. Name the problem.

2. Brainstorm solutions.

3. Say "Yes" or "No" to each possible solution.

4. Choose one or two solutions to try.

5. Set time to reevaluate solution(s).

EXERCISE # 7 - THE FOUR WHATS ☆

PURPOSE & BENEFITS:

Each time your child has had a new learning experience in life, spend the time exploring the experience with him. Unless a child has the opportunity to process his experiences – good or bad – you miss out on a wonderful "teaching" moment. Your child will begin to practice a learning process that he can continue to use throughout his life.

STARTING AGE: 5 years

TIME: 10 - 15 minutes

LOCATION: Anywhere

MATERIALS: None

INSTRUCTIONS:

1.   Parent finds a calm moment after child has had an experience you believe they could learn from.

2.   In peace and quiet (if possible) slowly ask your child the "4 WHAT" questions. Give your child time to answer the questions in his own way. Choose the best way to ask the question using the following choices. You will want to repeat

this exercise often with your child throughout the years. The more you work this exercise, the more relaxed you will be putting the "4 WHATS" in your own words.

3.   The "4 WHATS":

1. What happened ...
   ...the other day when ....
   ...when you ....
   ...when ....
   (Describe experience. Have your child talk about all the details)

2. What do you think ...
   ...caused it to happen that way?
   ...made it happen?
   (Challenge his thinking about cause and effect)

3. What would you have liked to have happened differently?

4. What could you do differently next time?

EXERCISE # 8 - FAMILY MEETING ☆

PURPOSE & BENEFITS:

To bring you family together regularly. To work together to solve problems and plan events. To give everyone in the family a sense of belonging and value as they share their ideas, opinions, and solutions.

STARTING AGE: 5 years (4 years depending on the child)

TIME: 20- 30 minutes maximum or children lose interest—plan family meetings weekly or every other week

LOCATION: Somewhere you can gather as a family without outside distractions—turn off family telephone ringer and put your cell phone on vibrate

MATERIALS: • a paper (8-1/2 x 11) titled "Agenda"

> • a piece of paper or notebook
> • a pencil or pen with which to take notes

INSTRUCTIONS:

1. The most successful family meetings have a structure, which is followed.

2. Before the meeting, a paper headed **AGENDA** is displayed somewhere in the home where each family member can write something they want to talk about at the meeting.

3. Each meeting is run by a chairperson whose job it is to start the meeting by giving the person on his or her left or right a compliment or appreciation. Then that person gives one to the next person and it follows around the family circle. An alternate way to begin the meeting is to say a prayer and ask family members to join in with special intentions or thankfulness.

4. Next the chairperson holds the agenda and names the first item listed on the agenda to be discussed. The agenda items should be discussed in the order they are listed. If there are many items listed, you may need to limit the discussion time by setting a timer. There may be meetings where you do not get to every item on the agenda. It is important that a parent does not skip an agenda items because the meeting then moves from a Family Meeting to a parent's meeting.

5. There is also a designated secretary at each meeting who takes notes. Although a 5-year-old can be a chairperson with a little help, the job of secretary needs to be someone who can write.

6. The jobs of chairperson and secretary should continue to change every meeting so every family member has a chance to experience each job over and over throughout the year.

7. Family Meetings are meetings to discuss agenda items. These could include problems that are happening in the family, or they could be suggestions to plan family events, parties, or outings.

8. Family meetings are not the time for parents to scold, criticize, or discipline their children.

9. Family meetings are a time to use the problem-solving techniques you have been practicing to solve family problems in a positive way. The last step of reevaluating solutions decided on could be set for five minutes at the next family

meeting.

10. Each family meeting should be followed immediately by a fun activity, playing a game together, or by serving a special treat.

11. You want your children to think of family meetings as an opportunity to have their opinion listened to and respected, a time when they can contribute to the family.

Suggested Agenda Items:

- How to eat dinner together with all the busy schedules
- How to plan a party together
- Plan a meal together
- Plan a trip
- Plan a camping trip
- How to get individual time with Mom and Dad
- What to get Mom, Dad, siblings for a birthday present
- Plan a surprise for someone
- How to get all the chores done – How everyone can help – How would it be fair
- Make a family play (as in a theater)
- Make a family movie, scrapbook, picture album

-14-

DECISION-MAKING

■ ■ ■

What You Will Learn in This Chapter

❑ Different personalities make decisions differently.

❑ Children need practice in learning how to make decisions.

❑ The foundation of our child's decision-making skills is laid from birth to age two.

❑ There are two types of decisions children face: immediate response and delayed response.

❑ Don't make decisions for your child (unless the decision she made is unsafe or unhealthy).

❑ Fear of making the wrong decision, or of being unable to undo a decision, can prevent a child from making any decision at all.

Every Day We Make Hundreds Of Decisions

Every day adults make anywhere from a hundred to thousands of decisions. Many of these we don't even think about; we just make them. Our life experiences have contributed to the way we can go about making so many decisions in a day without stewing over them too much. For instance, just going to the supermarket: we decide when to go, what to wear, and what to buy, which is the result of deciding what to have for breakfast, lunch, and dinner for the next few days or even for the whole week. Then if we decide to drive to the market, from the minute we step into our car and begin to drive, we are making decisions constantly. We must be alert, making decisions about when to stop and when to accelerate. We must judge what other drivers and pedestrians are going to do so we can be as safe as possible. Many decisions come naturally because our life experiences have taught us which decisions are the safest, most efficient, most productive, and most acceptable, Other decisions are more difficult to make. Yet over the years, we have each settled into a style of decision-making that fits us best.

Our children, no matter what age or stage they are in, are still learning how to make the best decisions. Our job as parents is to continue to teach them through role modeling, explaining, offering opportunities, and guiding them though learning experiences. We must also decide how we want to teach them to make decisions. Ask yourself what has worked well for you throughout your life. Are you a list maker? A "Pro vs. Con" person? Are you an information gatherer? Do you ask other people for their advice or do you make your decisions privately? There are many styles of decision-making. You know your child better than anyone else does, so you probably already have an idea of what will work successfully for your son or daughter. You also realize that if you have two or three children they will more than likely each have a different way of going about making decisions. While you work the exercises in this chapter, you will have the opportunity to observe your child's decision-making preferences.

Personality Types Make Decisions Differently

There are two personality types that make decisions differently. On two of the most popular personality assessments, The Meyer-Briggs Personality Assessment and The Kersey Temperament Sorter, these two decision-making personalities are referred to as the "J" - The Judger—and the "P" - The Perceiver.

A "J" or Judger Personality is characterized as someone who doesn't particularly like the decision-making process, but who moves on and lives with it once a decision is made. A "J" personality respects deadlines. If you talk to a "J" personality about completing a task, and agree on a deadline, she will probably accomplish the task on time. A "J" personality usually gets up when the alarm clock goes off, and is ready for school on time.

A "P" or Perceiver Personality, on the other hand, enjoys the decision-making process and is always gathering more information to make the decision. Once the decision is made, though, they might have a hard time living with it. You might hear a strong "P" personality question the decision almost as soon as it is made: "Do you think I made the right decision?", "I'd better rethink....", or

"I'm not sure if …." Since Perceivers are often unsure about the final decision, they may avoid finalizing it.

A child with a "P" personality has a hard time completing homework tasks. They tend to drag out an hour of homework into two hours. "P"s also have a difficult time being ready for school on time, and when they are old enough, they often use the snooze button three or four times before they get up. Parents of "P"s need to help them create a structure so they can successfully meet deadlines. As you work the skills in this chapter, become aware of whether your child leans towards a "P" or a "J" personality. This will help you teach him to make decisions in a way that is naturally comfortable for him.

We want to help our children become individuals who put some thought into difficult or important decisions they will make in their lives. For example, what peer groups to belong to, whether to tell the truth, whether to be angry with someone, whether to do a good job with your homework, and the list is infinite. The goal is not only to make sure children make wise decisions, but to ensure that they are comfortable with a decision once it's made, instead of ruminating over it.

Children continue to strengthen their decision-making skills through their life experiences.

An inability to make decisions and live with them can cause a person to become "stuck" in her life. "Stuckness" can paralyze a person at any age, and therefore cause the individual to question his or her ability to succeed. On the other hand, a person who rushes into a decision because he doesn't want to deal with the process of gathering information, often lives to regret the decision into which he rushed. An extreme of either of these personalities will lower your child's self-confidence and therefore his ability to make good decisions.

When an individual experiences several "bad" or "poor" decisions, she often becomes cautious or even hesitant to make more decisions. For instance, let's say your young child wants to have a friend over to play. She invites one little girl, who has to say no because of a dentist appointment. Then she asks a second friend who can't come because she's going to her grandma's birthday party. So your child asks a third little girl over, but this friend has already accepted a play date at another girl's house. At this point, your child is hesitant about asking a fourth little girl to play. Instead, fearful of receiving another no, which feels like rejection, she chooses not to ask anyone else. Her life experience of asking a friend over to play is clouded by one day's worth of negative experiences, which could cause her to avoid making the decision to ask friends over in the future.

This is where it is important for a parent to step in and help the child to see the experience in a new way, learn from it, and empower her to want to try again. Here's how this might go...

Mom: I bet that's disappointing that none of your friends can come over this afternoon.

Girl: I feel really sad, (starts to cry).

Mom: Why do you think they couldn't come over?

Girl: Because they don't like me.

Mom: Oh, I don't think so. I believe they like you very much. What did the first girl say?

Girl: She said she has to go to the dentist.

Mom: Does that mean she doesn't like you?

Girl: No, just that she has a dentist appointment.

Mom: What did the second girl say?

Girl: That it's her grandma's birthday and her whole family had to go to her grandma's house after school.

Mom: So, does that mean she doesn't like you or that her family was busy and she to be with them?

Girl: That her family's busy and she has to be with them.

Mom: What about the third little girl?

Girl: She was already going over to a friend's house.

Mom: It sounds like she planned ahead, and you just asked today after everyone had already made their plans. What could you do differently next time?

Girl: I could ask someone the day before.

Mom: That sounds like a really good decision to me. You let me know when you want to do that. Right now I would really like company going to the grocery store. Maybe you could be in charge of the list and tell me which aisles to go to?

Girl: Okay, Mom.

So How Do You Teach Decision-Making To Your Children?

If you have worked the Problem-Solving exercises with your child, it will be a smooth transition into Decision-Making exercises. Children make decisions differently at different ages and stages of their lives. The key to helping your child become confident about making decisions is to offer him as much experience at making decisions as possible and living with the consequences of the decision. Children build better decision-making skills as they get older as long as they are given the opportunity to practice along the way.

Ages 0-2 Years - Sensorimotor Cognitive Stage

We lay the foundation for our child's decision-making skills from birth to two years old. Remember, this is the *Sensorimotor Cognitive Stage*. An infant interacts with his environment during this stage and learns how his world works through his senses. What he feels is what he thinks. In the early part of this stage, he is simply reactive. His world is "NOW"—today, this moment. He is not aware of the past or the future. In other words he possesses an "out of sight, out of mind" mentality.

To help him develop decision-making skills at this stage, you need to interact with him as often as possible, offering him a variety of objects to touch and feel. As he moves though this stage, you will notice that he begins to show preference for a favorite toy, person, or sibling. He learns that if he pushes a button on his toy, it makes noise. If he pushes it again, it makes noise again.

As he grows, he will shift from reactive actions to decisive actions. He chooses to push the button to listen to the toy make noise. He begins to feel a sense of control in his environment. He learns through repetition, as well as through trial and error. In the scientific community, we would label his actions experimental. For your child, they are a natural progression in exploring his world as it consistently expands. You will also notice during this stage that your young child begins to move from "out of sight, out of mind" to making a decision to look for a missing toy. This doesn't happen overnight; the process is gradual. But when you are aware of the growth, it is exciting to watch.

Ages 2-7 - Preoperational Stage

The next cognitive stage is the *Preoperational Stage*, from two to seven years old. At this point, your child begins to think not only of today, but can recall yesterday and think about tomorrow. At the beginning of this stage what the child feels is still what he thinks, but he has new abilities. He is now able to verbalize his needs. He understands your words in response to his. He is getting a clearer understanding of the connection between cause and effect. By four years old the child has almost mastered his family's vocabulary. He still doesn't understand all the word meanings, but he uses his extensive vocabulary daily to the amazement of everyone around him.

When your child is four, you can give him as many opportunities as possible to make decisions. The more, the better—remembering to only give choices you can live with. The more your child experiences making his own decisions, the more ownership he will have over the results. He will learn that if he makes a decision he doesn't like, there might be an opportunity to change it, but not always.

You will notice tremendous growth during your child's fourth year. He will want to make more decisions for himself. Between the ages of four and seven, children are ready to learn from a decision they make. So you'll want to begin to explore with him, "If you do this, what do you think might happen?" Then, unless there is danger involved, let your child make his decision and follow through on it. Remember, our most powerful lessons are often the result of our failed plans. This is how we learn what to do differently next time. Play games with him where he has to make decisions and live with them, such as Jenga® or Tic-Tac-Toe.

As your child gets older within this stage and is used to your asking, "If you do this what do you think might happen?", you can begin to explore these three questions with him after a decision has been acted on:

1. What happened?

2. Is that what you expected to happen?

3. Would you do it differently next time?

Ages 7-11 - Concrete Operational Stage

At this *Concrete Operational Stage*, your child can begin to rationalize. His ability to use logic and problem-solving skills has increased dramatically, and when he makes decisions using these skills, you'll be amazed. Offer him as many opportunities as possible to join in making decisions that affect him. For example: When would he like to do his homework? How he would like his room set up? What chores he is willing to be responsible for? What kind of birthday party would he like? Who does he want to invite? What does he want to order for lunch at a restaurant? There will be thousands of opportunities during the next four years for you to work with your child to guide him into developing his own decision-making style. The style is not as important as his belief that he is capable of making a good decision.

Remember as you continue to work on raising his EQ, that his emotions should not overwhelm him as he accesses his cognitive brain to make healthy decisions.

Immediate Response Vs. Delayed Response Decisions

There are two types of decisions children are faced with: immediate response and delayed response. An *immediate response* decision might be something like, "What should I wear to school today?", "What toy do I want to play with?", "Should I hit my brother or not?", or "What do I want to eat?" In each of these decisions, the child gets the payoff right away: they wear the red sweater, choose the Legos to play with, decide not to hit the brother, and ask Mom for a peanut butter sandwich.

The second type of decision has a *delayed response* and thus involves a more sophisticated decision-making process. Rather than simply considering, "What do I want to eat right this minute?" A delayed response decision involves the repercussions of that decision. For example, "Mom said if I clean my room I can stay up an hour later tonight," "Dad said if I do all of my chores by lunchtime, he will play baseball with me after he gets home from work," or "If I eat all of my dinner now, even if I don't like it, I won't be hungry later. So should I eat it or not?"

The most difficult type of decision for children to make is one that involves a delayed response (delayed gratification). Very young children don't have a concept of delayed time. That's why, until about age seven, they will often choose to make a decision that has an immediate payoff. From seven years on, however, they are more able to understand the idea that, if I wait, the payoff could be better. In other words, "If I do my chores today, I'll get my allowance on Friday," "If I play nicely with my sister, my parents will be really pleased with me," or "If I do my homework tonight, I'll feel really good at school tomorrow."

Age and cognitive ability play a large part in decision-making. Your job as a parent is to offer your child the opportunities to make decisions that matter, both immediate and delayed, so he builds his confidence in his ability to make a decision. It is important for a child to experience successful decision-making on a regular basis so he builds this confidence.

Three Parent Traps That Undermine Decision-Making Confidence

1. The But Trap

As we talked about in the Self-Acceptance chapter, too often parents fall into the But Trap and unintentionally undermine their children's emotional intelligence. When our children make a decision and we say, "That's a good choice, but ...." we are sending the message that they made the wrong decision. For instance, we might say to our seven-year-old daughter, "Sarah, your outfit looks cute, but could you change to your black pants? They would look nicer with that great sweater you chose." Sarah doesn't hear that you like her sweater; she only hears that she made a bad decision in choosing the pants.

When a child repeatedly hears the 'but' phrase, she begins to believe that "Mom and Dad don't think I'm capable of making a good decision, so why bother—I'll just wait until they tell me what to do." Eventually her core belief becomes, "Why bother to try at all because no matter what I decide, it's not going to be the right decision."

I worked with a fifteen-year-old named Jason last year whose grades were much lower than his ability. His parents were very concerned about his lack of academic success because they saw college in their son's future. Towards the end of our first session together, I said to Jason "So, I know you are smart enough to get the B's your parents are asking for, yet you have C's in all your subjects. I also think you know why, so why don't you make my job easy and tell me what's going on." Jason calmly said, "No matter what I do, it's not good enough. If I get all B's, they'll (Mom and Dad) want all A's, so why bother?"

Report Card

Algebra I — C-
History — C+
Spanish — C
English — C-
Biology — C-
Art — C+

**"No matter what I do, it's not good enough. If I get all B's,
Mom and Dad will want all A's—so why bother?"**

Jason needed to feel successful about what he was accomplishing, and since he didn't, he made a decision that he could control. Letting his grades slip to C's, knowing the grades would upset his parents, gave him this sense of control. I met with his parents and explained what was happening. Jason was making a decision with a predictable outcome. It was hard for his parents at first because they felt that Jason was so capable, and it frustrated them that he wouldn't just decide to do what he needed to do to be successful academically. What was important for them to understand was that <u>all human behavior has a purpose</u>. Most children who succeed academically feel good about it, and their parents praise their efforts and successes. So everyone feels good.

For Jason, there was no payoff for getting good grades because he felt the B's still weren't good enough to please his parents. Jason had not experienced the joy of personally succeeding just for himself. His life belief had become "grades are about pleasing my parents, and since I never seem to please them why set myself up to work hard and then feel like I fail?" Jason got more of a personal payoff by being in control of upsetting and frustrating his parents. When his parents finally understood and bought into a plan to make Jason feel successful, Jason's grades started going up and everyone felt better. Today Jason has learned to take a pride in himself and to set personal goals for success.

2. The Assuming Trap

Another trap we fall into as parents is assuming we know what our children would choose to do in a particular situation. So instead of asking them for their decision, we make it for them. The decision-making might be as simple as ordering what we assume they want at a fast-food restaurant, rather than asking them what they'd like. It might be as simple as choosing a particular color T-shirt for them because it's their favorite color instead of asking them which T-shirt they'd prefer.

When we consistently make decisions for our children rather than asking their opinion, we send the message that we don't believe they are capable of making their own decisions. When we take the time to ask them to make a decision, even if they've responded the same way the last forty times, we are sending the message that we believe that they are capable to growing and changing. Who knows, today might be the day that they may want make a change. And if it is, we'll support them. When we take the time to celebrate who our children are today, and we encourage and support their ability to change and make decisions—even if it's in tiny ways—we send the message that we believe in them and respect them.

3. The Do It My Way Trap

The last decision-making trap that parents often fall into is being too directive. In other words, dictatorial or bossy. Children cannot become confident in their decision-making abilities if their parents send the message that there's only one correct decision: Mom's or Dad's. For example, when we ask our children to do a project and then proceed to tell them how to do it step-by-step "our way", down to the smallest detail, we're telling them that we don't believe they're capable of figuring out how to do this project, or any other project in the future, on their own.

Instead, beginning when your child is about four years old, give her a project, explore with her what she thinks you want her to do, and if her understanding is close to your expectation, let her do it her way. Throughout your child's life she will need to make many decisions on her own, so she'll need to start practicing as early as possible.

Children cannot become confident in their decision-making abilities if their parents send the message that there's only one correct decision.

If you need for things to always be "your way or no way" and are unable to allow your child to make decisions that vary from yours, she will likely become someone who lacks initiative, resourcefulness, and self-confidence. She will believe she must come to you to help her with every decision in her life. She will become a fearful, dependent adolescent who will be vulnerable to anyone who speaks to her authoritatively. In other words, she'll become a follower, not an independent thinker.

It's a good idea to take steps now to pave the way for your child's independence. Create projects where she can assert her individuality and develop her decision-making skills. You might ask her to arrange the vegetables "her way" on the appetizer plate, build a fort "her way" in the backyard, or set and decorate the table "her way" for her birthday party. You'll not only be helping to strengthen her decision-making abilities and raising her EQ, but you'll also be learning that there's more than one-way of doing things. It doesn't always have to be your way.

Most Decisions Are Not Forever

Believing that a decision can't be reversed may inhibit your child from making a decision. Some people don't make decisions because they're afraid of making the wrong one and then feeling uncomfortable. This fear of feeling uncomfortable is the basic reason for procrastination. So help your child under-stand the uncomfortable feeling of having made the wrong decision doesn't last forever, just for a short time. Also, let him know that it's often okay to change our minds after we've made a decision that doesn't make us happy. And help him to understand that even a bad decision becomes a good learning experience for the future.

Communicate to your child that a decision is usually not forever—and even if they can't change it, they will live through it and learn from it, so next time they'll make a different decision. For example, "wrong" decisions about the following can be easily changed next time around:

- What you ordered for lunch
- The friend you invited for a play date or a sleepover
- The theme for your birthday party
- A new haircut
- A new school binder

This set of exercises challenges you to get to know your child on a deeper level. You will learn how your child thinks and emotionally responds to people and situations. As you work the decision exercises with your child, it will be like looking through a window into your child's world of thoughts, emotions, and values.

EXERCISE # 1 - TALK ABOUT DECISIONS ☆

PURPOSE & BENEFITS:

To begin your child's awareness of his ability to make decisions. To empower your child to feel good about his ability to make decisions (choices).

STARTING AGE:　　4 years

TIME:　　10 minutes

LOCATION:　　Anywhere that is without distractions for 10 minutes

MATERIALS:　　None

INSTRUCTIONS:

1. Parent begins by asking child if he knows what a decision is. (In this exercise and throughout the chapter you can interchange the word choice for decision if that seems more understandable for your child).

2. Ask your child what decisions he made today. Count aloud as he names his decisions. If he gets stuck, go through his day and help him become aware of how many decisions he has made. For example: getting up, getting dressed (what to wear), brushing teeth, eating breakfast, combing hair (or not), tying his shoes, etc.

3. Ask him how many decisions he thinks Mom has made, Dad has made, his brother, and sister have made.

4. Talk about the different kind of decisions:
   - Ones we don't even think about: get up, brush teeth, etc.
   - Ones we think about: what to wear, what cereal to eat, etc.
   - Ones we ask advice for: Should I wear this outfit to Katie's party? Is this a good book for my book report?
   - Ones we gather information for: When can I have a play date? What will you let us do (swim, have lunch, or go to the park)?

EXERCISE # 2 - ALONG THE WAY ☆

PURPOSE & BENEFITS:

To become aware of conscious and unconscious decisions. Deepen your child's awareness of how many decisions he makes in a day.

STARTING AGE: 4 years
TIME: 5 to 10 minutes
LOCATION: Anywhere
MATERIALS: None

INSTRUCTIONS:

1. Parent ask your child to please go into another room and get something for you and bring it back to you.
2. When your child returns, the awareness begins.
3. Ask how many decisions your child made on his way to the other room, finding the item, picking it up, and bringing it back to you.
4. Help your child list a least ten decisions he made along the way and back.
5. Ask him if he is surprised at how he sometimes makes decisions that he isn't even aware of making.
6. Ask your child to go into a different room and pick up a different item and bring it back to you.
7. Discuss again how many decisions he made along the way.

EXERCISE #3 - 24 HOURS ☆

PURPOSE & BENEFITS:

To further develop awareness of the decisions your child makes. To build his confidence around his decision-making ability. To begin awareness of how he makes decisions. To empower your child with the knowledge that he makes good decisions.

STARTING AGE: 4 years

TIME: 5 to 10 minutes

LOCATION: Anywhere

MATERIALS: None

INSTRUCTIONS:

1. Parent asks child to tell about the decisions he has made since the last exercise. Parents count again the number.

2. Parent asks child to think about the decisions he will make during the next 24 hours.

3. Parent sets up a time to meet with your child 24 hours later.

4. Meet with your child at the set time (He will learn that what you say is what you do; you kept your commitment to meet).

5. Ask your child what decisions he made during the last 24 hours.

6. Discuss with him the ones he liked and the ones he didn't like.

7. Ask if he would make any decisions differently.

8. Ask how he would do it differently.

EXERCISE #4 - OTHER PEOPLE DECISIONS

PURPOSE & BENEFITS:

To become aware that everyone make decisions all-day long. To become aware that some people make decisions that affect us. Your child will deepen his awareness of what a large part decision-making plays in her life.

STARTING AGE: 4 years

TIME: 5 to 10 minutes

LOCATION: A quiet area without distractions so you can have a focused discussion

MATERIALS: • a piece of paper at least 8½" x 11" (to make lists)

• pen, pencil, crayon, or felt pen

INSTRUCTIONS:

1. Prepare ahead a piece of paper with columns so you can write

under the headings. Create your own headings or use the suggested ones:

Teachers	Police Officers	Bus Drivers	Mail Carriers	Waiters

2.   Ask your child what decisions she think each person written on the paper makes everyday.

3.   Someone then lists all of the suggested decisions on the piece of paper.

4.   When the time limit is up, discuss the decisions these people make. Any surprises? Discuss.

EXERCISE #5 - DECISION BASKET ☆

PURPOSE & BENEFITS:

To give your child the opportunity to share decisions he would make and to listen to the decisions other family member would make. Your child will begin to listen and learn different styles of decision-making.

STARTING AGE: 4 years

TIME: 15 minutes

LOCATION: Anywhere your family can gather around the basket with the least amount of distractions

MATERIALS:
- special decision basket (or bag or box)
- the following suggestions (or your own statements which ask for a decision) written on slips of paper and folded
- the folded slips then are put into the basket

INSTRUCTIONS:

1.   The family sits around the decision basket and decides on the order of who will begin.

2.   Each family member takes a turn choosing a slip of paper.

They read (or have help reading) the statement on the paper. After reading the statement, they share what they would decide to do in response to the statement.

3.   Accept all answers without criticism or negative judgment.

4.   The slip of paper is then folded and returned to the basket.

Suggested Statements:

- Your little sister took your toy. What do you do?
- You are mad at Mom. What do you do?
- Dad is upset with you for not picking up your toys. What do you do?
- It's your bedtime and you don't want to go to bed. What do you do?
- Your friend is being mean to you. What do you do?
- You are playing with your friends and the new student in class asks if he can play with you. What do you do?
- You know your sister/brother told a lie to your parents. What do you do?
- Mom told you not to eat anything before dinner, but you are really hungry. What do you do?
- Your neighbor left his toy on your front lawn. You really like the toy. What do you do?
- Your little sister/brother fell down and is bleeding. What do you do?
- Your favorite T.V. show is on and Dad asks you to do your chore now. What do you do?
- You don't like the dinner Mom just served. What do you do?
- You just got your haircut and you hate it. What do you do?
- Your little brother/sister just broke your favorite toy. What do you do?
- Mom and Dad are yelling at each other. What do you do?

EXERCISE #6 - HIGH - LOWS

PURPOSE & BENEFITS:

To observe how your child makes a simple decision. You will also be role modeling to your child good sportsmanship. You will be learning how he handles winning and losing.

STARTING AGE: 4 years

TIME: 15 minutes

LOCATION: Anywhere

MATERIALS: • a deck of cards

INSTRUCTIONS:

1. Divide a deck of cards into two even piles (three, four, etc. even piles according to how many people play).

2. Dealer begins by saying "high" or "low".

3. The dealer calls "high" then each player turns over a card; the player with the highest card wins all the cards turned over.

4. If the dealer calls "low", the player with the lowest card wins all the cards.

5. When the last card in the piles has been played, the winner is the person with the most cards.

EXERCISE #7 - STARS STEPS ☆

PURPOSE & BENEFITS:

To teach your child a decision-making formula that you can practice using with him. Visuals are helpful to children. The STARS acronym helps a child remember the steps to the decision-making formula. This exercise will teach your child there are important steps to take in all decisions.

STARTING AGE: 4 years

TIME: 10 to 15 minutes

LOCATION: Quiet location

MATERIALS: • piece of paper (to later post)

• pen, pencil, crayon, or felt pen

INSTRUCTIONS:

1. Ask your child what they think about when they are making a decision (choice).

2. Tell them you have a simple way of making decisions. It is called the STARS.

3. Draw a star.

4. Write the letters S–T–A–R–S, starting at any star point:

5. Explain what each letter stands for:

   State the decision (choice) to be made.

   Think about your choices, then choose one.

   Action and acceptance. Take action and accept the consequences.

   Review and learn. Review how the decision turned out. What did you learn? Would you make a different decision next time?

   Start again with your next decision.

6. Many parents like to make this chart ahead of time and have it ready to discuss.

7. Otherwise, write the letters and fill in the underlined parts when talking with your child.

☆	
S	
T	
A	
R	
S	

8. Choose some sample decisions and practice the STARS steps:
   - Who would you like to invite over for a play date?
   - When and how should we clean your room?
   - What is the best time to do your homework?

EXERCISE #8 - DECISION CHART ☆

PURPOSE & BENEFITS:

To give your child more practice thinking and making decisions. The more practice your child has making decision, real or in an exercise, the more confident she will become about her decisions.

STARTING AGE: 4 years

TIME: 15 to 20 minutes

LOCATION: Anywhere

MATERIALS:
- a decision chart
- spinner
- timer

INSTRUCTIONS:

1. Make ahead a decision chart – follow the directions below or be creative and make it your own way. Use statement on the following page for ideas.

2. To make the spinner, use a piece of cardboard from an old box, a piece of poster board, piece of wood, etc. You can also use one from an old game you might have or buy at a garage sale like the game Twister®, which has a large cardboard spinner.

3. Draw a circle and divide into eight pie slices. Assign a letter to each slice.

4. Make the spinner arm by using a piece of cardboard and pulling a fastener through it. Leave the fastener loose enough to spin the spinner.

5. Using a large piece of paper, poster board, a side of a cardboard box, etc. make the chart. Cut into a square or rectangle (or be creative).

6. List the statements below or make up your own and label as the diagram shown.

A	~~~~~~~~~~~~~~~~~~~~~~~~~~~~~~~~~~~~~
B	~~~~~~~~~~~~~~~~~~~~~~~~~~~~~~~~~~~~~
C	~~~~~~~~~~~~~~~~~~~~~~~~~~~~~~~~~~~~~
D	~~~~~~~~~~~~~~~~~~~~~~~~~~~~~~~~~~~~~
E	~~~~~~~~~~~~~~~~~~~~~~~~~~~~~~~~~~~~~
F	~~~~~~~~~~~~~~~~~~~~~~~~~~~~~~~~~~~~~
G	~~~~~~~~~~~~~~~~~~~~~~~~~~~~~~~~~~~~~
H	~~~~~~~~~~~~~~~~~~~~~~~~~~~~~~~~~~~~~

To Play:
- Decide who goes first and the order to follow.
- Each person takes a turn spinning the spinner.
- When the spinner lands on a letter, the person reads the statement and shares what they would do in the situation described.
- Next person takes his or her turn.

Variation:
- Family members can ask one question each about the decision.

Suggested Statements:
A. Your mom/dad told you to turn off the T.V. and pick up your toys.
B. Your little brother/sister keeps pestering you to play with him/her. You don't want to.
C. Mom/Dad is busy with some project, and you are bored.
D. Mom/Dad asks for your help with a chore, and you are watching TV.
E. You are angry/upset with your older brother/sister.
F. You want to go to your friend's house to play and Mom said she is too busy to drive you.
G. Mom/Dad asked if you did your chore. You didn't.
H. Two children are playing together at school and you want to play with them.

EXERCISE #10 - PLAY GAMES

> ## PURPOSE & BENEFITS:
>
> To give your child the opportunity to make immediate response decisions. You will have the opportunity to role model good sportsmanship.

STARTING AGE: 4 years (3 years depending on your child)

TIME: 10 minutes+

LOCATION: Anywhere

MATERIALS: • the games

INSTRUCTIONS:

1.   Follow the directions of any of the following games and enjoy.
   - Tic-Tac-Toe
   - Jenga®
   - Connect Four®
   - Perfection®
   - Old Maid, Fish, UNO® (any cards)
   - Chutes and Ladders®
   - Candyland®
   - Kerplunk®
   - Checkers or Chess
   - Yahtzee®
   - Dominoes

EXERCISE #11 - DELAYED GRATIFICATION ☆

> ## PURPOSE & BENEFITS:
>
> To give your child the opportunity to experience delayed gratification. To develop awareness and experience with waiting for something you want. Develop patience and tolerance.

STARTING AGE: 4 years

TIME: Varies

LOCATION: Varies

MATERIALS: Depends on activity chosen

INSTRUCTIONS:

1. Think about something your child might be willing to work toward earning: a new toy, a special outing, a special play date, a trip to the ice-cream Shoppe, special one-on-one time with Mom or Dad, etc.

2. Choose what action you want your child to do to earn the goal. It might be developing a new behavior: going to bed every night on time without a struggle, picking up toys with only one reminder, getting up on time, brushing his teeth every morning, helping you whenever you ask, using his manners of "please" and "thank you" without being reminded—the list is endless.

3. The parent can make the decision on what the goal or reward is to be.

4. For example:
   - The parents tells the child the number of successes needed to achieve goal: twenty times

   OR -

   - The parent can talk over possible goals and actions with the child and let the child decide what behavior he will do for what goal. The child can even work with his parent to determine the number of times needed to achieve the goal.

5. Post an ongoing tally sheet to show the number of successes. A tally sheet can be ✳ or −on a piece of paper on the refrigerator.

6. When the goal is reached, it is important for your child to receive the goal (reward) as soon as possible to motivate him to want to set another delayed goal.

EXERCISE #12 - CREATE DECISIONS (LONG-TERM) ☆

PURPOSE & BENEFITS:

To give your child the opportunity to experience decisions with time commitments (delayed responses) To develop awareness and life experience with how we need to live with some decisions whether we like them or not.

STARTING AGE: 4 years

TIME: Varies depending on decision

LOCATION: Varies

MATERIALS: Varies

INSTRUCTIONS:

1   Think about decisions you are willing to let your child make with a definite time commitment: 5 days (park and recreation class), two weeks (day camp), two or three months (soccer, baseball team, etc.), ten months (girl scouts, gymnastics, dance school).

2.   Discuss the decision. Use the STARS steps.

3.   Let your child own the decision. Write the decision and post somewhere in your house.

4.   Be patient throughout the time commitment: listening, supporting, especially if your child wants to quit. If possible, encourage your child to fulfill the commitment. There are more life lessons to be learned from fulfilling the commitment than by quitting halfway through.

5.   When the commitment is finished, review:
    • What did you like?
    • What didn't you like?
    • What did you learn?
    • What would you do differently next time?

-15-

ANGER MANAGEMENT

■ ■ ■

What You Will Learn in This Chapter

❑ Anger is a natural emotion.
❑ When anger is directed away from its source it is called *Displacement*.
❑ Even people with high EQ get angry.
❑ All children feel the tension and anger in their home.
❑ Children don't always know why they feel angry.
❑ Anger is always accompanied by at least three or four other emotions.
❑ All little monster type behaviors can be changed.
❑ Ten guidelines for parents to follow while practicing the Anger Management Skills.
❑ Anger at different ages and stages.

Anger Is A Natural Emotion

Anger is a natural emotion. Children often express it by yelling and screaming, perhaps even hitting, kicking, or biting. We don't want to stop our children from expressing anger; we just want to offer them safer ways to express it. Very young children can learn to talk about their anger to their parents, grandparents, teachers, or even their stuffed animals or pets. They can draw a picture about their anger and share it with an adult or give it to the person with whom they are angry. They can write about their anger alone or with help. They can bounce it out with a basketball, baseball, or a tennis ball, or kick it out with a kickball against a wall or the garage door. The parent's job through the exercises in this chapter is to help discover safer ways to express anger that work for your child.

When Anger Is Displaced Onto The Wrong Person

Psychoanalyst Sigmund Freud discovered that when people don't express their anger in the moment—at the person they're angry with—it oozes out later in different ways. He called this *displacement*. In other words, if a person feels angry towards someone but doesn't feel safe or comfortable expressing it toward that person, they will direct it towards someone else they consider much safer. For instance, let's say your child has a bad day at school, but instead of yelling at his classmates (he's afraid they might not play with him, or worse, they won't like him) he comes home and yells at you and at his siblings. In my own life experience, and through thousands of hours counseling children, I have consistently discovered that for children ages four through eighteen, Mom is usually that safe person. (Congratulations Mom!)

Children often displace their negative emotions on Mom.

Have you ever had the experience of picking up your child from school and saying something like "How was your day, honey" and having your son or daughter want to bite your head off? That's displacement. They experienced a build up of negative emotions, including anger, during the day and they held it in. Remember the balloon? Your child needed a safe place to dump his anger, and you were it. Moms and Dads are a great place to dump all of a child's negative emotions. This isn't low EQ—it's displacement.

Someone with high EQ realizes what's being done and finds a healthier way to vent that anger—most of the time. Remember: even high EQ individuals have low EQ moments. Have you ever experienced your spouse walking through the door when you've had a great day and can't wait to share it with him? All of a sudden ...whoosh! His body language is so grumpy, his greeting so curt, that in an instant your good mood—and the mood of the entire household—is changed. Chances are you haven't seen your spouse for eight or more hours, so he can't really be mad at you. More likely he had a bad day at the office, a bad commute home, a disagreement with someone on the phone, and now he just needs to let out his anger in a safe place—home being the safest place there is. If he had come home a half hour earlier and you weren't home yet, the entire sequence of events might have been different. He would have had time to unwind and relax, you would have walked in the door, and he might have met you with a welcoming hello and a hug.

There is another way that displacement happens in relationships. Freud talked about the individual taking negative emotions towards a person and directing them on to another person or object. I have learned within my own marriage and family, and in the families that I work with, that a unique phenomenon happens, which Freud didn't emphasize. A spouse or a child holding in negative feelings about not being listened to, not feeling loved, feeling disrespected and undervalued, will often choose some other issues to bring up rather than discussing what is really bothering him. For example, a spouse coming home after a long day, wanting to feel loved and nurtured, will walk through the door and see his wife on the phone discussing plans for tomorrow's school fundraiser. He notices that dinner isn't started and the children are running around. Instead of saying, "Honey, I've had the worst day, I could really use a hug right now and a little attention and then the rest of my evening is yours. Help me get the children settled down so we can talk and connect." What probably happens is more like this: The husband walks in picturing his wife waiting to greet him and the children tucked away quietly in the other room, and his mind flips a switch when he sees reality. Then he starts telling himself, "And this is what I go to work for? All I am is a paycheck to the family while everyone else gets to play all day. I live in stress. No one is cooking dinner. The children are running around and out of control. And she's probably been on the phone all-day gabbing." He has moved from "I had a bad day at work" to "Is this what my life is all about???" By the time his wife says "Hi Honey, I'll be off the phone in a moment," he's furious at life in general. He walks down the hallway, yells at the children to "quiet down" or just plain "shut up." When he gets to the bedroom and starts to change his clothes, his wife has caught up with him and says, "Honey, are you all right?" The truthful answer might be, "No, I've had a really bad day and I need a hug and some attention right now and I know I'll feel better in about ten or fifteen minutes." The wife, having a high EQ, might make a quick decision to support her husband knowing the fifteen minutes spent now will pay off all evening, and the evening would be happily ever after.

The reality of what probably happens is more like this:

WIFE: "Honey are you all right?"

HUSBAND: "No, I'm not all right. I go to work everyday. I work my butt off even though I hate my job, and what for? (WHINE, WHINE) So you and the children can play all day. Nobody even cares when I get home. You've probably been on the phone all-day because I sure don't smell dinner cooking and I can tell from looking around you sure haven't done any housework today (ATTACK, ATTACK). The children are totally out of control, running around. What kind of mom are you anyway? (ATTACK, ATTACK) It would be so nice to actually walk into my own home sometimes to peace and quiet and dinner cooking, but that's probably too much to ask! (WOE IS ME!)

We've all been there. If only the wife knew what was really bothering the husband or the husband could have talked about what was bothering him life would be smoother. Displacement in marriage and families goes beyond just dumping our negative emotions onto someone safe. Such scenarios too often end up with the angry person accusing or attacking the other. "You never...you always..." And when someone who is hurting and needing to talk about negative emotions ends up blaming or attacking the safe person, the situation often ends in conflict. The safe person usually doesn't understand why they're being attacked and takes it personally and gets defensive. The real issues are never addressed, and therefore the emotions are left to ooze out again in the future.

A person with a high EQ would recognize almost immediately from her husband's (or child's) body language that this person has a lot of negative emotions that will spill out one way or the other. A spouse or parent with a high EQ would know enough about reading someone else's body language to realize that now is not the time to share her great day. Now is the time to listen to the other person, who clearly needs to talk and vent his negative emotions, whose body language reflects how tense, angry, upset, depressed, frustrated he's feeling. So the high EQ person shifts from addressing her own needs to focusing on her family member.

And how might a high EQ child react to a parent's displaced anger? All children feel tension and anger in their homes, but the child with high EQ knows that there's a good chance her parents are not angry with her but with something that happened that day. She also knows she has the right to ask her parent if everything is okay. High EQ children understand that at some point in the evening or at bedtime, one of their high EQ parents is going to check in with them to see if they're all right. Children in a high EQ family feel much less fear, tension, or stress because they don't have to make up stories in their imagination about what is causing the negativity. At some point, a parent will be talking with them honestly, telling them about why one or both parents are upset, and assuring them that everything will be okay. This knowledge is a crucial security blanket for a child.

The goal of this chapter is not only to help your child manage his anger in a healthier way, but for each parent to become more aware of the difficult dynamics of anger. Anger can be a blatant outburst identifying the source of the anger or a cover up for the real source of the anger. Whichever way anger presents itself in your family if it is not acknowledged and discussed, it will continue to ooze out in hurtful ways doing damage to your family.

Do Children Always Know Why They're Angry?

Children and adolescents often have a hard time expressing what they really feel, mainly because they don't always know what they are feeling or why. Haven't you ever asked your six-year-old or even your sixteen-year-old, "Why are you angry?" and had them reply, "I don't know". They probably really don't know. Or perhaps you say, "Honey, you seem upset. Can I help?" and they reply, "No." They would probably love some help, but they don't have a clue why they're upset. And it's hard to ask for help when you don't know what's wrong and what you need to feel better.

Children often have a hard time expressing what they feel because they don't always know what they are feeling.

Almost all anger stems from being emotionally hurt. So when you are helping your child to explore why he is angry, always ask, "What do you think caused you to feel hurt?" Explore the answer. Then go on to discover the other three or four emotions your child is feeling. Look for frustration, hopelessness, helplessness, disappointment, and sadness. You will be surprised at how often these feelings accompany anger.

It's Important To Be Aware Of A Sudden Change In Your Child's Emotions

Take for example, seven-year-old Nicole who went off merrily to school on Wednesday and came home angry. Nothing Mom or Dad did seemed to be able to move Nicole from that place of anger. On Wednesday night, Mom and Dad went to bed hoping things would be better in the morning. Nicole woke up in a grumpy mood and announced she felt sick and didn't want to go to school. Mom took her temperature and nothing seemed to be wrong, so Mom and Dad insisted she go to school. Nicole cried and yelled in protest, but off she went to school. Mom called the school and spoke with Nicole's teacher at recess to see if she could explain Nicole's mood. Mrs. White, the second grade teacher, seemed as puzzled as Nicole's parents. She assured Nicole's mom that she would keep her eyes and ears open as the day went along and would let her know if she discovered anything that might have caused Nicole's anger.

Later that afternoon, Mom received a message from Mrs. White saying that she had learned that one of the little girls was having a small birthday party on Saturday. Only three girls were invited and they had been talking about how much fun the party was going to be. Nicole had not been invited but heard the girls talking about the party. When Nicole's mom picked her up from school that afternoon, Mom was prepared to use the techniques she had learned at one of my seminars to help Nicole.

They sat down together on Nicole's bed side. Mom began by saying she remembered once, a longtime ago, how hurt and angry she felt when she was left out of a classmate's birthday party. Nicole immediately started to cry and share with her mom about the party she wasn't invited to. Nicole and Mom together explored Nicole's feelings. She was: angry, hurt, sad, disappointed, lonely, and afraid. Mom understood most of the feelings mentioned and discussed. She was surprised to discover that Nicole was afraid she would never be invited to another birthday party in her whole life. Mom and Nicole began to talk about her own birthday party, which would be coming up in a couple of months. They discussed having a play date perhaps on the day of the classmate's party with one of the other girls who wasn't invited as well. They even talked about having a pretend birthday party that night at dinner and how they could sing Happy

Birthday to Daddy. Nicole began to realize that although she was angry, there were several other feelings and she did not need to stay stuck in anger.

Remember that we always experience four, five, or even six feelings at the same time in response to any situation. The strongest negative feelings are most often the ones to which we react. The strongest feeling is usually anger. If we are only trained to respond to the primary negative feelings without saying to ourselves, "What else is there?", we are always going to respond in anger and stay in anger. In this case "afraid" was the emotion which helped Nicole's parents understand Nicole's reaction.

Jennifer's Story

Once you have worked the exercises in this chapter with your child, they will be helpful in exploring for the other feelings. Take for example five-year-old Jennifer whose mom called to share this story with me. Over the Memorial Day weekend they had some friends over for a BBQ. Mom and Dad had decided to BBQ pork spareribs. When everyone sat down to eat, Jennifer refused to eat the ribs, in fact, she started yelling at her parents about what a horrible dinner they were making. Mom and Dad were stunned. They were also aware there was something hurtful under the anger. Mom offered to take Jennifer inside and explore for the root of Jennifer's outburst while Dad served the other guests.

When Mom and Jennifer sat down, they began the exploring process. Mom asked Jennifer to name her feelings. They had practiced this many, many times before. Jennifer said, "I am mad, I'm sad, I am hurt, I 'm scared, I feel sick to my stomach, I feel real mean." Mom chose one feeling to pursue. "Why do you feel mean?" Jennifer explained that her kindergarten teacher, Mrs. Boyle, had read Charlotte's Web to her class all week. Jennifer loved the story. She loved Wilbur. She didn't know how her parents could BBQ and eat pork ribs. Jennifer knew the pork ribs came from a pig just like Wilbur. Mom immediately understood Jennifer's feelings, and respected Jennifer's right to not eat the dinner that was being served. In fact, they went into the kitchen together and made a peanut butter and jelly sandwich for Jennifer. They also made a plan to talk about Charlotte's Web again after all the guests left later that night, or sometime the next day. The hard thing about anger is that it is cyclical. Anger just cycles around and around. It doesn't help you to understand your feelings, it doesn't resolve problems, it doesn't allow you to empathize, and it certainly doesn't allow you to be helpful to someone else. It is when we discover the other emotions accompanying anger that we can help our children come up with a plan to let the anger go.

Jason's Story

Anger is like a fire: it rages, sends off flames and sparks in all directions, eventually becomes reduced to hot embers, and then finally (hopefully) it's gone. Sometimes it goes out and sometimes it just simmers for hours, days, or even longer. Most other negative feelings, on the other hand, can lead to some kind of resolution. Another example involves eight-year-old Jason and his younger brother, Eric, who is six-years-old. Jason and Eric had always gotten along, so when Mom and Dad brought Eric into my office, they were at the end of their rope. For the past year, Eric had refused to play with Jason and he seemed angry with his brother all the time. Eric's parents were concerned because Jason, who had always treated his little brother kindly, was showing signs of frustration and impatience. Jason was tired of Eric's anger and had given up trying to play with him. As I sat with the parents exploring any changes that had occurred in their lives over the last year, we discovered the boys' grandpa, who is an avid fisherman, had retired just about a year ago. Since his retirement, he had been taking Jason fishing with him at least two or three times a month in a small boat the grandpa owned. Grandpa only took Jason because he was nervous about watching two boys and Jason was older and was a better swimmer than Eric. Eric had never shown any interest in fishing. I met with Eric in session and explored with him how he felt about Grandpa and Jason fishing. He began to cry and said that his grandpa didn't love him and that Grandpa only loved Jason because Eric himself had never been invited. Eric was hurt, sad, feeling unloved, not good enough, confused about why he wasn't good enough, and why his grandpa didn't love him as much as he loved Jason.

I brought Eric's parents into my office and helped Eric explain how he was feeling. The anger had presented itself so strongly and so nastily that it had not occurred to Eric's parents to look under the surface to discover the source. Once Dad and Mom understood what was causing the anger, the family immediately started to discuss a plan of asking Grandpa to spend some special time with just Eric. The last time I spoke with Eric's family, they had a regular miniature golf game set up with Grandpa and Eric, and Jason and his brother were playing together again. Eric's parents have learned the skills of exploring beyond and beneath the anger, and they told me they use the skills with much success.

Anger And Childhood Depression

Many psychologists believe there is a link between anger and clinical depression. A statement that is continuously being debated is that "depression is anger turned inward." Is anger the only cause for depression? I don't believe so.

I think depression can be genetic and environmental. There is also what I call "situational depression" where a situation is so traumatic or so frightening that it causes a person to fall into depression. Also, if you live with someone who is depressed, his or her mood tends to pervade the home, and I believe you can then feel what I call "secondhand depression."

What About Childhood Depression?

Young children often act out their depression through anger. When you follow the exercises in this chapter, your child will begin to deal with his anger in a much healthier way. If you have done all the exercises and your child is still throwing angry temper tantrums and seems out of control, you may want to consult a family therapist to have him assessed for *Childhood Depression, Oppositional Defiant Disorder, Anxiety Disorder*, or several other clinical disorders.

Overcoming Little Monster Behaviors

Our children learn their "How-the-world-works" rules from the first week they are born. All humans are born with an empty hard drive and begin inputting data about how the world works from that first week. They intake feelings and observations, but don't understand them. Still, they begin to learn what behavior is acceptable from birth. For example, if every time I cry I get what I want, then I will continue to cry. Or if I never hear the word no, then I learn to accept that my world has no place for no. If I then begin to hear no when I'm three or four, I will resist it, because it goes against the "How-the-world-works rules" I've learned earlier.

We can create problems for our children by thinking certain behaviors are cute when they're young and then thinking they will grow out of them. A child's belief system about how the world works and how he fits into it is set by the time he's three-years-old, even though he doesn't intellectually understand it. If you have created monster behaviors in your child, and are living to regret them, I want to assure you that it is never too late to reprogram a belief system. But it does take time, commitment, and consistency. Let's take the common example of a child having learned that "If I yell or cry loud enough in a store I usually get what I want." Usually the reason a parent has allowed this behavior is that it's a seemingly efficient way to stop the child's embarrassing tantrum and get him to be quiet. But again, giving the child what he wants to get him to be quiet simply reinforces the belief that, "I'll get what I want if I make enough noise—especially in a public place." So you're paving the way for more little monster behavior down-the-line.

Is a child really expressing anger when he has a tantrum like this? Actually, his singular focus isn't anger so much as it is, "I want something, and I know how to get it." What the parent often fails to think about is that, as soon as the child gets the reward for his bad behavior, he's verbally, physically, and emotionally content and calm. It's important to keep in mind that what may seem like anger in children isn't always genuine anger, but often a manipulative tool to get what they want.

Our children start to learn their
"How-the-World-Works" rules from the first week of life.

To change the "I'll get what I want if I have an angry tantrum" belief system, the parent has to be prepared to say "No!" and stick to it. It may mean weeks of walking out of stores, leaving half-filled carts behind, and going to the car to sit until the child calms down. Or it might mean going straight home where your child can cry without you feeling pressured to give him what he wants in order to quiet him down.

It normally takes only a couple of weeks for even the youngest child to reprogram his 'Tantrum = Reward' belief system. The new belief becomes: "When I cry or yell in a store, my mom or dad leaves and takes me straight home and puts me in my room to keep crying. I don't get anything out of it." Eventually, your child will try some new behaviors to get what they want, but once you understand how the belief system process works, you'll be so much wiser that you'll be able to nip the new manipulative behavior in the bud. All belief systems can be reprogrammed, even our own if we are willing to do the work.

Exploring Your Child's Anger

When children feel emotionally safe with their parent, they are usually willing to explore the reason for their anger. Be prepared for your children to blurt out reasons for their anger that range from childhood logic to absolute ridiculousness. I ask you to accept all answers even when you are aware of the mistakes in your children's perceptions. If you criticize or reject their attempt to explain the source of their anger, you will prevent your children from feeling safe enough to be honest about their anger. If you use their explanations as a starting place to explore, your children will feel listened to and respected. The rest of the exploring will probably flow easily and you will discover what is at the root of your children's anger. Children are great with labels, and they will likely apply different labels to their angry feelings. I'm going to ask you to accept all of these labels, even if they don't seem accurate. If you criticize or reject your children's perception, you will prevent your children from feeling safe enough to be honest about their anger.

Ten Guildlines for Parents

These exercises, more than the others, have to feel safe to your child. So to prepare yourself to guide him, I suggest you follow these ten guidelines:

1. Don't take your child's angry expressions personally.

2. Before you begin any of the exercises, say to yourself: "This isn't about me. This is about my child." Repeat this as often as needed so that you're in the correct frame of mind to deal with your child's anger.

3. Be prepared to feel a gut-wrenching or defensive reaction to some of the angry things your child might say. Don't allow yourself to get defensive, because then your child's issue will be about you and you won't be helping him understand what his anger is about.

4. When your child says "I feel angry when..." or " I feel angry because..." don't tell him, "You shouldn't be angry because...". The minute you do that, you discount his feelings; you devalue him as a person and teach him not to trust himself to label his own emotions. Even if the reason he says he's angry doesn't make sense to you, and you want to blurt out, "That's ridiculous. How could such a thing possibly make you angry?" DON'T!!! Our children feel what they feel. If we do not listen to them and respect their feelings and perceptions, they will not be open to sharing them with us.

Every individual's perception is unique. No two people ever have an identical perception of anything. When I hear someone say, "I completely understand." to someone, I often want to cringe because I know that's impossible. What we <u>can</u> do for those we love and care about is try to understand why they feel the way they do—in this case, why your child feels angry. Stephen Glenn, the author of <u>How To Raise Self-Reliant Children in a Self-Indulgent World</u>, states that one of the most wonderful things you can ever say to another person is "Let me make sure I understand what you just said." Wow. When we say this to our children (and our spouses!), we are really saying "I care enough about you as an individual, and I value what you have to say enough, that I want to make sure I really understood you." I agree with Stephen Glenn one hundred percent! Whenever I make that statement to anyone, I always learn more about that person. I send the message that I care about them and establish a sense of emotional safety.

5) Actively listen to your child; listen to his words and his body language. Try to listen as well for what he's <u>not</u> saying so both of you can discover the root of his anger.

6) Ask questions about what he's said. EXPLORE!!

7) State what you think your child might be feeling. Even if you say, "You sound hurt," and they say, "No, I'm not!" a child will often correct you by adding, " I don't feel hurt. I feel sad." Respect whatever they say.

Learning about your child's anger involves understanding her perception of the world.

8) Whatever you do, don't use this time of exploring your child's angry emotions to teach, preach, lecture, or moralize. If you do that even one or two times, they won't ever want to try to explain to you how they are feeling.

* Remember that children learn about life through observation and experience, not lectures.

* Remember also that 80% of children's morals are set by the age of ten. The other twenty percent is reached usually by their mid-twenties through trial-and-error of life experiences. So, if you feel compelled to lecture your child after the age of ten, do it once or twice at an appropriate time, but not while she's bearing her soul to you and trying to explain what's beneath her anger. And never give the same lecture more than twice!

9) Remind yourself that learning about your child's anger involves understanding his perception of the world. It's not about making him accept yours.

REMEMBER: "WHAT WE PERCEIVE WE BELIEVE."

In the early 1950s, Rudolph Driekirs, a child psychologist and author of <u>Children: The Challenge</u>, said, "Our children are great perceivers (of emotions), but poor interpreters." I think he's right, but I would go a step further and say, "Children and adolescents are great perceivers, but poor interpreters."

10) Listen, ask questions so you better understand your child's anger, name other possible feelings he might be experiencing, and most importantly: be there for him. If he wants help dealing with his anger, offer to help with a plan of action, but realize that even children as young as four years old are capable of coming up with their own plan to manage anger.

Anger Management From Birth To Ten Years Old

Birth To Two Years Old

Your child is learning about his relationship to the world during these two years. He is discovering that the sounds he makes cause you to respond in a certain way. In other words, he is learning basic communication skills through his actions and your reactions.

During this period, your child notices his feelings but doesn't understand them. He is, however, beginning to feel the difference between positive and negative feelings. For instance, "If Mom holds me, it feels good. If my big brother takes my toy away, it feels bad." Negative responses often feel more intense in the body. This is a good time for the parent to pay particular attention to the intensity of your child's responses. Listen to the difference between upset and anger from hunger and discomfort.

You will notice the more negative your child's emotions, the louder he will cry. You might even notice that around twelve months old his screaming sounds are different from even a month before. Such screaming is often his way of expressing anger. He is saying: "I don't like what is happening!" or "I don't like what you just did to me! (put me in my stroller, picked me up when I wanted to continue crawling or walking...)." If there is a payoff because of his screaming—for example, if his big brother gives back his toy—he learns there is certain power in his screaming. So, it's understandable why, when Mom takes his toy away for a good reason and he screams expecting to get the object back, and he doesn't get it back, he becomes confused.

Your child will continue to react to his emotions and to experiment with his own sounds and behaviors in response to what he is feeling. It is important during these two years to consistently use the self-soothing techniques mentioned. If you use these techniques regularly with your infant, they will pay off as he begins to feel anger. The more you work with your child to raise his EQ, the fewer out-of-control angry tantrums he will have.

Two Years Old To Four Years Old

Your child is trying to assert himself during this time. He is showing preferences for particular objects, food, people, and activities—and is also letting you know what he doesn't like. You may find him more negative and demanding and hear yourself say, "Where is my sweet little boy?" During this time the sense of predictability you were beginning to experience might be suddenly challenged. In fact, daily routines often become a source of conflict.

By four years old, your child is experiencing a range of emotions from loving and sweet to resistant and angry. This range can take place within an hour (or five minutes) like a strong gust of wind blowing through. You might say to yourself, "What just happened?" During these years, your child still equates what he is feeling with what he is thinking: "I feel upset, so I am upset." If he is feeling something negative—whether that feeling is disappointment, frustration, hurt, or anger—his behavior might look the same to you. For example, he might be yelling, screaming, crying, or kicking (or all the above!).

Your child is testing his world, and he needs you during this time to set boundaries and to help him understand what is going on within him. Two-, three-, and four-year-olds often scare themselves with their negative behavior, especially when it first begins. If inappropriate behaviors are allowed to continue, they soon become the little monster behaviors. If your child is going through this stage, you'll want to deal with the behavior as soon as it begins (maybe not the same day because you may be in shock!!!). Begin to set boundaries for the appropriate expression of anger. Is it okay to pound a pillow, but not okay to pound the door or your little sister? If you are part of a couple, make sure you discuss and agree with your partner about what is acceptable and unacceptable behavior for your child. And agree, too, to be consistent in your response to unacceptable behavior.

When Bill and I were raising our first two children, who were two years old and three years old at the time, the parenting experts of the day advised that we should be consistent with our discipline. We thought that meant make the consequence consistent for a particular behavior. So that's what we did. Our children were soon able to predict accurately the consequence of a particular behavior. What Bill and I found was that, as young as our children were, there were times when they decided to misbehave because they didn't think the consequence they knew they'd receive was so bad.

The lesson I'd like to pass on: Don't be so predictable with your consequences that you give your children the opportunity to misbehave because they think, "it's worth it." We set limits, rules, and expectations to teach our children self-discipline, respect, responsibility, and values. We don't want them to learn that it's okay to break a rule (and later in life, a law) if you don't mind the consequence.

It is necessary to be consistent with your behavioral expectations, not with particular consequences.

Once Bill and I caught on to what our children were up to, we kept them on their toes because they never knew what the consequence for a particular behavior was going to be. The more inconsistent we were with the consequences, the more consistent our children became about making good choices about their behavior.

Remember that, during the years between two and four, your child is exploring his boundaries, and your job is to teach him what the boundaries are. Children know they can wear us down when we're tired. But if you hold to expectations during these years, it will pay off.

It's natural for young children to get angry at times. It's not the anger you are trying to stop, it's the inappropriate angry behavior—such as yelling, kicking, and screaming every time they hear the word no. If you and your child are battling over such behavior, the exercises in this chapter will help you discover more workable solutions.

As we discussed earlier, if your child has had success acting out in anger, he likely holds the belief that, "If I get angry and yell and scream, I'll get what I want." Even if he only wins one time out of ten, he will continue to yell and scream knowing that the tenth time will be the charm. It's your job to be vigilant so his belief changes to: "It's okay to tell Mom or Dad that I'm angry, but if I yell and scream I won't get what I want. In fact, I'll get a consequence I don't want."

Five Years Old To Eight Years Old

Your child is now able to recognize what he is feeling and quickly name those feelings if you have been working the exercises. If not, you'll want to jump right in to it. It will take a little while to help your child understand that feeling angry is natural and okay. It is the angry behavior that's not okay.

Children at this age are capable of learning how to express anger in an appropriate way. This is the time for a child who has been hitting to use his words instead. Children between five and eight are experiencing a sense of independence. The anger often shows up when they want to be in charge, do things their way instead of following the rules or expectations of the parents. It is important in the "land of non-negotiables" that you hold your own, set the boundaries or expectations, and stick to them.

You will notice mood swings at times, where anger will turn into sullenness or sadness or, especially, frustration. Always use your communication skills to explore what your child is feeling. She is getting wise enough to manipulate you so she gets what she wants. Follow your instinct as to whether her sadness is credible or if she is using it to get you to change your mind about a no.

Your role modeling is extremely important at this time. If your child sees you yell, scream, swear, or punch doors, then it will be nearly impossible to prevent her from using this behavior as well. Your child loves you. She figures that if the negative behavior is good for you, it must be good for her, too. It only takes one parent acting out in anger to give a child permission to act out in anger and feel justified. Continue to encourage and explore what your child is feeling, and role model by sharing your feelings.

Nine Years Old To Ten Years Old

At this age, your children are able to rationalize and think about things. They are also able to hold on to small hurts and insults and simmer them until they become huge hurts or until your child becomes very angry. If they have learned throughout their lives to self-soothe and to talk about their feelings, their anger won't explode too often. Still, their lives at school and with their friends are becoming more complicated; throw puberty into the mix, and they're forced to deal with several challenging emotions. Seven hormones are needed to change a young girl or boy's body into an adult. These play havoc with a preteen's emotions during this transition.

Your daughter could be happy, sad, angry, and happy again all within thirty minutes—and you'll wonder what's going on with her. For some girls, puberty is starting as young as eight years old. Boys 11 to 14 still go through puberty a little later and don't seem to have the same range of emotions as girls—but they experience a lot of negativity and anger until they get through puberty.

Again, you want to let your children know that anger is a natural emotion. Talk to them about it, and make a plan to help them express it in a healthy way. It is not okay to yell, scream, kick, or hit anything or anyone. You must set the boundaries for respectful expression of anger in your home and keep the boundaries enforced. The bottom line is that, by the time they reach puberty, you want your children to carry a life belief that says, "Anger is natural, but I must be respectful of others in how I express it."

Children at this age can be wonderful at problem-solving. So, once you help them figure out "the what" or "the why" of their anger, you can help them formulate a plan to move beyond it.

Remember to always dig deeper than the anger for the other emotions your child is feeling. There are almost always four or five other emotions—such as hurt, frustration, disappointment, betrayal, and fear. These are the real clues to your child's perception of life at that moment.

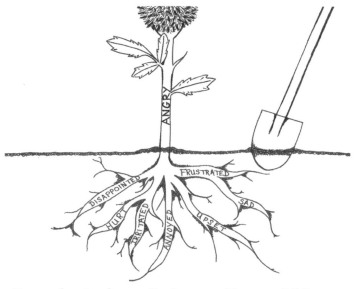

**Remember to always dig deeper with your children
for the correct emotions they are feeling.**

Anger is almost always the result of hurt, so if you get stuck while digging for the other emotions, say something to your child like, "You know every time I feel angry it seems like I always feel hurt at the same time. How about you?"

Relax and enjoy the next couple of weeks as you work with your child on the Anger Management Skills chapter. Keep a picture in your head of how calm your home will feel in a couple of months when these skills become the norm in your family.

EXERCISE # 1 - TALK ABOUT IT! ☆

PURPOSE & BENEFITS:

To begin to have your child become comfortable talking about anger; to teach your child that anger is a natural emotion. When a child begins talking about anger, they begin to realize that they can control what they do with it. Many children believe that anger is an outside power that controls them.

STARTING AGE: 4 years

TIME: 10 minutes

LOCATION: Somewhere you will be able to write a list

MATERIALS:
- a piece of paper
- pen, pencil, crayon, or felt pen

INSTRUCTIONS:

1. Tell your child that everyone feels angry at sometime. It is normal to feel angry.

2. Ask: Why do you think people get angry? List all the answers your child offers and remember; there are no wrong answers.

3. Ask: Why do you get angry? At who? List all the answers.

4. Ask: How do you know when someone is angry? How do different people show they are angry (Mom, Dad, teachers, coach, Grandma, Grandpa, brother, sister, friends)?

5. When you are finished discussing anger with your child, choose a place to put up the list of answers he suggested. The refrigerator or a bulletin board where everyone can see the list is always a good place.

EXERCISE # 2 - ANGER WORD LIST ☆

PURPOSE & BENEFITS:

To be aware of different words that you say or hear that sound like you are saying you are angry; to build your feelings vocabulary.

STARTING AGE: 4 years

TIME: 5 to 10 minutes

LOCATION: Anywhere

MATERIALS:
- a piece of paper
- a pen or pencil

INSTRUCTIONS:
1. Ask your child to tell you any words at all that describe being angry.
   - For example: anger, mad, upset, irritated, annoyed, frustrated, hurt, bugged, etc.
2. Go through the list and say each word. Have your child say the word and ask them if the word feels different in his body.
3. If he says no, accept his answer.
4. If he says yes, ask him how it feels in his body. Anger is usually a more intense reaction in the body than irritation or annoyed. When children notice their body feels differently when they are irritated or annoyed, or even frustrated, they will begin to label their feelings as anger less often. When a child, just as an adult, labels a feeling irritated rather than anger, the behavior response to the word is different – calmer.

EXERCISE # 3 - PICTURE ANGER ☆

PURPOSE & BENEFITS:

To continue to explore your child's perception of anger.

STARTING AGE: 4 years

TIME: 10 to 15 minutes

LOCATION: Somewhere you and child can draw

MATERIALS:
- paper
- crayons or felt pens

INSTRUCTIONS:
1. Ask your child what anger looks like.
2. Ask him to draw a picture of anger.

3. Draw your own picture alongside your child.

4. When you are done, talk about your drawings.

EXERCISE # 4 - BUTTONS AND TRIGGERS ☆

PURPOSE & BENEFITS:

To help your child identify people, situations, and events that make him angry. To teach the goal of shutting off his buttons. To begin the process of becoming aware of future triggering people, situations, and events.

STARTING AGE: 4 years

TIME: 10 to 15 minutes

LOCATION: Anywhere you and child can write

MATERIALS: • paper with six circles drawn on it.

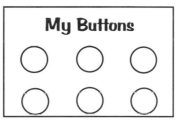

INSTRUCTIONS:

1. Give your child a piece of paper and ask him to draw six circles. - OR - You can prepare the paper with the circles already drawn if you choose.

2. Title the top of your paper MY BUTTONS.

3. Tell your child that everyone has people, events, or situations that upset them, even make them angry.

4. Tell your child the things that make us angry are like the push buttons on a soda machine. When our own buttons are pushed, out comes the anger—like the soda can. It almost feels like we have no control over it.

5. Tell your child to write things or people that make him angry in the circles (buttons) on the paper. If he is young, help him write.

6.   When the buttons are filled in, ask him one at a time why each person or thing makes him angry.

7.   Ask what would help him not have his button pushed by that person, situation, or event.

8.   Listen to all his ideas.

9.   Ask if he is willing to try any of his ideas so he doesn't get angry the next time his button is pushed.

10.   Write down his ideas and post them.

11.   Challenge your child to work on turning his buttons off with his ideas.

12.   Show him a Post-It® that says "Out of Order" on it.

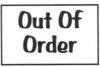

Out Of Order

13.   Tell your child that when his button no longer works (he doesn't get angry with that person or situation), you will give him an "Out of Order" Post-It® to put on his button.

EXERCISE # 5 - BLOW UP A BALLOON ☆

PURPOSE & BENEFITS:

A reminder that when we keep negative emotions inside us they don't go away. They continue to build up until they explode. A visual to impress the importance of talking about anger rather than hold it in.

STARTING AGE: 4 years

TIME: 5 minutes

LOCATION: Anywhere

MATERIALS: • a balloon

INSTRUCTIONS:

1.   Remind your child about blowing up the balloon when they were first doing the feeling exercises.

2.   Tell your child this time we are only going to blow up the

balloon with anger.

3. Ask all your family members to share situations that make them feel angry.

4. Each time someone shares an anger time blow air into the balloon.

5. When the balloon is almost filled, ask your child whom they can talk to when they are angry – let some air out.

6. Ask what else you can do to let go of some of your anger.
   - Talk to a friend, draw a picture, talk to stuffed animals, write the anger down in a book, bounce a ball, etc.

7. Each time a suggestion is given, let out some more air.

8. Then refill the balloon by asking for more anger times.

9. When the balloon is ready to pop, let it go and let it fly around.

10. Have a balloon ready to give your child to play with.

EXERCISE # 6 - HEALTHY SUGGESTIONS ☆

PURPOSE & BENEFITS:

To recognize and acknowledge people and situations that make you angry. To listen to suggestions from family members that might help reduce the anger or even turn off the button. Human beings do not change a response to a person or a situation until they have identified it, talked about it, and see a benefit to change.

Starting Age: 4 years
Time: 15 to 20 minutes
Location: Somewhere to hang a poster
Materials: • a large piece of paper or a poster board with a
                     large outline of a balloon drawn on it
                   • Post-Its® or small pieces of paper
                   • pens, pencils

INSTRUCTIONS:
1. Ask your child to tell you what she remembers about filling up

the balloon with negative feelings. Listen carefully.

2. Tell your child we're going to fill up this balloon on the poster with things that make us angry.

3. Ask your child to write something or someone who makes her angry on the Post-It®. Ask her to also write the reason they make her angry if she knows it. Everyone in the family can join in writing things that makes them angry.

4. A young child can draw a picture of what makes her angry. She can ask for help if she needs it.

5. Then have her put the Post-Its® inside the balloon drawing.

6. Next take turns having everyone in the family choose a Post-It® (either their own or someone else's), read it, and share why they think that situation or person would make somebody angry.

7. Then a member of the family gives suggestions of healthy ways to handle the anger next time.

8. Mom or Dad may need to begin this exercise so they can role model the reading and suggesting of ways to handle the situation to reduce the anger.

9. After the Post-It® is read and suggestions are offered, the Post-It® is removed from the inside the balloon and placed outside the balloon.

10. Continue to take turns until each person has had at least one of his or her Post-Its® read and suggestions given.

11. Set a time to come back together to report if anyone tried any of the suggestions with any success in reducing their angry response. If someone has had success reducing his anger, celebrate by removing the Post-It® from the poster and throwing it away. The parent may want to date the Post-It® and keep it in an envelope. The purpose of this would be to keep a record of events, situations, and people which anger family members.

12. Celebrate any successes and look for other possible solutions or suggestions from all family members for someone who didn't succeed.

13. Repeat this exercise until all the Post-Its® are gone.

EXERCISE #7 - DRAW ANGER SITUATION CARTOONS

PURPOSE & BENEFITS:

To develop continued awareness of situations that can cause an angry response.

STARTING AGE: 4 years

TIME: 20 minutes

LOCATION: Anywhere you can draw

MATERIALS:
- paper
- crayons, pencils, or felt pens

INSTRUCTIONS:

1. Fold the paper in four parts.

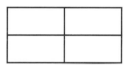

2. Ask your child to draw four times when she has gotten angry.

3. The parent can also draw four times she has gotten angry.

4. When the drawings are completed, take the time to share the drawings and talk about each picture.

    a. What happened?

    b. How did you feel besides angry (Remember there are always four to five feelings at one time)?

    c. What could you do differently next time?

NOTE: Variation: If your time is limited, fold the paper in half and draw only two pictures.

EXERCISE #8 - GOOD WAYS/BAD WAYS ☆

PURPOSE & BENEFITS:

To think about all the good ways to express anger. To become aware of all the bad ways people express anger.

STARTING AGE: 4 years

TIME: 10 minutes

LOCATION: Somewhere you can write

MATERIALS: • piece of paper or white board

                               • pen or pencil, felt pen

INSTRUCTIONS:

1.   Set up a piece of paper or a white board into two columns. Title the columns:

Good Ways to Express Anger	Bad Ways to Express Anger

2.   Ask your child to name all the ways she can think of that people express anger in Good Ways and list all the ideas. Then ask her to name Bad Ways.

Good Ways to Express Anger	Bad Ways to Express Anger
Time out	Hitting
Talk to someone	Yelling
Breathe deeply	Kicking
Counting to ten	Biting
Counting backwards from 100	Being mean
Distraction (T.V., book)	Hurting
Thought stopping	Throwing things
Avoidance	Rip things
Physical exercise	Break things
Write in a journal	
Draw pictures	

3.   Discuss the ideas listed under Good Ways.

4.   Ask your child to choose one or two ideas to try the next time she gets angry.

5.   Report back to Mom or Dad when she has tried any of the ideas.

            • What worked?

• What didn't work?
• What will she try next time?

EXERCISE #9 - BASKET OF ANGER WORDS ☆

PURPOSE & BENEFITS:

To have your child experience feeling safe talking about the times he feels angry. To bring the family together by listening respectfully to each other's anger stories. To offer the message the family cares about one another when they are upset. When a child learns to talk about his anger at a young age with his parents, he is much more likely to talk to them about it when he is older.

STARTING AGE: 4 years

TIME: 10 to 20 minutes

LOCATION: Anywhere

MATERIALS: • a basket: strips of paper (can be Post-Its®)
with the following words written on them:
Angry, Upset, Hurt, Frustrated, Mad, Irritated,
and Annoyed
• a timer

INSTRUCTIONS:

1. Prepare the strips of paper ahead with the words.
2. Fold the pieces of paper and put them in the basket.
3. Decide who will go first.
4. Each family member picks out a piece of paper and reads it.
5, Then, using a timer set for one minute, or up to two minutes, the person whose turn it is shares a time when he felt the feeling written on the piece of paper.
6. Everyone listens quietly—no put-downs or criticisms.
7. When that person is finished sharing, family members can ask supporting questions or offer support with positive suggestions.
8. It is important for the parent to role model support.

EXERCISE #10 - HEALTHY ANGER ☆

PURPOSE & BENEFITS:

To explore and practice healthy ways to express anger. The family works together to succeed in a goal.

STARTING AGE: 4 years

TIME: On-going

LOCATION: Everywhere

MATERIALS:
• a chart to post, which has each family member's name on it with a column underneath

Dad	Mom	Kim	Mike	Bob
5/24	5/26	5/21	5/22	5/19
5/27	5/27	5/23	5/28	5/21
		5/24	5/23	

• a pen or pencil to use on the chart
• the earlier list made of "Good Ways" to express anger posted

INSTRUCTIONS:

1. Each family member is to give herself credit for using a "Good Way" to express anger by writing the date under her name on the chart. Younger children may need help listing the date they used a healthy way of expressing their anger.

2. Next, set a family goal for the number of times anger was expressed in a healthy way. For example: twenty dates listed or when three out of five members list five successes.

3. Decide as a family what you want to do specially to celebrate the success. For example: Stay up later than usual and watch a special TV show or movie, go to McDonalds™ for a frosty ice-cream cone, play a favorite game, go to the park and play a family baseball, soccer, or Frisbee golf game.

4. THEN the next time set the goal higher: perhaps four out of

five family members succeed six times or a total of twenty-five times.

NOTE: The real goal is for your children to practice expressing anger in a healthy way.

EXERCISE #11 - ANGER WORD CHARADES

PURPOSE & BENEFITS:

For your child to recognize for himself that he feels different and looks different when he is experiencing different degrees of negative feelings. Encourage the family to be comfortable talking about anger in all degrees.

STARTING AGE: 4 years

TIME: 15 to 20 minutes

LOCATION: Anywhere

MATERIALS: • basket

• anger words written on slips of paper

INSTRUCTIONS:
1.   Write the following words on small pieces of paper, fold each one in half, and put in the basket: Anger, Upset, Mad, Irritated, Annoyed, Hurt, Frustrated, Disappointed
2.   Decide who will go first.
3.   Each family member takes a turn picking a piece of paper and acting out the feeling.
4.   Everyone else guesses what feeling is being acted out.
5.   When the feeling is correctly guessed, the piece of paper is put back in the basket.
6.   The person who guessed the feeling goes next in acting out.
7.   The parent makes sure everyone gets equal turns.

-16-

RESPONSIBILITY

■ ■ ■

What You Will Learn in This Chapter

❑ The definition of responsibility.
❑ When you work with your children to feel positive about being responsible, they usually do chores without much resistance.
❑ If a high EQ child is resistant to being responsible, there is usually a reasonable explanation.
❑ Seven steps to teaching your child responsibility.

What Is Responsibility?

Responsibility is a heavy word. It implies something serious and important, something that we must be cautious about or else something bad might happen. The word responsibility never seems to convey anything lighthearted, simple, or fun. On the contrary, it sends the message to young and old alike: "Behave, be good, work hard."

Can you even imagine what it would be like if the word responsibility elicited a response of feeling energized, eager, and motivated? Of feeling proud and good about ourselves? As parents, we can only dream that our children will come to us regularly and say, "Please give me more responsibility—I don't have enough and I really want more." What we can hope for, however, is that our children won't fight us when we ask them to take on new responsibilities. After you have done the exercises in this chapter—that will likely be the case. If most parents can just eliminate the struggle that often follows when a child is asked to do something, they would be happy. Isn't that so?

What do I mean by responsibility? I mean taking on a project or a chore, making a commitment or a decision, and then doing your best to complete what you have agreed to do in the best way you can. For example, suppose I have told my friend I will attend her fund-raising event on Tuesday night, but then Tuesday evening arrives and I'm exhausted and don't want to go. I want to stay home where it's warm and cozy. The responsible thing to do would be to go, even for a short time, because I have made the commitment. If I have committed to my husband that I will do two errands for him during the day, then the responsible thing to do is complete the errands even if it turns out that they were inconvenient. If I have to decide between watching my favorite TV show and writing a flyer for the PTA that is due tomorrow morning, the responsible decision is to live up to my commitment and do a good job on the flyer tonight rather than throw it together at the last moment in the morning.

When we make decisions, we know in our gut if they are responsible ones or not. So, when we say we are being responsible, we are saying to ourselves that we are doing the right thing according to our own set of values. It is important to remember that every human being has his or her own set of values. We develop them beginning in our childhood. And now, as parents, we have the opportunity to influence the values that our children will carry into their adult lives.

So my definition of responsibility is making a commitment to do something and following through with the commitment.

1. Accepting the job given to you by someone in authority (i.e., parent, teacher, boss, etc.), following through and doing it the best way you can.

2. Making a decision that is consistent with your values because it is the right thing to do.

3. Following rules - both official (i.e., traffic laws) and socially appropriate (i.e., don't let your children run around in a restaurant) - because it is the right thing to.

Feeling Good About Being Responsible

It's funny how we often think of responsibility and chores in the same sentence when we think about our children. The truth is that when we work with our children to feel good about—and even proud of—becoming responsible, they usually do their chores without much resistance. It's only when we make the idea of responsibility unpleasant and link it to "Do this or else you'll be a bad person or feel bad about yourself," that our children will resist doing things they wouldn't even mind doing. The chore then becomes about avoiding feeling bad.

**Responsibility can be a heavy word—connected
to chores and feeling bad.**

So how do you go about teaching your children to enjoy being responsible? It all revolves around feelings. Your goal is to teach your children that they can feel much better by being <u>responsible</u> than by being <u>irresponsible</u>. When we take the time to be involved with our children while we are teaching the new responsibility, we have the opportunity to make it fun, or at least enjoyable.

Children who are continuously increasing their emotional intelligence learn at a young age that it feels great to be appreciated and valued for what they have contributed. High EQ children are not afraid of new chores or requests. If there is resistance with a high EQ child, it usually has more to do with a reasonable explanation. For example, they might have a conflict and can't be two places at once—such as cleaning the garage and being at a classmate's birthday party. Or, the child may not know how to do the requested chore (i.e., weed the garden) or might be nervous or frightened about doing it (i.e., going next door and asking the neighbor to borrow something). There are many other reasonable explanations why a high EQ child might resist a particular chore. So if your child resists a job and you're not sure why, you'll want to explore with him why he is resisting it.

Seven Steps To Teach Your Children To Feel Good About Themselves When They Act Responsibly:

STEP 1 – Decide What You Want To Teach Your Child About Responsibility

Do you want to teach your child to...:
- always be honest?
- take the blame if he does something wrong?
- keep his word when he says he'll do something?
- do chores without a fight?
- do his homework without a struggle?

Be clear in your own mind what you mean by responsibility and what you want to teach your child.

STEP 2 – Do A Personal Assessment Of Your Own Behavior

The next step is to do an assessment of your own behavior. Do you role model what you want to teach your child about being responsible? If the answer is no, remember that parents are the child's #1 teachers and that parental role modeling is the #1 teaching tool. So, if there is anything you've wanted to change about yourself, now is the time to do it.

Perhaps you tell white lies, smoke, drink too much, often commit to doing something for your spouse or child and then put it off or never do it. Such behavior is irresponsible—and now is the time to change it so you'll be a better role model for your child.

Children today don't accept double standards. They don't buy into the old "Do as I say not as I do" rule. In fact, they look at their parents' behavior and tell themselves, "If Mom or Dad can do it, so can I."

Okay, I don't mean to scare you. This is actually a fun and a very productive chapter. As you begin teaching responsibility to your children, keep in mind the most effective teaching is *co-active*, so you'll be joining in with your child as he learns to feel good about being responsible.

STEP 3 – Be Aware Of Your Child's Capabilities And Be Available If They Need Help, Supervision, Or Encouragement

Be sure that you know your child has the ability to succeed in the task you are asking him to do. The best way to discourage our children from wanting to be responsible is to expect them to complete a job that is beyond their capability. If we then proceed to be angry, upset, or disappointed with them—perhaps even punish them for not meeting our expectations—children learn: "Why even try? I'm going to mess it up or get in trouble anyway, so I might as well not do it".

The chart on the next page gives the ages at which most children are ready to take on particular chores. The families I work with who use this chart as a guide always succeed in helping their children become responsible with their chores. Notice that most children still need reminding or supervision until the age of ten or eleven. I know this sounds like a lot of work for parents who'll need to be co-active until their children reach that age, but it pays off. Keep in mind that if you are involved with your child up through age eleven, helping him develop the necessary skills to become responsible and feel good about it, not only will he be ready to be responsible on his own when he reaches puberty, but your relationship with him will become even closer. When your child feels responsible at eleven, with good habits in place, the two of you will have an above average chance of making it through the preteen and teen years with much less conflict.

Household Jobs Participation Chart

Look at the Household Job Chart, and identify the chores your child currently does. Now think about how you interact with your child while she does those chores—or tries to do them or if you simply give a direction or an order and then disappear. I want you to look at the chart and see if your child is in the range of "H" or "R." Does your child need help with the task—or need reminding or supervising? If so, it's time to give up your disappearing act after you tell your child to complete a particular job. Instead, talk with her while she's making her bed or doing the dishes. Perhaps offer to do the job with her if she's having trouble. I promise you that if you do the chore alongside your child, you will not cause her to be lazy and quit. Quite the opposite will happen—she'll learn to do the chore more proficiently, willingly and will soon be ready to do it independently. When you're available to your child, you'll cause a dramatic shift in her feelings related to the chore and to responsibility in general

This chart, compiled by Elizabeth Crary for her book, Pick Up Your Socks... and other skills growing children need!, lists common household tasks, the percentage of Washington State children involved with the task, and the average age of children at different levels of involvement.

Symbols:
H means the child needs help with the task.
R means the child needs reminding or supervision.
A means the child does a task as needed without reminding or supervision.

Task	Percent children involved	3	4	5	6	7	8	9	10	11	12	13
						Ages and Involvement						
Dress Self	99%	H--	----	--	R--	----	----	----	----	-A		
Brush Teeth	99%	H-	----	----	----	----	----	R--	----	--A		
Bathe self	99%	H	----	----	----	R--	----	----	----	A		
Pick up belongings	99%			H--	----	----	----	-R	----	----	A	
Put dirty clothes away	99%			H-	----	----	----	R--	----	----	A	
Hang up clean clothes	97%			H-	----	----	----	----	--R	--	----	A
Make bed	93%		H	----	----	----	----	----	----	R-	-A	
Tidy room	98%			H--	----	----	----	----	----	R--	----	--A
Wipe spills	93%		H-	----	----	----	----	-R	----	A		
Vacuum floors	79%				H	----	----	----	----	----	-A-	-R*
Clean sink	75%					H-	----	----	----	----	A--	R*
Take out trash	72%				H--	----	----	----	----	----	A--	R*
Care for pet	72%				H--	----	----	----	-R-	----	-A	
Do laundry	54%							H	----	----	---	R/A (14 yr, 4mo)
Set table	93%		H-	----	----	----	----	----	----	R--	A	
Wash dishes	75%			H	----	----	----	----	----	R--	----	-A
Fix snack	89%		H	----	--	-R	----	----	----	----	--A	
Cook meal	71%					H--	----	R--	----	----	--A	
		3	4	5	6	7	8	9	10	11	12	13

Reprinted by permission of Parenting Press, Inc. and Elizabeth Crary, Copyright © 1990.

* Children require supervision again after becoming independent.

Here are some examples of how you can be co-active in teaching your child responsibility:

- You tell your child to brush his teeth, but he's resistant. He looks in the mirror and you are making funny faces behind him in the mirror. You both laugh. You thank him for brushing his teeth because it makes his smile brighter, saves you money at the dentist, etc. (Be creative!).

- Your son is carrying out the trash. You offer to open the door for him, or you pick up something he dropped along the way. As you pick up the dropped garbage, you tell him how much he's helping you by carrying out the trash and say "Thank you!"

• Your daughter is in her room taking the longest time possible to make her bed. You show up and start helping her without saying a word about the bed. Perhaps you mention a phone call you just had, a TV show you watched, or what you might make for dinner. You help her shift her emotion from "I'm all by myself and I don't want to make my bed because I don't care if it ever gets made," to "That was fun having Mom or Dad surprise me and help."

We often ask our children to do their chores or homework alone.
Most children like to be around other people.

Children like to be around other people. Most often when we ask our children to do their chores or homework, we send them off to do something alone that they are too young to care about or that has little value to them. Most children I know would never make their bed if they didn't have to. They'd just crawl back in it at bedtime and be as happy as can be. When we are present while they're working, whether we join in or just cheer them along, the child's experience shifts from "I'm all by myself doing something I hate." and "I don't care if this job ever gets done!" to "I like having one-on-one time with my mom or dad."

When we shift the child's expectation from tediousness to pleasant one-on-one time with her parent—and add in some heartfelt praise—she begins to think, "It feels good when I'm doing my job!" If this becomes their experience, children won't need to resist, because the pay off for doing their work is a positive one. In fact, when a child feels good about doing a chore and she notices that she likes how she feels, she'll often think to herself, "I might even look forward to doing this again!"

If you feel it is impossible to always be available while your child is doing a chore, remember that your presence is usually only needed for a few minutes. These few minutes will permanently shift your child's attitude towards helping out the family. It is important to mention to your child how much he is helping you and the family by doing his job. And always be willing to thank him for doing a good job.

Think about the bosses you have had throughout your career. There were those who never thanked you or showed any appreciation, and others who let you know that they valued your contribution. Now think about how you felt. Who were you willing to work harder for? And who made you feel better about the work you were doing?

As your child begins to shift his attitude and enjoy his chores, his self-acceptance and self-confidence will automatically rise—and he will like feeling responsible! ☺

Step 4 - Set Up Homework Guidelines That Help Your Child Feel Proud of His Accomplishments

Homework is often a child's first outside-the-home responsibility. Did you know that children who do household chores are better at doing their home-work? Also, children who do their homework do better at school, and children who do better in school are better at setting goals and motivating themselves in life. So let's see...being responsible for chores = being responsible for homework = succeeding in school = motivating yourself in life. It's an encouraging formula, right?

> **BEING RESPONSIBLE FOR CHORES ->**
> **BEING RESPONSIBLE FOR HOMEWORK ->**
> **SUCCEEDING AT SCHOOL ->**
> **MOTIVATING YOURSELF IN LIFE? ☺**

As a teacher and a school counselor for twenty years, I reached the conclusion that homework is not about mastering the subjects as much as it is about learning self-discipline. When we, as parents, have a positive, supportive attitude toward homework, it makes all the difference for our children. Still, I have to share there were many nights when I was so tired from a long day's work that I hoped my children had no homework. And when they told me about their workload for that night, I often felt like screaming, "There goes my night!! Yuck!!" In fact, there have been many nights when I thought of leading a nationwide protest against homework because I felt it takes away from a family's quality time together in the evening and adds extra stress which today's families simply don't need. With all that said, let's look at the benefits of homework.

Homework

Homework is the number one tool for teaching self-discipline and self-motivation throughout childhood. It is also the best way to teach children organizational and goal-setting skills. When children succeed in completing their homework, they feel prepared for their school day, which ultimately gives them a sense of control and confidence at school.

The parent's tasks when it comes to homework are: 1) to have a positive attitude towards the homework assignment: 2) to listen to and know your child well enough to provide the right environment for success. Some children need to be in their own quiet area to concentrate. Others need to be near other people—the kitchen table or the living room floor, for example.

Even though research tells us that about 50% of children can study with music on, 50% cannot. You may have both types of children, so help them figure out their best ways to study. Research also tells us that no one studies more productively with the TV on. That means if the TV is on in the room where your child is studying, it will be distracting. It is also distracting if the parent has it on in another room. Not only is it distracting, but also since most children would rather watch TV than do their homework, when they hear the TV on in another room, they'll want to watch it. This often causes children to rush through their homework and not do it well. Or if the TV is the reward when they are done, children will often rush through their assignments and say they are done even if they are not. I always recommend to the families I work with to agree on No TV Monday though Thursday evenings. When you eliminate the TV during school nights, you eliminate conflict over, "What can I watch? When can I watch? How late can I watch?" When there is no TV to watch, there simply isn't TV conflict. Of course, shows can always be taped for later viewing or exceptions can be made; for example, special events like presidential debates.

When parents eliminate TV on school nights, they eliminate TV conflict.

Again, the habits children develop through the process of doing their homework last a lifetime, so even if you can't go along with TV-free weekdays, consider not turning on the TV (even for yourself) during their homework time. If a child rushes though his homework, his pattern becomes one of rushing through chores, jobs, assignments, and responsibilities in general. He'll never learn to take pride in a job or to notice the "feel good" sense he gets from completing his homework and doing it well.

A parent's responsibility from kindergarten through third grade is to be available for their child, in most cases to be present in the same room while their child is doing her homework. Try to sound positive about the assignments. Don't make your child rewrite homework assignments if they're reasonably legible. Let the teacher ask your child to be neater. Your task is to help her develop a positive attitude toward doing the work and a sense of self-confidence that she understands it.

From fourth through sixth grade, it is still important to be present when your children do their homework. Be available and be interested in what they are doing. If they need help, offer it. It's better to take more of a coaching or consultant role than a teaching role at this stage. Check over the assignments, but again, don't make them redo their work for neatness if the content is okay.

In seventh and eighth grade, simply ask if they would like any help, but don't push to see their assignments. By this time, if you have done a good job training them, they should be able to do their homework responsibly on their own. Again, as in the earlier years, let them know you are interested in what they are doing and are available if they need help. It is important now that you set a limit on your availability so they won't use wanting your help as a means of staying up later and later. If your junior high child's bedtime is 9 p.m., for example, a rule of thumb is to state that you are available until 8 p.m. to help—and then you are off-duty as their homework coach. This let's you off the hook so you can begin unwinding from your day, and it also makes your child plan ahead. Set your "off-duty time" and stick to it.

You'll also want to explore what happens if your child forgets a book at school. Some children make this a pattern so they can borrow a friend's book, but what they really want is to visit with their friends. If this is a pattern for your child, it is important to stop it because it teaches him that irresponsibility (I forgot my book) has positive rewards (I get to visit with my friend).

Here are some grade-by-grade guidelines for homework time:
- K -> 1st grade: about ½ hour
- 2nd -> 3rd grades: 1-hour
- 4th -> 6th grades: 1½ hours
- 7th -> 8th grades: 2 hours

Remember: Provide a quiet setting, turn off the TV, and be available to your child without being in their face.

Classroom Learning vs. Homework Learning:

My estimates:	In Class %:	Out of Class %:
Kindergarten	95%	5%
1st & 2nd Grades	90%	10%
3rd & 4th Grades	85%	15%
5th & 6th Grades	80%	20%
Junior High: 7th & 8th	70%	30%
High School: 9th -> 12th	50%	50%
College	25%	75%
Graduate School	10%	90%

If you follow the above homework recommendations, your child's study habits should become second nature when she reaches high school.

STEP 5 - Provide A Safe Environment In Which Your Child Can Make Mistakes

Prepare a safe environment for your child to make mistakes on his pathway to learning responsibility. Remind him that making mistakes is often the way we learn. Thomas Edison conducted 9,999 experiments, attempts, or mistakes before he invented the light bulb.

There was a musical jingle from the TV program, Sesame Street, that we sang a lot in the Healy House when our children were young. It went like this: "Oops, I made a mistake, that's all!" If our son, Mike, spilled a glass of orange juice, we sang the jingle and he cleaned it up. If our daughter, Kim, forgot to wipe her shoes on the mat before she walked in the front door on a rainy day, we sang the song and she wiped up the floor. The point is to teach your children that it's not a big deal to make a mistake, and that they can turn it around by recognizing it, taking responsibility for it, and fixing it, if possible. A safe environment promotes honesty and responsibility.

> **A GREAT FAMILY MOTTO:**
> **MAKE A MESS—CLEAN IT UP!**

STEP 6: Set Goals And Celebrate The Accomplishments

The next step in building your child's sense of responsibility is to teach them to set short-term goals: "I'm going to dress myself today!" and long-term goals: "I'm going to help Mom put my toys in the toy box tonight before dinner. I'm going to make her happy!" ☺

When you work with your children to set goals, you teach them to think ahead, make a plan, make a commitment to accomplish the goal, and be responsible for their actions, which then leads to success or not. Teaching your children to set goals not only increases their sense of responsibility, it helps them to motivate themselves. Motivation results from having somewhere to go and figuring out how to get there. The "somewhere" in life is always a goal whether we call it that or not. When we have nowhere to go (no goal), we don't feel motivated. Motivation only exists when there is a destination! You can begin teaching your child to set goals as early as one-and-a-half or two by helping them to think ahead and make a plan. For example, you can say to your two-year-old:

- Let's play with your blocks today.

- What do we need to play blocks?

- Where shall we play?

- Let's go find the blocks, set them up on the kitchen floor, and play.

- Your young child will learn that taking responsibility for setting goals is fun and exciting!

Set goals with your child and celebrate his accomplishments.

STEP 7: Continue Your Unconditional Acceptance

The better our children feel about themselves (enjoying a high-level of self-acceptance), the more likely they will take responsibility for their own decisions and actions. High EQ children will believe they made the best decision at the time and will feel ownership of it. If their decision results in their plan not working out, they'll be able to explain why it didn't work out well, without fear of the consequences.

A parent's job in this seventh step is to continue to work on your child's self-acceptance by providing unconditional love and acceptance, especially when mistakes happen. Your child needs your acceptance and support when he succeeds and when he fails. When he receives it, he is encouraged to continue being a responsible individual, adhering to his commitments regardless of hardships, and taking responsibility for his decisions, regardless of the outcome.

Guiding your child to be a more responsible person is all much simpler than it sounds, because you have already laid a strong foundation by working through the previous six chapters with him.

So once again, relax and have fun.

EXERCISE #1 - ADULT – WHAT IS RESPONSIBILITY? ☆

PURPOSE & BENEFITS:

The parent takes time to think about what being responsible and responsibility means. If you have a spouse, a partner, or someone who is co-parenting with you: discuss the definitions with them if possible.

STARTING AGE: Parent

TIME: As long as it takes

LOCATION: Anywhere

MATERIALS: • a chart with either of the following statements:
- • "Being Responsible is Making Good Decisions"
- • "Responsibility is Making Good Choices"

INSTRUCTIONS:

1. Ask yourself the questions and take the time to think about your answers.
   - • What does responsibility mean to me?
   - • What does being responsible mean to me?
   - • What is your vision of a responsible child at the age of 4, 6, 8, 10, etc.:
     - • What qualities?
     - • What expectations?
   - • Agree with your co-parent what qualities of responsibilities you want for your child.

2. When are you responsible? Make a list for awareness.

3. Make a chart of either the following statements and post in your home:

Being Responsible Is Making Good Decisions	Responsibility Is Making Good Choices

EXERCISE #2 - CHILD - WHAT IS RESPONSIBILITY? ☆

PURPOSE & BENEFITS:

To begin to explore what your child thinks of responsibility. To become aware of when your child acts responsibly. To become aware of when your child thinks he is being responsible.

STARTING AGE: 4 years

TIME: 10 to 15 minutes

LOCATION: Anywhere

MATERIALS:
- chart you made in the last exercise
- paper to make a list

INSTRUCTIONS:

1. Ask your child what he thinks the word responsible means. Listen to all answers.

2. Ask your child when he is responsible. Make a list of all the times he believes he is being responsible. If he feels he is in situations you disagree with, still list them. Remember, perception is unique to each individual. You don't want to discourage your child from wanting to become more responsible.

3. Ask whom else your child knows who is responsible: Mom, Dad, preschool teachers, doctors, firefighters, police officers, Grandma, Grandpa, etc.

4. Show your child the chart you made and put your child's responsible list next to your chart on the refrigerator or bulletin board you have used in other chapter exercises.

EXERCISE #3 - SHARED ACTIVITY ☆

PURPOSE & BENEFITS:

To begin to have your child be aware of responsibility and enjoy it.

STARTING AGE: 4 years

TIME: Varies according to the activity chosen

LOCATION: Varies

MATERIALS: Varies

INSTRUCTIONS:

1. Choose an activity you would like to do with your child. <u>For example:</u>

    1) prepare and cook a meal

    2) plan a family night (a game, choose a movie and snack)

    3) plan a meal and make a list to go to the grocery store with your child; or

    4) prepare for your child's Little League or soccer game

2. Whichever activity you choose, sit with your child and explore with him what you need to think about in planning the activity.

    <u>For example:</u> Family Movie Night:

    Choose a movie, go rent the movie, choose a snack, what food is needed, how to prepare it, how to serve it, how much clean up there is, and who cleans up.

3. When you have finished the planning, ask your child what parts of the plan he wants to be responsible for, and ask what he will need to do to be successful.

4. When the activity time arrives, let your child do the parts he has offered to be responsible for and do not rescue him unless he specifically asks for help.

5. The day after the activity, ask him:

    - How do you think it went?

    - What would you do differently next time?

EXERCISE #4 - SET GOALS ☆

PURPOSE & BENEFITS:

To begin having your child set goals and work towards accomplishing them. Whether your child succeeds or fails, he will learn from the experience.

STARTING AGE: 4 years
TIME: 5 to 10 minutes
LOCATION: Anywhere
MATERIALS:
   • a piece of paper
   • a pen or pencil

INSTRUCTIONS:

1. This exercise can be done individually with your child or all together as a family.

2. Each member of the family chooses two goals to work on during the week, including Mom and Dad. Encourage your child to choose something he can do on his own. Prepare a chart titles: Family Goals. Write everyone's name on the chart.

3. Write down the goals next to the person's name.

Family Goals	
Dad	1. To exercise 3x during the week. 2. To help Mom with dinner.
Mom	1. To exercise 3x during the week. 2. To yell less.
Kimberly	1. To do all of her homework by 8 p.m. 2. To fight less with her brothers.
Mike	1. To be on time for school in the morning. 2. To not fight with brother and sister.
Bob	1. To pick up his room without being asked 2. To fight less with brother and sister

4. Post the goals where everyone can see them.

5. Parent, check in with your child during the week to see how things are going.

6. Gather together in a week. Give each family member the opportunity to report on how he did. Celebrate any successes.

7. If there have been failures, this is a good time for family members to offer support and suggestions.

8. Set two new goals and repeat exercise.

EXERCISE #5 - COOK A MEAL ☆

PURPOSE & BENEFITS:

For your child to share responsibility with his parent. To have your child experience fun along with being responsible. For your child to spend some one-on-one time with parent.

STARTING AGE: 4 years

TIME: 30 to 45 minutes

LOCATION: Kitchen or BBQ outside

MATERIALS: Whatever is needed to make the meal

INSTRUCTIONS:

1. Parent sits with child and discusses what meal they would like to cook for the family. This exercise is done best with only one parent.

2. Set a date to cook the meal.

3. Once the meal is chosen, sit with your child and make a list of what will be needed: shopping list, pots and pans to cook, stove, oven, BBQ, setting the table, etc.

4. Next, talk about the preparation and cooking of the food. Assign the tasks–individual and shared. Write down the assigned tasks and post, even if your child doesn't read yet. When you write down a child's accepted responsibility, it is more difficult for a child to say, "I never said I'd do that!"

4. If possible, grocery shop together.

5. When the date arrives, go over the plan with your child. Relax and have fun.

6. Relax and enjoy the meal.

6. Review the day after:
   - How do you think it went?
   - What would you do differently next time?

EXERCISE #6 - CHOOSE A FAMILY CHORE ☆

> ## *PURPOSE & BENEFITS:*
>
> *To begin to have your child contribute to his family by having a chore that benefits everyone. To be aware of his accountability to the entire family, not just himself.*

STARTING AGE: 4 years

TIME: 10 to 20 minutes

LOCATION: Somewhere the family can gather to talk without distractions.

MATERIALS:
- paper or white board
- pen, pencils, or felt pens
- basket, bag, or box

INSTRUCTIONS:

1. Parent prepares ahead by thinking of chores that each family member could be successful (one per person) at.
    For example:
    - folding towels
    - setting the table
    - emptying the dishwasher
    - cleaning bathroom sink and counters
    - taking out the recycling
    - picking up dog poops
    - dusting living room and family room
    - sweeping kitchen floor

2. Be creative and age appropriate with your list.

3. You are only going to start with one family job per person because you want your child to get used to helping the family without being overwhelmed with two or three jobs with which to start.

4. Each individual should still be responsible for his or her own clothes, toys, bed, hygiene, homework, room, etc., so to start with only one family chore is realistic.

5. Parent either presents the list of chores (four for a family of four) or a list of six to ten chores.

6. Write the chores on small pieces of paper; fold the papers and put them in a basket, box, or bag.

7. Each family member draws his or her chore for the week from the basket.

8. Repeat each week or every two weeks.

NOTE: Family members are allowed to give feedback on how well the jobs were done.

EXERCISE #7 - PLAN A FAMILY EVENT ☆

PURPOSE & BENEFITS:

To work together with each family member contributing with a responsible task. To experience working together as a family unit, provide a special family memory. To teach your child the preparation and planning that goes into having family events. To set goals and work to accomplish them.

STARTING AGE: 4 years

TIME: Varies (this exercise can be repeated several times throughout the year)

LOCATION: Varies

MATERIALS: • a white board or piece of paper

INSTRUCTIONS:

1. Parent make a list of possible events you would be willing to do, or choose an event yourself, and have your family join in the planning (Look at suggestions on the next page).

2. Parent may want to choose the event the first time you do this exercise.

3. Gather the family together (this can be done at a formal family meeting) and announce the event you would like their help planning.

4. Ask the family the following questions and write the responses on a white board or a piece of paper:

- What needs to be done to make this event happen? (before, during, after—make a list)
- What do we need to make this event happen (equipment, food, etc.—make a list)

5. Look at the list of <u>jobs</u>, which need to be done to make this event happen.

6. Ask each family member to take on as many jobs as they think they can do well (there can be job-sharing).

7. Make sure all the jobs are as fairly divided as possible so everyone joins in the work.

8. Parent meets with each child individually sometime after the meeting and explores with them what they think they need to do to be successful with their jobs. Ask and decide when and how they need your help.

9. Enjoy the event!

10. Sometime during the week after the event, meet with the family and discuss:

- How do you think the event went?
- What would you do differently next time?

11 Parent acknowledges and compliments each individual for his or her contribution of the job.

12. Repeat exercise.

<u>Suggested Family Events:</u>

- A family picnic
- A family fun night
- A day at the beach
- An overnight camping trip
- A birthday party for a grandma, grandpa, aunt, uncle, etc.
- A trip to an amusement park, baseball, football, basketball, or soccer game
- A visit to a museum
- A fishing trip
- Planting a family vegetable garden

NOTE: There are thousands of possibilities!

EXERCISE #8 - INVITE A FRIEND ☆

PURPOSE & BENEFITS:

To take on the responsibility of having a play date.

STARTING AGE: 4 years
TIME: One-hour or more
LOCATION: Home
MATERIALS: Varies

INSTRUCTIONS:

1. Ask your child which friend he would like to have over.
2. Parent decides when and how long.
3. Explore with your child what he thinks needs to happen:

    a. **before** his friend comes over. For example: think of what to play; do you have all the game pieces, what should you have as a snack, etc.

    b. **during** the play date. For example: household rules still hold while friend is over: no running or screaming in the house, no hitting, clean up after your snack, etc.

    c. **after** his friend leaves. For example, if you and your friend have made a mess, it's your child's mess to clean up, if he wants to have future play dates, etc.

4. Review after the play date:
    • How do you think it went?
    • What would you do different next time?
5. Take this time to compliment your child if he lived up to most of the expectations discussed before the play date.

EXERCISE #9 - HOW PROUD I AM ☆

PURPOSE & BENEFITS:

To give your child a chance to feel "good" about being responsible. To give the family the opportunity to celebrate the child's success.

STARTING AGE: 4 years
TIME: At a meal or during a family meeting
LOCATION: Anywhere
MATERIALS: • a special button, hat, or tokens(of some kind)
INSTRUCTIONS:

1.   When the family gathers together, go around the group and give everyone the opportunity to describe a time during the week they were proud of themselves for being responsible.

2.   If it would be fun in your family, let the person who is describing a time he was proud wear a special button or hat, or perhaps hold a special token while he is telling his story. The token can be a magic wand, a special teddy bear, a special rock, toy, or even an old trophy (be creative!).

3.   When the child is finished sharing his story, it is important for the family to celebrate the success.

EXERCISE #10 - BE A FINDER ☆

PURPOSE & BENEFITS:

To surprise your child with an appreciation or a compliment. When a child is acknowledged and complimented for doing positive behaviors, he will tend to repeat the same behavior because it felt good.

STARTING AGE: 4 years
TIME: 10 to 20 seconds
LOCATION: Anywhere
MATERIALS: None
INSTRUCTIONS:

1.   Parent is on the lookout every day to find something the child is doing well (in a responsible way).

2.   When the parent sees the child doing something well (anywhere!!), the parent takes the time to compliment the child.

3.   If the parent forgets to compliment the child in the moment, it's never too late—even if it's a few days later.

4.   A child will continue to do behaviors he is encouraged to feel good about.

EXERCISE #11 - RESPONSIBLE HONOR ROLL

PURPOSE & BENEFITS:

To acknowledge your child for his positive behavior in a public way.

STARTING AGE: 4 years

TIME: 5 minutes

LOCATION: The refrigerator or bulletin board (be creative)

MATERIALS:
- paper or poster board
- pen, pencil, or felt pens
- paper titled "Responsible Honor Roll"

INSTRUCTIONS:

1.   Create a chart or scroll that you can post somewhere in your home.

2.   Title the paper Responsible Honor Roll.

3.   Surprise your child by writing his name, the date, and the responsible decision he made on the chart.

4.   Point out the successes written on the chart to other family members.

5.   Make an effort to show guests to your home the Honor Roll and let your child overhear you complimenting him on his behavior.

6.   If you have more than one child, be on the look out for responsible behavior from each child.

-17-

FRIENDSHIP

■　■　■

What You Will Learn in This Chapter

❑ Your child's friendships are an indicator of his future relationships.

❑ Children need to be taught social skills.

❑ Children first learn their social skills at home.

❑ It is important to offer our children as many social opportunities as we can, beginning at birth.

❑ There are three basic childhood personalities: shy, slow-to-warm-up, and aggressive.

❑ There are six personal skills necessary to enjoy healthy friendships.

Friendships Are Important

Your children's friendships are an accurate predictor of their future relationships, including their marriages. That may be scary, but it is true. Our entire childhood is about gathering knowledge and growing in wisdom from our life experiences so when we are ready to leave the nest, we are prepared for what life will throw at us. How to get along with people and enjoy their company is one of the most important life skills your child can learn.

Many parents believe that if their son or daughter doesn't have any friends or seems to lack social skills, "It's just the way he is." The truth is that children are not born with excellent social skills. They are born with certain personality traits and preferences, and their environment influences them as well. But they have to learn how to be sociable. Unfortunately, our society tends to throw children into the deep end of the social skills pool and let's them sink or swim, with no previous training. That haphazard method works for some children, but for most children it is more painful than it needs to be. And of course, if the parent is aware of their child's difficulty making friends, they feel the sting of his pain as well. In this chapter, you'll learn about the necessary skills that healthy friendships require, so you can help your child develop them.

**Our society tends to throw children into the
deep end of the social skills pool.**

Children with high EQ have more friends and are more secure in their friendships. They are able to read other children's body language to recognize if the other child is happy or unhappy. Children with high EQ have a solid sense of self-acceptance. They like themselves and just take for granted that other children will like them too. They've learned to recognize their own feelings and not be overwhelmed by them. If a conflict comes up with another child in elementary school, for example, they recognize that conflicts are just problems to be solved. They have learned that every problem has a solution, so they are not thrown by social conflict at school.

Regardless of your child's personality, this chapter will help her develop important social skills that she will continue to use for the rest of her life.

How Do Children Learn About Friendship And Social Skills?

Remember the day our children are born, they begin inputting life experiences into their brains. It is similar to someone entering data onto the hard drive of a computer. Children do not understand the data (information); they just put it in. The information comes from their everyday experiences, and since infants and young toddlers have no other information stored in their "computer", their experiences become their source of reference or their life beliefs. Some of these beliefs can become must beliefs about relationships.

How Does A Child's Early Experiences Influence How She Approaches Friendship?

If every time a child cries she is picked up and held, she learns that crying = attention. Later in a social setting when she wants attention, she might cry and expect someone to come and comfort her. On the other hand if every time she cries she is either held, changed, fed, moved, patted, etc., then what she learns is that crying has an effect, and it can be any of the previous things mentioned. She begins to learn cause and effect, but not necessarily always the same effect. Then as the child grows, if she learns that, "Every time I cry or throw a temper tantrum, I get what I want," her life belief becomes: "whenever I want something all I have to do is cry or have a temper tantrum and I'll get what I want." We have all seen children on the playground or at preschool try this behavior to get a toy they want from another child. Although this behavior may work at home or on her family with some success, it usually backfires in a social setting. In fact it may cause a child with this particular life belief to be shunned by the other children as early as preschool.

Let's say a child has an older sibling. He might learn that all he has to do is cry or tell Mom or Dad that "Big brother is being mean to me and won't share his toy," and he'll get the toy. His life belief then grows into, "It's okay to cry or lie to get what I want." On the other hand, if every time the child cries or lies to get his brother's toy, his parent confiscates the object which angers the older brother who then directs his anger at the younger brother. This then teaches the younger child, "It's not worth trying to trick Mom by lying to get my brother's toy." His new belief becomes: "I might as well just wait my turn."

Here is another example of friendship life lessons: An older sibling might think, "If I want to take a toy away from my little sister, all I have to do is grab it away, and give her some other toy to play with. Then when she starts to cry, I'll act concerned and tell Mom I don't know what she's crying about because she was just fine a minute ago." If Mom buys this, the life lesson becomes: "I can use force to get what I want, and then lie and pretend I really care about my little sister. Boy is Mom dumb!!!" If instead, Mom is wise enough to take both toys away because she's not sure what just happened, the older brother learns it's not worth grabbing a toy and lying because "Mom's too smart and I'm going to lose."

Our children learn their first social lessons with either their siblings or playmates at day care during the first couple of years of their lives. Whether the parents or caretakers have been on top of what's going on, or have been duped into being manipulated at times, the child brings these early lessons into the social arena of preschool or kindergarten.

We need to decide how we want our children to act socially and then set out to teach them as though it were a subject in school. Is sharing an important value to you? Or is protecting your personal belongings from the possibility of getting broken or ruined an important value? Is it important to you to include everyone in an activity? Do you favor doing things in small selective groups? Are manners in small children important to you? Or do you believe manners are something to be taught at a later age? Is it more important to win a ball game or is it more important that each child has an equal opportunity to play? Our difficult challenge today, with so many working moms and dads, is that we're often unaware of the life lessons our children are learning when they are not with us. As a family therapist, I am constantly struck by the fact that parents are so often surprised by their children's life beliefs. Nine out of ten parents are surprised to learn that the source of sibling rivalry, low self-acceptance, or low self-confidence, anger, acting out behavior, etc. has its roots in an early life experience—whether in or out of the home—that went unnoticed by the family. And because the life experience turned into a life belief, it became part of the child's everyday world.

For instance, Emma brought her brand-new Barbie® to school for show and tell when it was her turn. After she had told her kindergarten class about getting her new doll and showed off Barbie's® accessories, her teacher insisted she pass her doll around the class for the other children to see it up close. When it came time to return Emma's Barbie® to her, three of the accessories were missing and they were never found. Also someone had put a crayon mark on Barbie's® face. I met Emma when her parents became concerned that she refused to share any of her toys when she had her friends or cousins over to visit.

Another example was three-year-old David, who wandered into the bathroom at preschool while four-year-old Brian, was already in there. Brian told David, "If you ever walk into a bathroom again while anyone is using it, you are going to get beaten up." From that day forward, David was afraid of older boys, as well as going to the bathroom anywhere, but at home, for fear that he might be beaten up. One unpleasant incident can stay with a child for his or her entire childhood—or a lifetime. Such an experience can be the source of an irrational belief, which will then affect how a child acts in the world.

That's why it's important for parents to be vigilant and to notice if there is any abrupt change of behavior in their child—for instance, a young child refusing to go to the restroom anywhere but at home. Explore with your child to see if you can find the source of the change. More likely than not, you will discover an irrational thought that has become part of his belief system. In the above example, once David's parents learned that classmate, Brian, caused his bathroom fear, they might talk with a preschool teacher to help David feel safe again. It would also be important for the teacher to provide opportunities for David to interact with some of the older boys at preschool so David wouldn't be fearful in his future of making friends with older children.

If you want your child to enjoy the pleasures and benefits of friendship, my general advice is to offer as many interactive social opportunities as you can, beginning at birth. For instance, infants who grow up with people around them—parents, siblings, and others—and who learn to accept the noise and normal confusion of life, will be more comfortable in a school setting because of their life belief that: "It's normal and okay to have people and noise around me all the time." This holds true even for children whose natural temperament is to be shy, which leads me to our next topic: childhood personalities.

When I went through my California Teacher's Credential Program years ago, I was trained to be sensitive to the variety of children's personality styles. Over the years, I have explained children's personalities to the parents I have worked with by describing three basic types: the Shy Child, the Slow-to-Warm-up Child, and the Aggressive Child. Children seem to arrive in this world with one of these three preferences. They are not good or bad. Each of these preferences can be worked with and changed, if the child wants to change. But it is important to accept your child for who she is—as she is—and not push for change unless she wants it. Once you consider the following descriptions, you'll get a better sense of which type your child most resembles.

The Shy Child

The Shy Child is most comfortable at home playing by herself or with her parents or siblings. When she's at school, a family gathering, the park, or a birthday party, she is usually withdrawn and feels insecure. She might stay near an adult as though seeking safety and protection. The Shy Child is comfortable in familiar settings, but can become nervous or anxious in unfamiliar ones.

If your child is in this group, don't force her to be more outgoing. Even if she's not participating in all the activities at the family picnic, she may be enjoying herself by simply watching everyone else. Check in with her occasionally throughout the event. If she says she's happy just watching, let her be. Unless her shyness prohibits her from going to school, family events, etc., don't be overly concerned. As she grows continue to observe her in social settings. By the age of five you might want to ask her if she would like to be more outgoing. If she says no, don't worry; just accept her the way she is. If she says yes, the exercises at the end of this chapter will help her begin to relax in social situations.

The Shy Child can become nervous or anxious in unfamiliar situations.

The Slow-To-Warm-Up Child

The Slow-To-Warm-Up child arrives at a family party and stays close by you until she checks out who is there and what everybody's doing. She takes her time joining in the activities, but eventually does join in when she's ready.

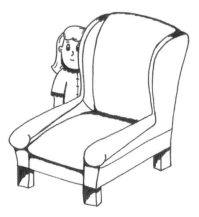

The Slow-To-Warm-Up child takes her time joining in activities.

This is the child who enters a swimming pool at the shallow end, one step at a time, but when she's ready can swim the length of the pool and back with confidence. This is the most common personality among children falling somewhere within a range of one to ten on a scale of slow to warm.

The Aggressive Child

When the Aggressive Child jumps into social situations, you definitely know she has arrived. While the Shy Child tends to sit by the side of the pool and think about going in, and the Slow-to-Warm-Up Child tries the shallow end first before swimming into the deep end, the Aggressive Child acts first, and thinks later. She dives into the deep end without even checking how deep it is! Aggressive children need to be taught to be more aware of their boundaries and their surroundings. They need to learn to slow down, to think first, and then to make a choice.

The Aggressive Child jumps into social situations—you definitely know she has arrived.

Each of these personalities presents a challenge to parents, especially if the child's personality type is the opposite of the parent's. Each of these personalities presents a challenge when it comes to friendships. Always remember that every child has unique gifts and talents, and one of a parent's responsibilities is to recognize the child's strengths and to encourage and develop them. This will not only help to build self-acceptance, but it will also help build friendships. When we as parents are aware of our child's personality type, we can help prepare our child for social interactions. For example, when the Shy Child wants to have a play date, you can help him by discussing possible activities he could suggest playing. You can set up an emergency plan if your child becomes uncomfortable while the friend is over, perhaps taking a planned snack break so he can check in with Mom.

The Slow-To-Warm Up child might also feel more confident with a plan of activities talked about before the friend's arrival. The planned activities might not even happen, but they would help your child feel more confident about the time he will spend with his friend.

How Birth Order Affects Friendships

Birth order can affect friendships in several ways. For example, a child who is the youngest of three or four children may be comfortable with being teased and not be hurt by it. On the other hand an only child may be sensitive to teasing and have her feelings hurt more easily than a child with a sibling. The oldest child in a family may have the tendency to be bossy in friendships whereas a middle child might have more patience and be more flexible than an oldest child. A younger child in a family may learn how to bully if an older sibling has bullied him, and may go to school and bully classmates because he has had expert training in this area.

The influence of birth order on friendships can be endless.

Six Personal Skills For A Healthy Friendship

Whether your child is shy or aggressive, the only child, the youngest of five, or the oldest of two, he or she will need to develop six personal skills to engage in healthy friendships. These are:

1. Self-acceptance (You like yourself)

2. Empathy (Willingness to understand what others are feeling)

3. Patience (You can't always go first)

4. Flexibility (You can't always play what YOU want to play)

5. Willingness to try new things (Often new friends do things differently)

6. Respect for others (Treat others the way you want to be treated)

1. Self-Acceptance

The number one requirement for a healthy friendship is self-acceptance, which you have been working on since Chapter Twelve. This is important in friendships because for your child to grow and be happy within a friendship, she must be able to say "Yes" to an activity she wants to do and "No" to one she doesn't.

If your child's self-acceptance is low, she will not stand up for herself in a relationship and will be influenced by peer pressure. It's okay to occasionally be a follower in a friendship—if it is your child's choice. But if she is always a follower because her self-acceptance is low, it will likely get even lower as her friend feels the power of control, which erodes mutual respect. As the stronger child loses respect for the child with the low self-acceptance, the low self-accepting child begins to tell herself, "I'd better do everything my friend tells me to do or she won't be my friend."

I find this scenario sad because it paves the way for a cycle of abuse. Individuals with low self-acccptance tell themselves, "I don't believe in myself so I'd better do whatever my partner tells me—otherwise, I'm afraid he will leave me, and I'm not strong enough to be on my own."

If your child's self-acceptance is low, go back and review Chapter Twelve and continue working the exercises.

2. Empathy

The second personal skill your child needs to develop and enjoy healthy friendships is the ability to empathize. Empathy involves being able to read social cues. Imagine a six-year-old boy who hasn't developed any empathy skills walking up to a child on the playground who is obviously "down in the dumps" and asking the child if he wants to play in a cheery voice. At this point, the other child responds with a big loud "NO!"

In Chapter Ten you learned about developing your child's ability to read other people's feelings and how important that is for the relationships into which he enters. You may want to revisit some of those exercises. The exercises in this chapter will give you additional practice in this area.

3. Patience

Some children are born with a great deal of patience and others were not present when the patience fairy was handing out everyone's share. For these children, I have included exercises in this chapter to help them develop this important skill.

Children need to have patience in a friendship because they're often called on to listen to a friend's problem, to put up with a friend's habits, or to wait for their turn in a friendly game. For example, if two little boys are playing together on the climbing dome and one zooms to the top and starts yelling for the other to hurry up, the slower boy is likely to feel bad because he's not fast enough or good enough to keep up with his friend. If the faster boy had more patience, he wouldn't cause the slower boy to feel bad. In fact a child with patience might even encourage the other child.

Children with strong self-acceptance will choose people to be their friends who make them feel good, not bad. If a fourth grade girl lacks patience and therefore makes her friend feel bad for not doing her math homework fast enough so they can go out and play, she may risk the friendship. The girl who needs more time to do her math homework will likely resent the pushy girl and will definitely think twice about doing homework with her again. A young girl with patience, if she finished quickly, might offer to help the other child in a kind way.

A lack of patience can also inhibit preschool friendships and turn the impatient child into an unlikable outcast. Let's say a group of children are engaged in a creative art project, and the impatient child rushes through the project while the others are taking their time and enjoying the creativity. The impatient child begins annoying the other children, hoping to get someone to abandon the art project and play with him instead. But the other children just think he's a pest. Chances are this child's impatience will be an ongoing stumbling block in his quest for friendship.

**A lack of patience can inhibit preschool friendships
and cause a child to be looked at as a pest.**

4. Flexibility

Children who can adjust to a change in plans have the ability to make and keep friends. Children who are not flexible take a change of plans personally and often resist it with anger, crying, or a passive-aggressive response. They demonstrate low EQ and cause the person who has requested the change to feel badly, uncomfortable, guilty, or attacked.

Again, no one chooses someone to be their friend who makes them feel bad on a regular basis. Life is always changing, therefore plans change regularly. Children who have said yes to a play date often have to cancel because of family circumstances. For example, two girls decide at lunch to play together after school. When their moms arrive to pick them up, the inflexible girl's mom tells her she can't play today because she has a dentist appointment. The inflexible girl throws a temper tantrum, which causes the other little girl to feel uncomfortable and awkward. Is she likely to want the tantrum-throwing girl for a friend? Or let's say the other mother says her daughter can't play today, and the inflexible girl becomes angry or mean, causing the girl who can't play to feel bad. Will she want to be friends with someone who makes her feel bad?

On the other hand, a flexible child might say, "I am so sorry we can't play together today, but we'll do it as soon as we can." These two girls will play again in the future.

5. Willingness To Try New Things

Another requirement for making friends and maintaining friendships is a willingness to try new things.Let me clarify what I mean, until the age of ten, children believe that the way things are done in their homes is the right way. It is not unusual to hear a young child say, "Mom, they don't set the table right at Michelle's house. They put the napkin under the fork instead of on the plate." The implication is the way we do it in our house is the right way.

The willingness to try new things goes way beyond the way things are done in our house versus my friend's house. We all know children (and even adults) who will resist trying anything new—from a new food Mom has just cooked, to a new activity. This unwillingness to try new things can often limit a child's ability to make a friendship work.

For example:
- A fifth grade girl asks an acquaintance—who might become a friend—to go to the library after school. The unwilling girl says no because she thinks the library is boring. So the girl asks someone else, and the unwilling girl misses an opportunity to make a new friend.
- An eight-year-old boy gets invited to a friend's house for dinner. The mom cooks something he's never eaten before. He won't try it because he doesn't think he'll like it. The friend's mom feels badly, but this is all there is for dinner. The boy won't eat, but mentions that he feels hungry. The other boy and his mom decide not to invite the unadventurous eater over for dinner again.

On the other hand, a child who is willing to try new things can take advantage of new opportunities to make friends. For example:

- A nine-year-old girl gets invited to an ice-skating party where she won't know many of the guests. She also doesn't know how to ice-skate and is nervous about it, but she finds out there will be others there who don't know how to skate either and that there will be an adult to teach them when they arrive. She's excited about learning a new sport, having fun, and making new friends.

It is important to encourage our children to be open-minded and to try new things—new foods, new activities, new friends. We primarily do this by role-modeling our willingness to try new things and by making the situations as safe as we can when our children are willing to try something new. The more we can expose our children to diverse experiences, people, and places, the richer their lives will be. And they will also benefit from becoming an open-minded person that others will want as friend.

6. Respect For Others

When our children respect their friends, they treat them with kindness and fairness. They don't yell and scream at them or call them names. When they know what respect is, they don't talk behind their friends' backs, gossip about them, or make fun of them with other children. Treating other children with respect means that a friend can trust that they will feel safe with your child. Even very young children can learn to respect one another. For example, three-year-old Tony was riding his tricycle at preschool when the bike fell over. Some four-year-old boys started laughing at Tony. Bobby, Tony's friend, went over to see if he was hurt. He treated Tony with respect while others were laughing. Bobby knew at three how to be a good friend.

Too often children bad-mouth their friends to show off, gain points with other children, or to be accepted by the popular group. Such behavior is flat-out disrespectful. Respecting your friends doesn't mean you always agree with them; it means that when you disagree, you do so in a way that respects their feelings. Nine-year-old Gina had her feelings hurt by a classmate. Gina went up to the girl who hurt her feelings and yelled at her. Bella, Gina's best friend, didn't agree with Gina yelling, but she respected her friend and wanted to help her friend feel better so she asked her if she wanted to talk about what happened.

"Treat others the way you want to be treated." This Golden Rule is as effective today as it was two thousand years ago when it was first said.

Help Your Child Develop The Six Personal Skills For Healthy Friendships!

So, again, here are the six personal skills that will help your child enjoy healthy, rewarding friendships (Interestingly these are also the personal skills needed for a successful marriage!):

1. Self-acceptance

2. Empathy

3. Patience

4. Flexibility

5. Willingness to try new things

6. Respect for others

Have fun and enjoy the exercises. You are helping your child to become a friend others will treasure.

Your children's friendships are an accurate predictor of their future relationships.

EXERCISE #1 - FRIENDSHIP CHART ☆

PURPOSE & BENEFITS:

To develop awareness about how friends interact with one another. To encourage your child to be more aware of the choices he makes with his friends. To learn whom your child sees as his friends. To learn how your child treats his friends.

STARTING AGE: 4 years

TIME: 10 to 20 minutes

LOCATION: Somewhere quiet without distractions

MATERIALS:
- paper or poster board
- pen, pencil, or felt pens
- a paper titled Friendship Do's/Don'ts

INSTRUCTIONS:

1. Sit with your child in a comfortable place where you can make eye contact.

2. Tell your child you want to talk to him about friendships.

3. Begin by asking your child who his friends are. Ask him what he likes about each of the children named. If you hear the name of either a child you don't like, or who you know your child never plays with, do not disagree with him—just listen and explore. Remember that exploring questions are non-judgmental, non-critical, and not sarcastic.

4. Tell your child you think it would be fun to make a chart about friendship. If you have worked the other chapter exercises, your child is comfortable with charts and lists by this time.

FRIENDSHIP	
DOs	**DON'Ts**

5. Ask your child what he thinks makes a good friend. List the qualities and characteristics he names.

6. Ask your child what kind of behaviors children do whom he would not want as friends.

7. Ask what your child does that makes him a good friend and add his answers to the list.

8. Ask your child if he does any of the behaviors listed under the DON'T column.

9. Ask your child if there is any behavior he would like to change. If he says yes, help him make a plan.

10. Post the list and tell your child he can add to it during the week if he would like to.

EXERCISE #2 - GAMES ☆

PURPOSE & BENEFITS:

Childhood friendships always involve play. This exercise gives your child the opportunity to practice being a good sport at play. Children who have a lot of friends are good at winning and at losing. Playing games in a safe home environment develops the skills of good self-acceptance, patience, respect, and flexibility. As new games are introduced, the skill of willingness to try new things is developed.

STARTING AGE: 4 years

TIME: Varies

LOCATION: Wherever the game chosen can be comfortably played

MATERIALS: • Games

INSTRUCTIONS:

1. Parent role models good sportsmanship, respect, patience, flexibility, and willingness to try new activities and empathy during the game.

2. The first few times you play games with your child, you may want to choose the game to be played. Choose a game you want to play so you can enjoy yourself with your child.

3. The following is a suggested list of games to get you and your child started.

Cards:

• Fish	• Uno®	• War
• Hi-Low War	• Old Maid	• Rummy
• Double Solitaire	• Poker	• Malice
• Blackjack (twenty one)		

Games:

• Connect Four®	• Mancala®	• Battleship®
• Jr. Scrabble®	• Tic-Tac-Toe	• Hangman
• Perfection®	• Candy Land®	• Jenga®
• Simon Says	• Scattergories®	• Sorry®
• Boggle®	• Checkers	• Chess
• Backgammon	• Yahtzee®	• Dominoes
• Chutes and Ladders®		

4. Play and have fun.

EXERCISE #3 - CHANGE THE PLAN ☆

PURPOSE & BENEFITS:

To teach flexibility. The more positive experiences children have with plans changing, the more accepting and tolerant they become. The more often you do this exercise with your child, the more likely his life belief will become "I am disappointed about the change of plans, but I know it wasn't done to hurt me. If I want to talk about it later, I know Mom or Dad will probably check in with me about how I felt about the change." The second life belief we want to develop in our children is "Change happens in life and we survive it and move on. It's okay."

STARTING AGE: 4 years
TIME: Varies
LOCATION: Varies
MATERIALS: None

INSTRUCTIONS:

1. The first time this exercise is done, be prepared for the regular response. If the expected response is upset, anger, or disappointment, then prepare yourself for that reaction.

2. Tell your child you "think" you are going to:

    > ...go out to lunch (then eat at home)
    >
    > ...go over to visit a friend (then stay home)
    >
    > ...go out for pizza (go somewhere else)
    >
    > ...order pizza in (fix dinner instead)
    >
    > ...arrange a play day Tuesday (change it to Thursday)
    >
    > ....buy your child a requested toy this afternoon (go tomorrow instead)
    >
    > ...rent a particular movie (get a different movie)

3. As you tell your child about the change of plan, remind your child you had only said you "think" the event might happen.

4. At some point, either immediately or later that day, find a quiet time to explore what your child felt when they heard the change of plans. Ask:

    - What did you feel when you heard the change of plan? Just listen to his answer, don't criticize or judge.
    - Is it hard for you when plans change? Just listen.
    - Do you think that happens a lot in people's lives? Just listen.
    - What would make it easier for you to accept changed plans? Just listen.

5. It is important to let your child express his feelings around the changed plans. The primary reason is because children who become too upset with a change of plans often feel disrespected and devalued when the change happens. They feel they had no voice or control over the change. Many children feel powerless, which often leads to acting out behavior, which presents itself in anger. When we explore with our child how he felt over the change of plans and genuinely listen to his feelings, he may still be disappointed, but he'll feel respected and valued.

EXERCISE #4 - GUESS WHAT PEOPLE ARE FEELING ☆

PURPOSE & BENEFITS:

To continue to develop empathy in your child. To give you insight into how well your child reads social cues.

STARTING AGE: 4 years

TIME: 1 to 2 minutes

LOCATION: Anywhere, anytime

MATERIALS: None

INSTRUCTIONS:

1. If you have continued to talk about feelings with your child, which you began in Chapter Ten, this exercise will be easy and fun.

2. Everywhere you go, notice a person of any age and ask your child what they think the person is feeling.

3. Remind your child that everyone feels at least four or five feelings at any given moment.

4. If you do this exercise as a family, accept all answers.

EXERCISE #5 - SCAVENGER HUNT ☆

PURPOSE & BENEFITS:

To have your child work as part of a team. Children are often assigned to work in groups throughout childhood. This exercise continues to develop the skills needed to work successfully with others: respect, patience, flexibility, willingness to try new things, empathy, and self-acceptance.

STARTING AGE: 3 years (2 years, depending on the child and the teams)

TIME: 20 to 30 minutes

LOCATION: Home or backyard (a safe environment)

MATERIALS: • a prepared scavenger list

• a bag to hold discovered items

INSTRUCTIONS:

1. Parent prepares a list of two to twenty items to be found around the house or backyard.

2. The first time this exercise is done, the parent decides the teams so each team has an equal chance to win.

3. The parent sets the rules although the children can suggest rules they feel are needed.

   For example:

   • Time to be announced and a timer set. When the timer goes off everyone stops looking for items and gathers in a predetermined area.

   • No yelling or put-downs among team members or the whole team gets disqualified.

   • No damage can be done to get an item.

   • No one can go into another person's room, dresser drawers, desk drawers, or closet to get an item.

4. Choose the parent(s)—or designated adult(s)—to be the judge to decide the winning team.

5. The emphasis is on working as a team, not the prize. Make the prize simple (choose the family movie to watch, an ice-cream bar, choose the dessert for dinner, paper crowns to wear for the evening—be creative).

6. This is a fun game to play when you or your children have friends over.

EXERCISE #6 - TEAM GAMES ☆

PURPOSE & BENEFITS:

To develop strengths in areas of self-acceptance, respect, flexibility, willingness to try new things, patience, and empathy.

STARTING AGE: 4 years (a 2- or 3-year-old can be teamed with a partner and experience of being part of a team)

TIME:	Varies
LOCATION:	Wherever the game chosen can be comfortably played
MATERIALS:	• Game chosen

INSTRUCTIONS:

1. Parents choose the game the first time this exercise is done.
2. Parent role models good sportsmanship throughout the game.
3. Parent determines the teams. Make sure to balance the teams so they each have an equal chance to win.
4. Set a specific time to play when you will have a minimum amount of interruptions.
5. If your family is small, consider inviting extended family members, friends, or neighbors.
6. Choose a game, explain the directions, accept questions for clarification, relax, and have fun!

Suggested Team Games: (These can be played in teams)

- Pictionary®
- Balderdash®
- Charades
- Trivial Pursuit®
- Hoopla®
- Taboo®
- Cranium®
- Outburst®

EXERCISE #7 - PLAY DATE ☆

PURPOSE & BENEFITS:

To give your child social experiences. To give you the opportunity to observe your child in a social setting. To give your child the opportunity to learn and experience her social skills in a safe environment.

STARTING AGE:	4 years
TIME:	1-hour to overnight
LOCATION:	Home, park, etc.
MATERIALS:	Whatever is needed for the play date.

INSTRUCTIONS:

1. Parent thinks about whether they are comfortable when it

comes to having the responsibility of watching another child.

2. Consider asking a child from the neighborhood, preschool or school, a relative, or a friend's child to come over for a play date. Do not limit yourself to only offering play dates to a same age child as your own. Our children grow in their social skills when they have developed relationships with older and younger children.

3. Once you have decided what type of play date you want to offer your child, sit and talk to her about the possibility.

4. If your child agrees, talk about both of your expectations, length of play date, activities, snack or meal, house rules, etc.

5. After the play date, explore with your child:
   - How do you feel the play date went?
   - What would you do differently next time?

EXERCISE #8 - HOW WOULD YOU FEEL IF...? ☆

PURPOSE & BENEFITS:

To help your child continue to develop strong empathy skills. To continue to increase your child's awareness of her own feelings.

STARTING AGE: 4 years

TIME: 10 to 15 minutes

LOCATION: A quiet location

MATERIALS:
- the question cards "How would you feel if...?" made on index cards or pieces of paper
- pen

INSTRUCTIONS:

1. Parent prepare the "How would you feel...?" cards from the suggestions on this page or make your own.

2. Make at least ten "How would you feel...?" cards.

3. Put cards in a pile.

4. Sit with your child, or with the whole family, and put the pile of card in the center.

5. Decide who will go first.

6. The first person picks the card on the top of the pile and reads it. If the child can't read yet the parent or older sibling can read it.

7. The child then answers the questions with at least two or three feelings. Accept all answers.

8. When the child is finished, the card is put back anywhere in the pile.

9. Rules:

    • Accept all answers.

    • No put-downs.

10. The following is a list of questions to copy onto the cards. Write out the whole sentence on each card.

11. How would you feel if...

    • ...your best friend came over to play with you?

    • ...your friend was mad at you?

    • ...you had to choose between two friends' birthday parties?

    • ...your friend was crying?

    • ...your friend was playing with someone else at recess?

    • ...there was a new child in your class?

    • ...you didn't know how to play the game your friend wanted to play?

    • ...your friend was yelled at by his mom?

    • ...your friend yelled at you?

    • ...your friend told you to be mean to another child?

    • ...you won the game you were playing with your friend?

    • ...your friend couldn't come to your birthday party?

    • ...your friend's mom called and said he couldn't come over for the planned play date?

    • ...your mom told you that she had to cancel your play date?

    • ...your friend laughed at you when he won the game you were playing together?

- ...your friend hurt himself while you were playing?
- ...your friend was being laughed at by some of your classmates at school?
- ...your friend told you you were his best friend?
- ...your friend told a lie to his mom?
- ...your friend asked you to tell a lie?
- ...Your brother/sister was nice to you?

EXERCISE #9 - NEW GROUPS

PURPOSE & BENEFITS:

To give your child many opportunities to meet other children and practice his social skills. To help your child to discover and develop his interests and talents.

STARTING AGE: 4 years
TIME: Varies
LOCATION: Varies
MATERIALS: Varies

INSTRUCTIONS:

1. Parent decides what group activities you are willing to let your child try.
2. Consider cost, time involvement, and transportation.
3. Remember, we all have limitations in our life and we simply cannot offer some activities to our children even if they want them for practical reasons.
4. It is more difficult for a child when a parent says, "Yes, I'll sign you up. No problem," and then discovers it isn't possible to allow the child to participate in the activity.
5. Do your research before you make a promise or commitment to your child.

Possible Group Activities:

- Local Park and Recreation classes and programs
- Organized sports teams

- Boy and Girl Scouts
- Church youth group activities
- On-going lessons: ballet, gymnastics, music, art, drama, etc.
- Junior museum programs
- Science and nature programs
- Hi-tech programs and classes

EXERCISE #10 - FRIENDSHIP ROLE PLAYS ☆

PURPOSE & BENEFITS:

To give children the opportunity to prepare themselves for possible life experiences while in a safe environment. To receive feedback to alternative ways to respond to possible life situations.

STARTING AGE: 5 years (4 years old depending on the child)

TIME: 20 to 30 minutes

LOCATION: Where a stage area can be created

MATERIALS:
- role play cards
- basket, bag, or box

INSTRUCTIONS:

1. Parent copies the suggested role plays onto pieces of paper. Fold them in half and put them in basket, bag, or box.
2. Determine who goes first.
3. The first child to go picks a role play paper from the basket and reads it aloud. If your child needs help, read it for him.
4. Your child chooses someone with which to role-play with.
5. The two actors take a minute to discuss how they are going to act out the role play.
6. If necessary, set a timer for 2 or 3 minutes for the role play.
7. The actors act out the role play in front of the family.
8. If it is only one parent and one child, still follow the same procedure. You do not need an audience for your child to benefit from this exercise.
9. After the role play is completed, or the timer goes off, the

actors stop.

10. The parent then explores how the actors felt while they were role-playing.
   - What were you feeling while you were acting?
   - Were you surprised at how you felt?
   - What would you do the same or different if the situation happened in real life?

Suggested Role Plays:

1. You are playing a game with a friend and they start getting mad and yelling at you because they are losing. What do you do?

2. You are planning on having a play date today. Mom tells you that she needs to cancel the play date because Grandma feels sick and you are going over to take care of her. What do you do?

3. You are playing Legos® and your brother keeps coming by and knocking them over. What do you do?

4. You are playing ball at school with a group of classmates. One of the children keeps bumping into you. You are getting upset. What do you do?

5. You got into a fight with one of your friends today. You just arrived home. You are mad and sad at the same time. What do you do?

6. Mom or Dad is yelling at you for being mean to your brother or sister. You don't think they were being fair. What do you do?

7. You are playing out in your front yard and one of the older boys who lives on your block keep coming over and teasing you. What do you do?

8. You and your friend are playing basketball in your driveway. Your friend isn't very good at basketball. You are getting frustrated. What do you do?

9. You are at school. You go up to your friend and ask her if she wants to play. She tells you to go away. She doesn't want to play with you. What do you do?

10. You are at school and a group of girls are playing together. You want to play with them. What do you do?

EXERCISE #11 - FAMILY, FRIENDS, AND NEIGHBORHOOD GET-TOGETHERS ☆

PURPOSE & BENEFITS:

To give your child the opportunity to socially interact with different ages. To build a long-term support group in your child's life.

STARTING AGE: 3 years
TIME: Varies
LOCATION: Varies
MATERIALS: Varies

INSTRUCTIONS:

1. Parent be open to attend or plan potluck get-togethers, whether they are at your home or another home, at the park, the beach, at the school your child attends, on your block, etc.

2. Before you attend the social function with your child, go over your expectations for your child's behavior—any rules or boundaries that need to be set because of the location (i.e., beach).

3. Ask your child if he has any questions.

4. Share with your child your family's contribution: food, games, tables, chairs, etc.

5. Ask your child what he is willing to do to help.

6. Depending on your child's personality, make a plan to help him feel comfortable during the function.

7. Set up a check-in plan.

8. During the following week, explore:
   • How do you think the event went?
   • What would you do differently next time?

EXERCISE #12 - SHARE A GOOD FRIEND STORY ☆

PURPOSE & BENEFITS:

To continue to develop awareness for your child about the qualities of a good friend.

STARTING AGE: 4 years
TIME: 2 to 3 minutes
LOCATION: Anywhere
MATERIALS: None
INSTRUCTIONS:
1.   Parents ask your child to share a time when someone was a good friend to her or when your child was a good friend to someone.
2.   Parent listens and compliments child on being a good friend.
3.   Parent shares a similar story.

EXERCISE #13 "OUTDOOR GAMES"

PURPOSE & BENEFITS:

To give your child more opportunities to develop good sportsmanship skills and a willingness to try new activities.

STARTING AGE: 5 years (4 years old depending on the child)
TIME: Varies
LOCATION: Varies
MATERIALS: Varies
INSTRUCTIONS:
1.   Parent chooses the game to be played.
2.   Parent gives the directions and answers any questions.
3.   Parent clearly points out any additional rules to be observed beyond the basic directions.
4.   Parent and child have fun!!

<u>Suggested Outdoors Games</u>

    1. Frisbee Golf (all ages) – Individual play

- Any number of players; team up young children
- Each player has a Frisbee
- This played similar to golf
- A target is identified (a tree, a bush, a rock, etc.)
- All players try to hit the target with the least number of throws
- The player with the lowest number of throws is the winner for that round
- Each target can have a winner. Celebrate the win and move on, or you can play any number of holes (targets). If you play nine holes, assign one person to keep score. When all holes (targets) are completed, the scores are added. The player with the lowest score wins.

    2. Touch Football – Team play

- Divide the group into two teams
- Discuss and decide on the rules
- In touch football, there is no tackling
- Decide whether you are playing for a designated amount of time or to a determined score
- Explain the rules to the players

    3. Basketball (any age) – Individual play

- Around-the-World or Horse
- Any number of players
- Designate specific spots on the basketball key—for example:

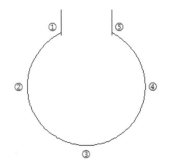

- Each player takes one-shot starting at the number one

spot (H or W)

- If the player misses the basket, the next player takes a turn
- If the player makes the basket, he moves to the second spot (O) and takes a turn
- Repeat (Number three spot for R, number four spot for S or L, and number five for E or D)
- The first player to complete the word HORSE or WORLD by making five baskets is the winner

4. Friendly Soccer (any age) – Team play
    - Any number of players
    - Divide the group area into two teams
    - Determine the goal area (i.e., between two garbage cans) and the outside boundaries
    - Decide whether to play for a designated set time or a predetermined score
    - Parent clearly explains the rules
    - Anyone who breaks a rule is asked to leave the game for a certain amount on time 2, 3, 4, or 5 minutes
    - Rules:
        - No kicking
        - No tripping
        - No hitting
        - If a ball is kicked out of bounds, the other team kicks it back into play
        - A point is earned by kicking the ball into the goal area

5. Baseball With a Pinch Hitter/Runner (any age) – Team play
    - Any number of players
    - If Grandma wants to hit, but not run, her team can use a pinch runner
    - If a three-year-old wants to run, but not hit, his team can use a pinch hitter
    - Divide the group into two teams
    - Determine the number of innings to be played (i.e., four, six, or nine)

- Choose a pitcher and a catcher
- Choose a lineup
- Flip a coin to see which team is up first
- Play by baseball rules

6. Kicker Friendly Kickball (any age) – Team play
   - Any number of players
   - Divide the group into two teams
   - Choose a pitcher and catcher
   - Mark the bases
   - Decide on a lineup
   - The pitcher throws the ball to the kicker who kicks, runs to first base, and then on to second if he thinks he can make it
   - The opposing team catches the ball and either throws to a baseman to tag the runner out or throws to the pitcher
   - The play stops when the pitcher has the ball
   - The next kicker is up
   - The kicking team continues to kick until they have three outs
   - Outs:
     - If a kicked ball is caught on a fly ball
     - If a runner is tagged out by a baseman with the ball
     - If the baseman catches the ball before the kicker arrives on base

NOTE: There are many other outdoor games:
   - Volleyball
   - Badminton
   - Kick-the-Can (Backyard version)
   - Build a sand sculpture
   - Races (hopping, skipping, three-legged, etc.)

APPENDIX

■ ■ ■

Faces and Feelings Questionnaire

This is a picture of me when...

I AM HAPPY

I AM DISAPPOINTED

I AM MAD

I AM HURT

I AM FRUSTRATED

I AM UPSET

<u>Children's Feelings List (Ages 5-7)</u>

Happy	Hurt Feelings
Sad	Good
Silly	Loved
Scared	Confused
Mad	Lonely
Glad	Proud
Angry	Surprised
Bad	Joy
Embarrassed	Disappointed
Kind	Nice

Children's Feelings List (Ages 8+)

Put an "X" by the feelings you feel everyday.
Put an "✓" by the feelings you feel once a week.
Put an "☺ "by the feelings you feel once a month.

Accepted	Fearful	Patient
Afraid	Frightened	Playful
Angry	Frustrated	Pressured
Ashamed	Funny	Puzzled
Awful	Good looking	Rejected
Bad	Guilty	Sad
Bored	Happy	Scared
Brave	Hateful	Shy
Caring	Helpless	Smart
Confident	Important	Special
Confused	Jealous	Surprised
Concerned	Kind	Terrible
Curious	Lonely	Terrified
Depressed	Loved	Tired
Different	Mad	Ugly
Disappointed	Mean	Uncomfortable
Discouraged	Miserable	Understood
Disgusted	Mixed-up	Upset
Disturbed	Nervous	Uptight
Embarrassed	Nice	Wonderful
Excited	Not good enough	Worried

Adult's Feelings List

Abandoned	Caring	Dreadful	Glad
Accepted	Cheerful	Dumb	Gloomy
Accused	Cold	Dumfounded	Good
Afraid	Comfortable	Eager	Grateful
Agitated	Compassionate	Ecstatic	Great
Alone	Competent	Edgy	Grieved
Ambitious	Concerned	Efficient	Guilty
Amused	Confident	Elated	Hampered
Angry	Confused	Embarrassed	Happy
Anticipate, to	Content	Empathetic	Hateful
Annoyed	Cool	Empathy	Heartbroken
Anxious	Cowardly	Encouraged	Helpful
Appreciated	Crushed	Energetic	Helpless
Appreciative	Curious	Enjoy	Honored
Approval	Daring	Enraged	Hopeful
Ashamed	Defeated	Enthusiastic	Hopeless
Attracted	Defensive	Envious	Horrified
Awful	Deflated	Exasperated	Hostile
Bad	Degraded	Excited	Humble
Bashful	Delighted	Exhausted	Humiliated
Belittled	Dependent	Failure	Hungry
Bent out of shape	Depressed	Fascinated	Hurried
Betrayed	Deprived	Fearful	Hurt
Better	Detached	Feel like giving up	Impatient
Bewildered	Difficult	Floored	Important
Bitter	Different	Flustered	Imposed upon
Blah	Disappointed	Fond	Impressed
Bored	Discontented	Foolish	Inadequate
Bothered	Discouraged	Frantic	Incapable
Brave	Disgusted	Free	Incompetent
Bugged	Disrespected	Friendly	Indifferent
Burdened	Distracted	Frightened	Inexperienced
Calm	Distressed	Frustrated	Infantile
Capable	Disturbed	Funny	Infatuated
Captivated	Doubt	Furious	Infuriated

Inhibited	Optimistic	Riled	Tense
Insecure	Ornery	Roused	Terrified
Inspired	Overcome	Rushed	Thrilled
Intense	Overwhelmed	Sad	Ticked off
Interested	Pained	Satisfied	Tight
Intimidated	Panicky	Scared	Tired
Irritated	Paralyzed	Self-conscious	Tolerant
Isolated	Passionate	Selfish	Trapped
Jazzed	Patient	Self-pitying	Ugly
Jealous	Peaceful	Sensual	Unappreciated
Joyous	Peeved	Sensitive	Uncomfortable
Kindly	Perplexed	Sentimental	Understood
Knifed in the back	Persecuted	Serene	Uneasy
Lazy	Perturbed	Serious	Unfair
Left out	Pessimistic	Shaky	Unhappy
Let down	Pitied	Shocked	Unimportant
Like a fool	Plagued	Shook	Unkind
Lonely	Playful	Shy	Unloved
Lost	Pleased	Silly	Unmoved
Loved	Precarious	Slow	Unprepared
Loving	Prepared	Smart	Unsure
Low	Pressured	Sore	Untrusted
Lucky	Protective	Sorrowful	Unworthy
Mad	Proud	Sorry	Upset
Mean	Provoked	So-so	Uptight
Miserable	Put down	Special	Used
Misused	Puzzled	Staggered	Useless
Mixed-up	Rejected	Startled	Vindictive
Modest	Relaxed	Strong	Violent
Moody	Relieved	Struck	Vulnerable
Mortified	Remorseful	Stupid	Want to get even
Moved	Resentful	Submissive	Weak
Naïve	Respected	Subdued	Weird
Needed	Restless	Superior	Wild
Neglected	Revengeful	Sympathetic	Worried
Nervous	Ridiculous	Tender	Worthless

GLOSSARY

absolute thinking - declares that what I am saying must happen, and if it doesn't, my world will not be okay; when these words are a part of anyone's core belief system, they set up the person for disappointment

absolutes - perfect in quality or nature; complete; not to be doubted or questioned

active listening – being listened to in such a way that we know the listener is trying to understand what we are saying

A-ha Moment – the moment when a light goes on and you have an understanding of something new

amygdala - an almond-shaped mass of gray matter in the anterior portion of the temporal lobe; our emotional database

anger management – ability to control your anger

Anxiety Disorder - is much more than the normal anxiety people experience day to day. It's chronic and exaggerated worry and tension, even though nothing seems to provoke it. Having this disorder means always anticipating disaster, often worrying excessively about health, money, family, or work. Sometimes, though, the source of the worry is hard to pinpoint. Simply the thought of getting through the day provokes anxiety.

assessment - to determine the value, significance, or extent of

autonomy – the condition or quality of being autonomous; independence; self-determination

belief - mental acceptance of and conviction in the truth, actuality, or validity of something

belief systems – a collection of our own personal beliefs

Childhood Depression - depression is an illness that involves feelings of sadness lasting for two weeks or longer, often accompanied by a loss of interest in life, hopelessness, and decreased energy. Such distressing feelings can affect one's ability to perform the usual tasks and activities of daily living. This is considered to be clinical depression. It is very different from a temporary case of "the blues" triggered by an unhappy event or stressful situation.

co-active – interacting with another person

cognition – the process of knowing in the broadest sense. including perception, memory, and judgement; to know

cognitive stages – cognitive stages identified and labeled by Jean Piaget; his research showed that cognitive development involved a predictable sequence of stages that are never skipped

common sense - as "ordinary good sense or sound practical judgment"; sound judgment not based on specialized knowledge; native good judgment

communication - the exchange of thoughts, messages, or information, as by speech, signals, writing, or behavior

comparison trap – when the act of comparing produces a negative emotional response

conscious - having an awareness of one's environment and one's own existence, sensations, and thoughts.; mentally perceptive or alert; awake

Concrete Operational Stage – ages seven to eleven; children can use symbols and engage in mental activities; they are able to classify in more sophisticated ways, seriate, conserve, and understand part-whole relationships and terms.

decision making – the act of making a choice

decisive actions – actions that have an impact on a particular consequence

defensive - constantly protecting oneself from criticism, exposure of one's shortcomings, or other real or perceived threats to the ego

delayed response – a response which demands a person wait a designated amount of time

Depression - a psychiatric disorder characterized by an inability to concentrate, insomnia, loss of appetite, anhedonia, feelings of extreme sadness, guilt, helplessness and hopelessness, and thoughts of death.

dialogue - a conversation between two or more people; an exchange of ideas or opinions

disconnected - to sever or interrupt the connection of or between

displacement - is the process that happens when the unexpressed negative feelings you felt toward a particular person or event are then expressed towards someone else

egocentric - caring only about oneself; selfish; holding the view that the ego is the center, object, and norm of all experience

emotional cutoff – represents a flight from unresolved emotional conflict and may mask unexamined fusion

emotional databank – holds a memory of our emotional experiences

emotional intelligence - is the ability to recognize and label what one is feeling at any given moment, and to make a reasonable guess about what others are feeling and to respond in a healthy way; emotional intelligence regarding the emotions, especially in the ability to monitor one's own or others' emotions

emotional quotient (EQ) – a new perceived ability to measure our emotional intelligence

emotional reactivity - refers to making a decision based on the intense feelings one is feeling at that moment

emotion - a mental state that arises spontaneously rather than through conscious effort and is often accompanied by physiological changes; a feeling; the part of the consciousness that involves feeling; sensibility

empathy – the ability to understand what another person is feeling

ethics - is the way we live our lives; the rules or standards governing the conduct of a person; the study of the general nature of morals and of the specific moral choices to be made by a person; moral philosophy

family of origin (FYO) – the family we grew up in; how we think and behave is in large part due to the accumulation of experiences we had in the family we grew up in

feelings - an affective state of consciousness, such as that resulting from emotions, sentiments, or desires

feeling labels – words used to describe feelings

feelings vocabulary - is our accumulation of feeling words; are unique to each individual.

Formal Operational Stage – from ages 11+; individual is able to think abstractly and relatively—if given a premise, he or she can deduce logically as well as test the premise

friendship - the quality or condition of being in a platonic relationship

fusion – inability to distinguish thoughts from feelings

Golden Rule - treat others the way you want to be treated; the biblical teaching that one should behave toward others as one would have others behave toward oneself

grading statements – a statement which infers a judgment in response to a behavior

ideal self-image - an unrealistic picture one holds of oneself which involves irrational beliefs which must be met in order to feel okay

immediate response – a response which occurs immediately after an activity has ceased

influence - a power affecting a person, thing, or course of events, especially one that operates without any direct or apparent effort; power to sway or affect based on prestige, wealth, ability, or position

informational databank - holder of information needed in order to make rational decisions

intelligence - as the ability to acquire and retain knowledge; the capacity to acquire and apply knowledge

intelligence quotient (IQ) - as a number showing how intelligent you are compared to others

irrational - marked by a lack of accord with reason or sound judgment

irrational beliefs – a belief held which has no evidence to prove it to be true

irrational thought – a thought without any basis in truth

irresponsible - lacking a sense of responsibility; unreliable or untrustworthy; not mentally or financially fit to assume responsibility

I-Statement – a communication statement which shares the speaker's feeling

klunk – an emotional fit when a feeling word matches the feeling being experienced

life beliefs – beliefs one holds to be true about life

Limbic System - a group of interconnected deep brain structures, common to all mammals, and involved in olfaction, emotion, motivation, behavior, and various autonomic functions

memory – the mental faculty of retaining and recalling past experience; the act or an instance of remembering; recollection

meta message – an underlying message often non-verbal about another message

mixed-message - a situation in which a person is receiving verbal or nonverbal cues that seem to contradict each other, from another person; typical reactions to this behavior are confusion, anger, and a willingness to cease communication with the person

morals - are defined as the difference between right and wrong; teaching or exhibiting goodness or correctness of character and behavior: conforming to standards of what is right or just in behavior; virtuous

must beliefs – a belief which must happen or failure is inevitable

neocortex - the dorsal region of the cerebral cortex, especially large in higher mammals and the most recently evolved part of the brain

nest - a place in which young are reared; a place or environment that fosters rapid growth or development; a place affording snug refuge or lodging; a home

one-way communication - one person speaking and the other person (hopefully) listening; moving or permitting movement in one direction only

Oppositional Defiant Disorder – an ongoing pattern in children of uncooperative, defiant, and hostile behavior toward authority figures that seriously interferes with the youngster's day to day functioning.

perception - recognition and interpretation of sensory stimuli based chiefly on memory; the neurological processes by which such recognition and interpretation are effected

Preoperational Stage – from ages two to seven; symbolic function develops. This allows use of language, symbolic play, and imitation. There are two sub-stages: preconceptual (2-4 years) and intuitive (4-7 years). Limitation on preoperational thoughts are: (1) egocentrism: inability to see from other's perspective, (2) animism: giving human characteristics to inanimate objects, (3) centrism: focus on only one aspect of a situation or object, and (4) irreversibility: unable to see that actions can be reversed.

problem-solving – recognizing a problem and seeking a solution

quelled - to put down forcibly; suppress; to pacify; quiet

Rage-aholic - is someone who feeds on expressing rage. Like the alcoholic, the rage-aholic is addicted to blowing up. This is usually caused by the rage-aholic stuffing back real feelings and emotions until it builds up the point that the rage-aholic snaps. Stress of any kind can be a trigger. It is a cry for love, but a fear to accept it. A person who is addicted to blowing up; a person who is addicted to the expression of anger.

rational beliefs – a belief based in truth

rational thought – a thought based on logic

rationalize - to make rational reasons for one's behavior

reactive actions – actions taken without much thought

real self-image – an image representing the person

reframing – changing the original perception of an event or situation and thereby altering the way the event or situation is viewed; giving new labels or perspective to an old pattern of behaviors thereby changing the original emotional response

repair - soothing and calming the body's response; to restore to sound condition after damage or injury; fix; to set right; remedy

responsibility – able to answer for one's conduct and obligations; trustworthy; able to choose for oneself between right and wrong

role model - a person whose behavior in a particular role is imitated by others; a person who serves as a model in a particular behavioral or social role for another person to emulate

ruminating – to go over in the mind repeatedly and often; to reflect on over and over again

rupture - fear and intense body reaction; the process or instance of breaking open or bursting

self-absorbed - excessively self-involved; absorbed in one's own thoughts, activities, or interests

self-acceptance - is liking ourselves just for who we are

self-centeredness - concerned solely with one's own desires, needs, or interests; engrossed in oneself and one's own affairs; selfish

self-confidence - confidence in oneself or one's own abilities; confidence in oneself and in one's powers and abilities

self-image - the conception that one has of oneself, including an assessment of qualities and personal worth

self-worth - feeling a sense of value

Sensorimotor Stage - from birth to age two; child perceives objects in terms of how they look, feel, or taste and what can be done with them. There are six sub-stages in this period when behaviors become more goal-directed and responses to objects and events increase.

solution – the method or process of solving a problem; an action or process of solving a problem

stress – a state of extreme difficulty, pressure, or strain; a mentally or emotionally disruptive or upsetting condition occurring in response to adverse external influences and capable of affecting physical health, usually characterized by increased heart rate, a rise in blood pressure, muscular tension, irritability, and depression

sympathy the act or power of sharing the feelings of another; inclination to think or feel alike; the act or capacity of entering into or sharing the feelings or interests of another; the feeling or mental state brought about by such sensitivity

thalamus - a large void mass of gray matter situated in the posterior part of the forebrain that relays sensory impulses to the cerebral cortex and amygdala; the largest subdivision of the diencephalon that consists chiefly of an ovoid mass of nuclei in each lateral wall of the third ventricle and functions in the integration of sensory information

thought – the act or process of thinking; cognitation; product of thinking; the faculty of thinking or reasoning

toxic - poisonous

two-way communication - involves two people taking turns being the speaker and the listener

unconscious - the division of the mind in psychoanalytic theory containing elements of psychic makeup, such as memories or repressed desires, that are not subject to conscious perception or control but that often affect conscious thoughts and behavior; lacking awareness and the capacity for sensory perception; not conscious; without conscious control; involuntary or unintended; not knowing or perceiving; not aware

unconscious beliefs – beliefs which a person is unaware of

unconscious thoughts - thoughts which a person is unaware of

vagus nerve - the tenth and longest of the cranial nerves, passing through the neck and thorax into the abdomen and supplying sensation to part of the ear, the tongue, the larynx, and the pharynx, motor impulses to the vocal cords, and motor and secretory impulses to the abdominal and thoracic viscera;

values - what is important to you; to regard highly; esteem; worth in usefulness or importance to the possessor; utility or merit: the value of an education; a principle, standard, or quality considered worthwhile or desirable

whoosh - the unfiltered emotional response is based on the amygdala's databank of past emotional experiences; to make a soft sibilant sound; to move or flow swiftly with or as if with such a sound

You-Statement – a statement directed at the listener which states the listener is responsible for the speaker's feelings

RECOMMENDED READINGS

■ ■ ■

Altman, M., R. Reyes, and A. Bitton, comps. <u>Developing Your Child's Emotional Intelligence, Self-Control by Age 3 in 10 Simple Steps</u>. Gretna, LA: Wellness Institute Inc., 2003.

Anesko, K. M., F. M. Levine. <u>Winning the Homework War</u>. New York: ARCO, 1987.

Biddulph, S. <u>The Secrets of Happy Children</u>. New York: MJF Books Fine Communications, 2002.

Crary, E., P. Casebolt. <u>Pick Up Your Socks . . . and Other Skills Growing Children Need!</u> Seattle, Washington: Parenting Press Inc., 1990.

Dreikurs, Rudolf, et al. <u>Children: The Challenge</u>. New York: Hawthorne Press Inc, 1964.

Eastman, M., S. Rozen. <u>Taming the Dragon in Your Child: Solutions for Breaking the Cycle of Family Anger</u>. New York: John Wiley & Sons, Inc., 1994.

Elkind, D. <u>The Hurried Child: Growing Up Too Fast Too Soon</u>. Cambridge, Massachusetts: Perseus Books Group, 2001.

Ekman, Paul and Richard Davidson, eds. <u>Fundamental Questions About Emotions</u>. New York: Oxford University Press, 1994.

Elias, M., S. Tobias, and B. Friedlander, comps. <u>Emotionally Intelligent Parenting: How to Raise a Self-Disciplined, Responsible Socially Skilled Child</u>. New York: Three Rivers Press, 1999.

—- comp., <u>Raising Emotionally Intelligent Teenagers: Parenting with Love, Laughter, and Limits</u>. New York: Harmony Books, 2000.

Gardner, Howard. "Cracking Open the IQ Box." The American Prospect, Winter, 1995.

Gibbs, Nancy. "The EQ Factor." Time Magazine, 5 October 1995: 60-68.

Glenn, S., M. Brock. 7 Strategies for Developing Capable Students. Roseville, CA: Prima Communications Inc., 1998.

Glenn, S., J. Nelsen. Raising Self-Reliant Children in a Self-Indulgent World: Seven Building Blocks for Developing Capable Young People. Roseville, CA: Prima Communications Inc., 2000.

Goleman, D. Emotional Intelligence. New York: Bantam Books, 1995.

—- comp., Working with Emotional Intelligence. New York: Bantam Books, 1998.

Gottman, J., J. Declaire. The Heart of Parenting: Raising Emotionally Intelligent Children. New York: Fireside Book, published by Simon & Schuster, 1997.

Greenspan, Stanley, et al. Building Healthy Minds: The Six Experiences That Create Intelligence and Emotional Growth in Babies and Young Children. Cambridge, Massachusetts: Perseus Publishing, 1999.

Hallowell, E. The Childhood Roots of Adult Happiness: Five Steps to Help Kids Create and Sustain Lifelong Joy. New York: Ballantine Book published by The Random House Publishing Company, 2002.

Leach, Penelope. Your Baby and Child from Birth to Age Five. New York: Alfred A. Knoff, 2000.

LeDoux, J. The Emotional Brain: the mysterious underpinnings of emotional life. New York: Touchstone Books, Published by Simon & Schuster Inc., 1996.

Massey, Morris. The People Puzzle. Reston, Virginia: Reston Publishing Company, Inc., 1979.

Merlevede, P., D. Bridoux, R. Vandamme, comps. 7 Steps to Emotional Intelligence. Carmarthen, Wales, UK and Williston, VT: Crown House Publishing LTD., 2003.

Nagy, A., Geraldine Nagy G. How to Raise Your Child's Emotional Intelligence: 101 ways to bring out the best in your child & yourself. Texas: Heartfelt Publications, 1999.

Nelsen, J. Positive Discipline. Fair Oaks, CA: Adlerian Counseling Center, 1981.

Nelsen, J., L. Lott, and S. Glenn, comps. Positive Discipline A-Z: from toddlers to teens-1001 solutions to everyday parenting problems. Roseville, CA: Prima Communications Inc., 1999.

Piaget, J. The Child's Conception of the World: A 20th Century Classic of Child Psychology. Savage, MD; Rowan and Littlefield publishers, 1951.

Rosemond, J. Six-Point Plan Raising Happy, Healthy Children. Kansas City, Missouri: Andrews and McMeel, Universal Press Syndicate Company, 1989.

Shapiro, L. How to Raise a Child with a High EQ: A Parents' Guide to Emotional Intelligence. New York: Harper Collins Publishers, Inc., 1997.

Simon, Sidney. I Am Loveable and Capable. Hadley, Massachusetts: Values Press, 1988.

ABOUT THE AUTHOR

Eileen Healy, a mother of three children, she is also a Licensed Marriage, Family Therapist as well as a Parent Educator. She has been a guest speaker at national conventions, pre-schools, elementary, junior high, and high schools. She has been an invited authority, on both TV and radio shows, discussing marriage, family and relationship issues. She has a lifetime California Teaching Credential and was a classroom teacher, a vice-principal, and a school counselor. Eileen is the founder and developer of the successful Personal Skills Workshops Program© designed to increase children's emotional intelligence. She is also the Founder and CEO of Familypedia.com.

Eileen and her husband, Bill, have raised their daughter, Kimberly, and two sons, Michael and Robert, each with whom they have a wonderful relationship and close friendship. They are enjoying love and gifts their son-in-law, Chris, and daughters-in-law, Caitlin and Valerie, have brought into their family. They are feeling blessed with the birth of their first grandchild, Kaylene Rose and are looking forward to the birth of their second grandchild, Abbey Rose, in January 2006. Their grandchildren are officially beginning the next generation of high EQ children.